Princess Grace

Other books by Gwen Robyns

The Friendly Potato
Light of a Star—a biography of Vivien Leigh
Royal Sporting Lives
Royal Ladies
Wimbledon
Agatha Christie (winner of the Edgar Allan Poe Award, 1980)

Also, in collaboration

Margaret Rutherford
My Book of Flowers by Princess Grace

Princess Grace

Gwen Robyns

W. H. Allen · London
A Howard & Wyndham Company
1982

Copyright © Gwen Robyns 1976, 1982
Printed and bound in Great Britain by
Biddle's Ltd, Guildford & King's Lynn,
for the publishers, W. H. Allen & Co. Ltd,
44 Hill Street, London W1X 8LB
ISBN 0 491 03221 8

Little Flower, you're a lucky one
you soak in all the lovely sun
you stand and watch it all go by
and never once do bat an eye
while others have to fight and strain
against the world and its every pain of living.

But you must, too, have wars to fight
the cold bleak darkness of every night
of a bigger vine who seeks to grow
and is able to stand the rain and snow
and yet you never let it show
on your pretty face.

Written by Grace Kelly as a child

Foreword

Whenever I begin work on a biography I search for the key. The key that will unlock the character of the person I am writing about . . . so necessary if one is to understand the motivation of his or her life.

There is no point in asking the person concerned. They have no way of knowing. No extra perceptory equipment to be able to stand apart and recognise such a deliquescent characteristic.

With the actress Vivien Leigh I found the key in her own words—searing, ruthless, honest—'Scorpions burn themselves out and eat themselves up and they are careless about themselves—like me.'

When I wrote Margaret Rutherford's autobiography for her this beloved woman had already slipped into her own autumnal world of shadows. One day as she sat in the garden in lonesome, depressive silence she suddenly leaned forward in her wheelchair and spoke:

'Do you believe in fairies? When did you last see a miracle?'

I smiled gratefully. I had the key.

With Her Serene Highness Princess Grace of Monaco it was different. The canvas was broader, blurred by international barriers and indefinable royal obstructions.

Once upon a time she was an ordinary little American girl with knobbly knees and a shy whimsical smile. Now she is a royal princess—a world beauty and personality. How and why did this metamorphosis take place?

For a year I searched. Day after day listening to her family.

Absorbing the atmosphere of the streets of Philadelphia, New York and Los Angeles where once she walked freely.

Sitting long into the night talking to friends. Mingling with the film world who had worked, and played, with her. Consistently probing trusted members of her staff who over the years have observed her in the family life of the palace in Monaco. Sifting the Princess's own elusive and oft-times original thoughts.

As people talked the platitudes and clichés tumbled out. All perfectly true—but no clue. It was not until I sat in the cool luxury of producer John Foreman's house in Beverly Hills that I suddenly knew my quest was over.

It was nearly midnight on a Sunday in June 1974.

Hollywood is a crisp early-to-bed city in contrast to Rome's decadent night hours. In Los Angeles Sunday is a day for barbecueing round the swimming pool, catching up with parental duties and boozing with friends.

By 9 p.m. when the last guests have left in the blue twilight the curtains are drawn. Already the movie-makers' minds are stretched into the hazards of Monday morning. Monday morning's dawn rising. Monday morning's 'shooting' problems. Monday morning's money troubles.

I knew this. I knew it all. Selfishly I sat on sipping wine and fencing with words. At 11.50 p.m., when Foreman's brown beauty and pale blue denims were beginning to crumple, there came a revealing moment.

I almost wept with gratitude. He had given me the key.

Thank you, John Foreman.

There are so many others who have helped in this book. Because it is not an official biography their help was vital. They do not need to stand up and be counted. Their words are there, testimony to the charismatic affection Princess Grace arouses among everyone who meets her.

To the Kelly family, one and all, I am grateful for bringing to life her happy childhood.

I would like especially to thank Madame Nadia Lacoste of the Monaco Palace Press Bureau; Gant Gaither for permitting me to quote from his book *Princess Grace* (Holt) which was written at the time of her marriage; to Peter Hawkins for permission to quote from his authorised biography of Prince Rainier (William Kimber); to the editor of the *Philadelphia Bulletin* for allowing access to their fine library.

But one person stands out beyond everyone. When all doors were closed, all hopes abandoned, all dreams unfulfilled, he alone trusted me.

I owe so much to Vane Ivanovic, the distinguished Consul General for Monaco in London. He never once failed me.

London, New York, Philadelphia,
Los Angeles, Paris, Monaco . . .
Oxfordshire

One

'There is a mystique that surrounds Grace and always has from the beginning. It is the act she put together for survival.'

Producer John Foreman was talking to me late on Sunday night in the intimacy of his den in his home in Beverly Hills, Los Angeles.

'Only Grace could have created Grace Kelly. It must have been a concept in her head. No one else did. No manager, no agent, no producer, not even her family.

'She made up the idea of Grace Kelly and having made it up she was the only one who knew how to make it operate. She can make Grace Kelly do Grace Kelly things that nobody else can do. She did it then and she does it now. She is unique.'

Foreman has known Princess Grace of Monaco since she was a young actress in full rebellion in New York and had watched her survive and conquer the toughest pinnacles in Hollywood by her sheer will-power.

'To have one's act together is the best thing anyone can possibly have in this business of surviving. It means a colouring in personality that you have put on yourself to afford the best protection.

'Grace's act, which has stood her in good stead all these years, is one of the most efficient I have ever seen because it affords her the chance to make friends immediately and have people help her instantly and be glad of the opportunity. She is also absolutely consistent in her behaviour and utterly dependable. For quite a few of us, and for many years, she gave us a perfect place that one can relate to and this is why we admire her so.'

'Having one's act together' is not only a consistency of character but also a combination of knowing your own limitations and never breaking your own code of behaviour at whatever level you have set for yourself. Thus it becomes the essence of good manners since it protects other people from outbursts of emotion.

Princess Caroline was untruthfully quoted in an English magazine article as saying: 'My mother is a nordic beauty. She is very beautiful but this type of beauty can sometimes be rather cold.' To begin with, Princess Caroline has never said this about her mother, whom she admires tremendously. Also nothing is further from the truth as seen through my eyes which have spent a lifetime studying the world's most beautiful women. Her economy of emotion in public is part of her act and her own personal way of never embarrassing anyone; of keeping the situation within an enclave that she can control. Her golden colouring is never cold.

In private she is warm, out-giving, conscientiously thoughtful and loves to giggle. Few of her staff or friends have ever seen her visibly angry. 'I go away to be horrible by myself,' she says.

As a child it was called 'the sulks'. Now it is more likely to be described as 'one of her moods' which everyone around her is fully aware of—and respects.

This then is the clue to the character of Princess Grace. It began when as a child, with a maturity far beyond her years, she conscientiously set a pattern for the life-style that she intended to follow—and from which she has never deviated.

It was coincidental, but also brilliant timing, that she arrived in Hollywood at a period when many life-styles were going through an untidy period.

It was the era of Ava Gardner, Elizabeth Taylor and Marilyn Monroe. With courage and abandon their lives spilled over daily into the gossip columns and left them pathetically vulnerable.

Marilyn had her act together on one level. She knew how to exploit the sexuality act better than anyone before or after her. But as a human being her life was a mess. So many days were wasted simply because she was unable to cope with even the smallest problems of living. She was totally incapable of any kind of administration in her own life and personal affairs.

If you walked into a room to meet her you never knew what to expect. She was slovenly, sloppy, dirty, disagreeable, funny, bewitching, sensuous, beautiful, enchanting. She was so inconsistent that her friends found it unnerving because they never knew where they stood.

Grace Kelly could, and still can, always be counted on for an optimistic, enthusiastic and humorous reaction to the circumstances she finds herself in.

Elizabeth Taylor had her professional act together as no one else since Garbo. She knew her acting capabilities and within those boundaries kept strictly to her limitations. It has made her a very rich woman, but it has not ensured a smooth marital path.

Ava Gardner did not care. Once she had the Hollywood situation summed up she used it like a piece of lingerie and threw it away when the lace began to fray at the ends.

With Grace Kelly it was different. She alone created her public and private image, maintained it and has never tarnished it by a word or gesture. Her consistency and professionalism of temperament made her if not the most gifted film actress in Hollywood, at least the most respected.

She not only chose the most difficult career, the most competitive and the most heart-breaking, but she climbed to the top in Hollywood strictly on her own terms. She never conceded—it was a gamble that paid off.

Grace Kelly deliberately left behind the security of a wealthy family life in Philadelphia, scorned financial help from her parents and, with only her act to protect her, in five brief years left an indelible mark on Hollywood history.

There were other girls just as pretty—she had not yet acquired real beauty—just as talented, just as hard working. Why did she succeed where others failed?

Why was she also mentally, physically and emotionally able to slip into the role of royal princess in one of the oldest, and one of the most difficult, ruling houses in Europe without any outward signs of stress?

One comes back to this key—this act—that never lets her down, plus her own resilient toughness.

Though both would deny it, Princess Grace and Queen Elizabeth II of England have much in common. Outwardly they are reserved, shy, sincere and lonely to a point of almost being misunderstood on certain occasions. But privately, within their own chosen world, they are fun, sensitive, quick-tongued and can be wildly funny.

Both, too, have accomplished the almost impossible task of being full-time royal personages as well as involved mothers concerned with every aspect of family life. Each in her own way, too, is a perfectionist although the Queen's canvas is broader and her personal interests less feminine than Princess Grace's.

Their main difference is that the Queen is a dedicated country woman and all her real interests revolve round rural living while Princess Grace is a fringe country girl enjoying the theatre, ballet, film and art worlds and the people of metropolis living.

Princess Grace, who is now forty-five years of age, has not made a film in twenty years, but her impact does not diminish. She still keeps up with all the American picture news through trade magazines and is still regularly sent scripts which she reads avidly. If she were to break her self-imposed vow not to act in commercial films again she could still command the highest financial deal of any film star alive today.

As John Foreman explained: 'The producer who could go to the studio or bank with a commitment for her to appear in a film would get immediate finance. There is not one actor in the business, from Marlon Brando to Paul Newman, who would not be enchanted to work with her.'

For twenty years after her retirement Garbo remained the in-cult among her fans but to the young people of today she would rate little more than as an interesting curiosity. With Princess Grace it is different. Her glamour is still gleaming bright.

The four great women stars created since the last war—and they may well be the last of the 'greats'—were Grace Kelly, Marilyn Monroe, Elizabeth Taylor and Sophia Loren.

Oddly enough, Grace Kelly and Marilyn Monroe never met although they were a stone's throw apart on at least two occasions. Once they were both on the same plane flying from New York to Los Angeles.

While Marilyn was being given the star treatment in a sleeping compartment up-forward in the plane, Grace sat up through the night in the economy class reading a book. It was the kind of scoop that every Hollywood reporter would have given his eye teeth to get. It also proves the truth in what Grace Kelly used to say about herself: 'When Ava Gardner gets into a cab the driver knows straight away that she's Ava Gardner. I'm sure it's the same with Marilyn Monroe and Elizabeth Taylor. But not me. I'm never Grace Kelly. I'm always somebody who looks like Grace Kelly.'

In New York when her engagement to Prince Rainier had been

announced, and they were both appearing in public for the first time at the dazzling Monte Carlo gala ball, Marilyn was a block away at Madison Square Gardens—riding a pink elephant in the Barnum Bailey Circus.

Next morning the New York newspapers had double headlines recording the event.

It is strange, too, that both Grace Kelly and Marilyn Monroe appeared as story-book princesses in movies. Grace in *The Swan* with Alec Guinness, and Marilyn in *The Sleeping Prince* which was to be renamed *The Prince and the Showgirl* in America.

The difference was that Grace married a real live prince and now lives in a palace and Marilyn died a mysterious, lonely death in a rented nondescript house in Los Angeles.

Grace had her act together . . .

The marriage of Prince Rainier of Monaco to Grace Kelly, the golden girl of America, hit a tired, disillusioned world like a galaxy of stars. No one disputed the Prince's urgent need to find a bride and bear an heir to the throne of Monaco. No one debated that an injection of healthy American blood was not a desirable addition to the house of Grimaldi. But the undeniable and sheer creditability of this romance between the dashing prince and beautiful girl made a sugar-spun fairy-story come to life.

It is what every little girl dreams of when she sits alone in her own private world. For Grace Kelly who used to beg her older sister Peggy, 'Please let me be the princess' when they played 'let's pretend' games, it was a dream come true.

What makes Princess Grace into the remarkable woman she is, is her ability to have transcended the sugar line and made herself a unique niche as a world figure. And this she has done as few, if any, other women could have bettered.

The esteem she commands in Monaco is remarkable. The fact that she is always referred to by Monegasques as 'Our Princess' is understandable after twenty years, but so deep is their love and respect for her that they totally resent anyone who knocks her image. Any criticism of the Princess immediately becomes a personal insult to the citizens of Monaco.

When *Time* magazine last year wrote a professionally slick article on Princess Caroline called 'The Super Kid from Monaco', which also included some snide remarks about Princess Grace, it was the talk of Monaco.

'How could they do this to our Princess—and her own country people too?' they questioned me.

Princess Grace also brought to Monaco a profound sense of responsibility. It is part of her act. The Monegasques found in her a sincere person who was prepared to give even more than what she was to get in return for her royal status. This they had not expected.

'She brought us life. The whole place changed from the moment she arrived. Her ideas were fresh and charming. For instance, she arranged that every Monegasque mother who gives birth to a baby is sent a medal commemorating the event. Her daily personal interest in running the Red Cross as its president is astonishing and even when she is abroad she is in constant contact making decisions by telephone. A day nursery for the children of working mothers, help for the old, our wonderful International Flower Show, the crafts centres, the formation of the International Arts Festival, to which top artists from all over the world are invited, are all due to the Princess.'

Behind the scenes she is full of unobtrusive acts of kindness.

Being a Princess of Monaco is also a form of role playing and because of her strict personal discipline as an actress these are the roots which make her present royal situation tenable, habitable and livable. She is doing another job only this time with the help of a loving husband, Prince Rainier.

Princess Grace has also brought Monte Carlo glamour. She spares no efforts to dress up for the galas and be seen on every possible occasion. Despite being such a private person she considers this all part of her job, and when at all possible likes to be accompanied by the Prince and her children.

The Grimaldis are a family in every sense of the word.

Princess Grace does not have an easy self-assurance but what she has acquired over the last twenty years is a deep well of defensiveness on which she draws when the need is there.

At forty-five years of age Princess Grace is probably more beautiful than at any time of her life. Her bone structure is inherited, but knowing her responsibility she works hard at keeping herself at the pinnacle of health and form.

She looks about ten pounds heavier than when she married and if she gains a pound or so is distraught and immediately goes on a diet.

'Whenever I gain weight people always think I am pregnant. Then I know it is time to diet again. I don't know whether it is a compliment or not, but when I read how many times the Continental Press wrote that Queen Elizabeth was pregnant I manage to take it light-heartedly as I am sure she does.'

Her skin is flawless without a trace of lines and the eyes clear blue and frank. The Hollywood highlights have disappeared from her hair, which is now a soft butter-scotch. No photograph does her beauty justice.

As the searing fierce sun of Monaco upsets her she tends to wear dark sun-glasses in the summer or floppy straw hats.

Walking through the streets of Monaco to the hairdresser Alexandre or her favourite *patisserie*, as she frequently does, the Monegasques allow her the privacy she craves and only recognise her if she stops to speak to them.

In Paris she is always recognised and has a special quick-step technique. The second she sees a crowd gathering she quickens her walk, rushing from one counter to another where her own assistants help her quickly. She is in and out of the shop before there is time for real chaos. Hovering discreetly in the background she is always watched by a family chauffeur who behaves towards her like a faithful nanny.

She has a hatred of crowds and like many women forced to live much of their lives in public suffers from claustrophobia. She has developed a routine whereby people are not allowed to come too near her. She is mindful of the time early in her marriage when people tried to snatch a button from her coat, or worse when she was expecting Caroline and a woman rushed forward to lay her hands on the Princess's body 'for good luck'.

What she dislikes intensely are the paparazzi who flood in from Italy and pester the family wherever they go.

She enjoys the anonymity of shopping in London, where she says the people have 'such good manners'. In New York she has comparative freedom and spends hours in her favourite shop, Bloomingdales.

I spoke with a taxi driver in Monaco as we drove up the winding road to the palace. Perhaps he above all summed up the feelings of the Monegasques about their American Princess.

'Is good princess,' he said. 'The first year we did not know if Hollywood princess or real princess. Now we know she is real princess.

'But she is more than that. She is good mother and she lives her religion. That is more important than being princess. We all family people and we know she has to be in Paris to be with daughter Caroline and visit her mother in America. But it is not the same when she not here.

'Princess Grace belongs to us and we belong to her.'

Two

Much of the tensile strength and moral fibre that we see in Princess Grace today goes back to her early forebears. On both sides of her family she comes from energetic, rugged and resolute stock.

On her father's side there are the Kellys, who brought to America not only the vivid, handsome looks of Ireland but a splendid capacity for hard work.

Grandfather John Henry Kelly, a twenty-year-old County Mayo farm-boy, sailed across the Atlantic on the *City of Boston* in 1867 to a new life in America. Soon after his arrival he caught the eye of seventeen-year-old Mary Costello, also from County Mayo, who had been sent to America to live with her grandmother and aunt at Rutland, Vermont, when she was only eight years old. They married.

Mary Costello Kelly matured into a woman of strong principles, a strict belief in the principles of the Roman Catholic Church and an invincible Irish tongue. To the ten strapping children she bore she was always known as 'The Dowager'.

Soon after the birth of her first child, named John, who died at the age of ten with sunstroke, they moved from Rutland to Mineville in New York State, later to Vermont and finally to Philadelphia, where the family settled down for the next hundred years. Mr John B. Kelly, the Princess's father was named after his late uncle, who died before he was born.

Although John Henry Kelly began his married life as a labourer, a job that his magnificent body could easily cope with, he went on to build a flourishing insurance business.

But it is Mary Kelly's blood in Princess Graces's veins, and her fierce family loyalty, that is deeply etched in the royal family life in Monaco today.

When a neighbour once asked Mrs Kelly: 'Do you have more love for your sons or your daughters?' Mary Costello Kelly puffed up like an outraged pigeon.

'That's no question to put to a mother,' she replied. 'But since you have asked I will tell you the truth. There's a great pride in the love I have for my sons, God bless them. But there's a special tenderness and understanding in my heart for my girls.'

It could have been Princess Grace speaking today.

In his book *That Kelly Family* (A. S. Barnes and Company) John McCallum quotes Mary Kelly as saying:

'The trouble is that in most families the mother is afraid of her children. I have never stood in fear of mine even though I would have given my heart's blood for them. They are the whole world to me. But I've never been afraid of them. Why should I be? For their own good they must be taught to respect me as their superior. Not that I demand their respect just because I happen to be their mother. You can demand a *show* of respect, as long as you are the stronger. But the thing itself must be *earned*. I will never stop trying to earn the respect of my children.'

Just a hundred years later her granddaughter Princess Grace of Monaco was to tell English journalist Dennis Holman: 'Handling a child you love is based on instinct, on your own upbringing and on the up-bringing of others you have known.

'You just try to do your best.

'There are no rules except to help your children to realise that you are not perfect and that you, too, can make mistakes. Let them see your weaknesses so that they realise that you are human and forgive you.

'All of us when we are young think our parents are perfect. It is better that, as we grow older, we do not get a rude awakening.'

Though Mary Kelly disliked personal publicity, in 1924 the *American Magazine* chose her to write an article titled: 'Oh, There Ought to be a Million Mothers Like Mary Kelly'. And of Princess Grace in 1974 *New Reveille* wrote 'No One Rules this Royal Roost!'

The spirit is the same.

Of Mary and John Henry Kelly's family one daughter Grace, an actress and after whom Princess Grace is named, was to die of a heart attack at a skating party when she was only twenty. Four of their six sons were to become celebrated figures each in his own right.

Patrick Henry, the eldest, became a leading figure in the construction business and made his mark as a polished after-dinner speaker.

The second oldest in the family, Walter, became known in England and in America as *The Virginia Judge* due to his original vaudeville act.

Princess Grace was only nine years old when Walter Kelly died, but such was his fame that the whole Kelly family were brought up on anecdotes about Uncle Walter.

Uncle Walter was considered one of the funniest men in America. He could tell a story in such a way that he had his audience in stitches.

His celebrated act *The Virginia Judge* was created from a chance visit to the Newport News police court where he sat enthralled as Judge Dudley Brown, a serious looking Virginian, dispensed justice with a whimsical blend of homespun philosophy and humour. Walter was so entranced with the hilarious repartee that went on between Judge Brown and 'the accused', often Negroes, that he spent the next days in court jotting down notes. From this then was born the act that was to bring him fame throughout America, Australia and England.

Walter's turning-point in his career was the night he substituted for Marie Dressler on Broadway. He had been engaged to act with this great comedienne in a musical production but on the opening night she was ill with an acute attack of laryngitis.

Just a quarter of an hour before the curtain went up the producer Percy Williams grabbed Walter and said that he had to go out in front of the curtain and do his *The Virginian* act.

The management offered the customers their money back or suggested that they stay and see 'the brilliant new comedian Walter Kelly'. Most of them remained in their seats and that night as he went into his patter and brought to life all the warm-hearted characters of the Newport News Court history was being made on Broadway and Walter Kelly became a star overnight.

Walter first brought his act to London in 1908, the year the Olympic Games were staged in England. Highlight of his whole trip was the afternoon when the Olympic Marathon was run and Walter Kelly was invited to see it in a box in the company of those two great sportsmen, Lord Dewar and Sir Thomas Lipton.

Some of Walter Kelly's gift for patter has rubbed off on his niece.

Princess Grace has a keen ear for dialect and can give an impromptu performance with superb mimicry of any event that amuses her. She also has that rare gift of being able to repeat almost verbatim any conversation that she has heard recently. Learning lines as an actress was never any problem to her.

Perhaps the uncle who was to influence the young actress Grace Kelly most of all was George. Along with all the sons of Mary Costello Kelly, George had a body of steel. Before the 1914-18 war he worked in an iron works but his heart was on the stage. After the war he stuck out his job for three months while he took a night course in acting.

From then it was just a step to behind the footlights. But it is not as an actor that America remembers George Kelly today but as a playwright of considerable talent. From writing his own vaudeville sketches he developed into full-length plays. His first, *The Torchbearers*, in which young Grace Kelly was years later to give a pleasing performance at Bucks County Playhouse, was an instant Broadway hit. This was followed by even greater successes—*The Show Off* and *Craig's Wife* which won the Pulitzer Prize.

All George Kelly's plays were inspired by everyday neighbours in The Falls and their appeal was that every small community in America could identify with his characters.

When *The Show Off* opened on Broadway the whole Kelly clan arrived in New York from East Falls. There was Jack Henry Kelly, mother Mary Kelly, Walter, Mary, Ann, Elizabeth, Jack and his new girl friend Margaret Majer.

It was a tradition that Jack and Margaret Kelly were to continue whenever their own daughter Grace had an opening night.

George Kelly made his home in California for many years and whenever she had time Grace Kelly used to enjoy hours sitting with this grand old gentleman listening to his advice, not only as a playwright but also as a human being.

During the preparation of this book I had hoped to speak with George Kelly. He was by then old and frail and had gone back to Philadelphia to be with his own folk. On the day we were to meet he was not well but took great pains to send me this message:

'I am so proud of my niece Grace. She was not only a very fine actress but is a human being with considerable qualities. Had she stayed on the stage and continued her career I think we would have seen some very fine performances from her.'

He was to die a few weeks later.

Jack Kelly, so good looking that President Roosevelt was to say he was the most handsome man he had ever seen and who was once invited to Hollywood to take a screen test, made several names for himself—in business, sport and politics.

As a young boy he worked for his brother Patrick carrying hods in his brick-contracting business. In the evenings he spent his time on the Schuylkill where he became so proficient at sculling that he ended by winning the Olympics. His rejection at Britain's Henley Regatta on the grounds that, as a former labourer, he was not a gentleman made sporting history.

When Philadelphia's democratic party was reviving in 1935 John B. Kelly ran for Mayor. He lost by 47,000 votes and never ran for office again, but he always retained an interest in politics.

John B. Kelly was twenty-three when he first clapped eyes on a pretty blonde, blue-eyed schoolgirl, Margaret Majer, at the Philadelphia Turngemeinde Athletic and Social Club. He came from the East Falls section and she was Strawberry Manson. Neither took each other very seriously but Jack sometimes picked Margaret up from school or the club and walked her home. She told him that she intended to enrol at Temple University and study physical education and he confided in his ambitions to become an international sculler. But it was not until after Jack returned from serving with the U.S. Army during the 1914-18 war that their courtship began in earnest.

In 1924, nine years after they had first met, Margaret Majer and John B. Kelly were married at St Bridget's Church and the whole of the Falls of Schuylkill turned out for the event. By then Margaret had become a magazine cover girl as well as gaining a degree in physical education. She had just been signed up with the University of Pennsylvania as the first woman physical education instructor of co-eds.

Today Margaret Kelly is a remarkably pretty seventy-seven-year-old. She has the looks and energy of a woman twenty years younger and keeps her hair slightly more golden than her daughter's. The eyes are still china blue and the skin as delicate as an apricot. Princess Grace has inherited her mother's clear-cut bones which come from the Majers' Teutonic background.

During the summer when she moves to the old family house at Ocean Beach, 'Ma Kelly', as everyone still calls her, rises with the sun, swims every morning and keeps fit by daily jogging along the beach.

Mrs Kelly had just returned from a visit to Monaco when I met her.

She was sitting in her luxurious Germantown apartment in Philadelphia surrounded by flowers and much prettiness. We talked about Princess Grace:

'If I did give my daughter anything it is very hard to say what it was, you know. I think perhaps discipline played an important part. I had a good stiff German background. My parents believed in discipline and so do I . . . no tyranny or anything like that but a certain firmness.

'Grace was so timid as a child that she was reluctant to go downtown by herself. She would say to me, "Mommy, please come with me. I am afraid to go. I don't know anybody."

'I think she is still a bit timid but now she goes out and gets things done—mostly by an act of will. She is very determined. I'm terribly proud of her, you know.'

To understand the environment of the Kelly family it is necessary to know about Philadelphia itself. Princess Grace does not, as popularly believed, come from an old Philadelphia Main Line family, like the Biddles or the Stotesburys or Cadwalladers. Nor do the Kellys rate in the social structure like that other great family. The Kennedys are a clan. The Kellys are a family.

The affluent families of the eastern seaboard towns of America are largely descended from the first English settlers, and to this day there remains a well-defined inbuilt class system.

They consider themselves to be better than the rest of America not only because of birthright but because of their own splendidly isolated culture. In the hierarchy Bostonians place themselves above the rest, but the Charleston, Baltimore, Philadelphian and New Orleans families will not accept this and any family who can trace its ancestry in the United States for 200 years is aristocracy indeed.

Pennsylvania was founded by that eccentric Quaker aristocrat William Penn in 1682 and his influence is still felt today. Though Philadelphia had in fact a Catholic population way back in the eighteenth century it is still in the minority. Boston did not have its Catholic community until the nineteenth century.

In discussing the anomalies of the Philadelphian social structure with Professor E. Digby Baltzell of the University of Pennyslvania, and one of America's foremost sociologists of the upper classes, he told me:

'The Kennedys have far more ability since that came from a culture that stressed the intellect, stressed leadership, stressed dominance. For all his ability you did not feel that Jack Kelly had any dominance here in Philadelphia.

'I think he could very well have been a great political leader in the City if he had come from Boston—but he did not. I think by the same token only a Philadelphian would have given up a top career in the movies to become the wife of a minor royalty in Europe. I could not visualise a Kennedy doing this.'

Although the Kellys are about as conspicuous in Philadelphia as the 30th Street Station, the difference between them and the Kennedys is that the Kellys are a great athletic family whereas the Kennedys gained their status in politics.

It is interesting to note that in Professor Baltzell's scholarly book *The Philadelphia Gentlemen—The Making of a National Upper Class*, though hundreds of families are mentioned by name, there is no entry about the Kellys who have given so much to the city of Philadelphia.

The Philadelphia Social Register is itself also a feudal phenomenon in which the name of Kelly does not appear. It has certain basic filters through which names have to pass and one of them is against anyone who is not essentially white Anglo-Saxon and therefore Protestant.

The Kellys were originally Irish immigrant and the stigma remains to this day.

One of the strangest anachronisms is the Assembly Ball that Philadelphians have been going to since Washington attended it. As it is an historical institution it is therefore mostly Episcopalian and Protestant and is not related to Catholicism, which in Philadelphia is not so much a religion but is based on ethnicism and race.

For all their beauty, good manners and intelligence, the Kelly girls never attended the Assembly Ball. The only way they could have been invited was to have married into one of the founding families, or to have taken up residence in another county when they could have received an out-of-town invitation for one year.

Grace Kelly would have undoubtedly been invited had she married an early beau, Bill Crozier, which many people had predicted. He came from one of the socially acceptable families. It is birthright and breeding, not money, that counts in the old families of Philadelphia.

Equally curious is the fact that one does not mention being on the Assembly list as it is tantamount to announcing your rank in a country of hereditary titles.

All this may have been important to the Kelly family twenty-five years ago, but knowing their disdain of snobbism I doubt it.

John B. Kelly's dream was to celebrate the 200th anniversary of the founding of Philadelphia by bringing the Olympics to his doorstep. Margaret Kelly has carved her name in pure gold in the city by her incalculable contribution to Women's Medical.

This then is the background to John B. Kelly's remark after the announcement of the engagement of his daughter Grace to Prince Rainier of Monaco: 'I told the Prince that royalty didn't mean a thing to us. I told him that I certainly hoped that he wouldn't run around the way some princes do, and I told him that if he did, he'd lose a mighty fine girl.'

Three

Grace Patricia Kelly was a puny little girl. From early babyhood she was susceptible to colds, had sinus trouble and was constantly troubled with asthma. She was in fact sickly a great deal of her babyhood and because of the asthma spoke in a whiney voice which did not leave her until she took speech-training lessons. Today her voice is low and gentle with transatlantic overtones.

There were many days at the family's fifteen-roomed brick house in Henry Avenue, Germantown, when Grace had to be kept in bed while her rumbustious brothers and sisters were allowed out to play. If she minded, she never showed it.

'We all knew from the beginning that there was something special about Grace,' her mother, Mrs John B. Kelly, told me. 'She was a shy child but there was a kind of inner tranquillity and quiet resourcefulness. She never minded being kept in bed and would sit there with her dolls for hours on end. When you passed near you could hear her talking very quietly to them. She was making up little plays for the dolls. Grace could change her voice for each doll, giving it a different character. Yes, she was a very patient and calm child. She loved attention but did not cry if she didn't get it.'

All the Kelly girls loved dolls and each amassed a large 'family' during their girlhood.

'Grace loved her dolls,' recalled Mrs Kelly, 'but somehow managed to play with Peggy's and Lizanne's and keep her own in brand-new condition—she just did not want to dirty them.'

Lizanne was not only the challenger but the holy terror of the family. To tease her bigger sister she used to steal Grace's family of dolls until Peggy intervened. Once in a fit of temper she locked Grace in a closet and went off to play. It was not until some time later that Mrs Kelly became suspicious about Grace's disappearance and looked in the cupboards. There she found her completely happy. She had found some dolls in the cupboard and was quietly playing 'mother-and-baby'.

From those early days Grace was always a squirrel and hoarded everything that made up her personal life—letters, badges, programmes, snapshots and even old clothes. These traits remain with her today and she still wears clothes that she had, including one much-loved skirt, before her marriage twenty years ago.

One of the favourite family stories about Grace is that when she wanted to stay away from school she would solemnly announce the fact at breakfast. She then sat back and waited for the family to talk her out of it. The point being that she did not really want to skip school.

Neighbours in Germantown remember Grace as an ordinary American child with knobbly knees, skinny legs, a shining smile but less pretty than her two sisters, Peggy and Lizanne. There was certainly none of the true beauty that was to show in her face in later years and make her today one of the most arresting women in the world. It was a round little face with plump cheeks, calm lollipop-sized eyes and straight, ash blonde, silky hair pulled starkly to the side, as was the fashion at the time, and held with a big ribbon bow.

The Kelly home was an exceptionally agreeable atmosphere in which to bring up children. There was sufficient money to give the children the security they needed, but much more than that Margaret and Jack Kelly were passionately involved and active parents and although kind and concerned they did not fuss their children. Each child was allowed to develop naturally like maple saplings in the forest.

Indeed, if there were any marital differences in the Kelly family—and Jack was quite a lad—they were never aired publicly. Above all it was a united and wholesome Catholic family. They were also a family of 'Beautiful People', long before the jet set discovered and mutilated the phrase. They had the same healthy charisma of the Kennedys but none of the built-in arrogance nurtured in Boston. In later years the two families were often to be compared but they are as unalike as *bœuf tartare* is to the wholesome hamburger.

The Kelly back garden was always filled with the sounds of children —their own and all their friends east of the Schuylkill River. The back yard had a family vegetable plot which all the children worked in during the war years, a swing, sandbox, tennis court, walk-in dolls' house, boys' den, plenty of bats, rackets, glasses of milk, cookies and fruit. It was in the days before the ubiquitous swimming pool.

Mrs Kelly was always known even to the children as 'Ma Kelly'. The Kelly family world was not made up of blacks, yellows or whites; it was made up of human beings and all children were welcome.

It was a lesson so indelibly printed in the Kelly children's minds that fifteen years later when an American television crew moved into the Principality of Monaco, Princess Grace never hesitated and reacted true to the family standard. There was a scene using the children of friends and members of the staff. The director noticed three little black children, the family of one of the palace staff, who had intermingled with the others playing on the slides. Someone immediately went over to Princess Grace and explained:

'Your Serene Highness, the film is to be shown in the South and it won't do to have black children playing with white children. At least while we are filming we don't want them there.'

'We do,' Princess Grace answered, and there were no more complications.

Sister Peggy, now Mrs Conlan, lives in a luxurious house in an undistinguished part of Philadelphia called Aspen Street. Her front door is constantly receiving small knocks and I have watched an endless stream of children—black, brown, ochre, pink, white—solemnly hand her a treasure they have found or sit on the floor beside her telling of their innermost secrets.

Keeping a kindly eye on the Kellys' back yard in Germantown was Godfrey Ford—'Fordie' to all the children. 'Fordie', who was black, was hired as a handyman in the Kelly house, but by his sheer force of personality he became almost part of the family. He was part-time parent, nursemaid, father confessor, referee, chauffeur and the complete confidant. His daughter Ethel shared all the Kelly children's playhours.

When Grace Kelly became a famous film actress 'Fordie' obliged with his reminiscences of her to *Newsweek* magazine.

'Every Thursday night when the nurse was off I used to put the kiddies to bed. Before bedtime Gracie used to ask my opinions. I'd tell her what I thought, and she'd usually follow my advice. She still consults me on a lot of important things.'

It was 'Fordie' who taught Grace to drive in front of the house. Chuckling with delight, he loved to tell how she finally got her licence 'but she was never any good at parking'. Even today Princess Grace hates to drive a car, and just as 'Fordie' said is not very skilled at parking!

When Grace Kelly married the handsome Prince of Monaco and became a part of the royal household of Europe no one was less surprised than 'Fordie'. His girls were only fit to be princesses.

'Fordie's' other proudest boast was driving President Roosevelt when he came to Pennsylvania during the Democratic campaign in which Mr Kelly was involved.

When Godfrey F. Ford finally 'passed over to the other side' in 1968 he went to the sound of glory. 'Fordie' looked extremely well lying in his satin-lined casket, his chest emblazoned with a magnificent wide ribbon to which was attached a huge gold medal. On his face was the smile of one who was out to meet his Lord knowing that down here on earth he had done his best. Angels in white robes with drawn swords embellished the ends of the casket. There were four preachers and many of the ladies in the choir had bought new wigs for the occasion. Place of honour in the church was given to the Kelly family and a magnificent wreath from 'Grace and Rainier de Monaco'. There was singing and parading and the whole church was filled with joy. How 'Fordie' would have loved it.

The girls had a large dolls' house in the Kelly back yard where they held court and the boys had a kind of den at the bottom of the garden. This was to become headquarters of the 'Tomato Men' who were to play a significant part in Grace's childhood. They were a bunch of brother 'Kell's' friends who took their gang-name from the fact that a large patch of the garden was given over to the growing of tomatoes for the family's daily use and home preserving. As some boys today use snowballs, bicycle chains, or even knives, the Tomato Men used tomatoes.

Opposite the Kelly house lived Howard Wikoff, who formed his own band called the Potato Men. When the rival gangs came into combat, small sisters were apt to get in the way. On one such occasion Gracie caught a tomato right between her eyes. In an instant this tiny waif turned into a fighting shrew and went straight in, slamming the boy who had fired it. Only the swift action of 'Fordie' saved a first-class fist fight.

When 'Kell' decided to turn the shed at the bottom of the garden into the headquarters of 'The Tomato Men' it was Peggy who immediately retaliated by pinning a notice on the outside of the dolls' house 'No Boys Allowed'.

It was 'Ma Kelly' herself who was responsible for the breaking up of the Tomato Men. One morning she went out into the garden to find a sizzling fight in action between the boys and the girls. They had all raided the tomato patch and with armfuls of tomatoes were pelting each other. Their faces and clothes were stained with red tomato juice and the garden bare. 'Ma Kelly' roared into action and read the riot act. The Tomato Men were no more.

Both Mr and Mrs Kelly were keenly interested and knowledgeable about building healthy bodies. Jack had gained his experience during his rowing days and Margaret Kelly during her period as women's physical education instructor at the University of Pennyslvania. Apart from advocating plenty of sun, fresh air and exercise as a means of keeping fit, they kept a sharp eye on the children's diet.

Mrs Kelly worried most over 'little Gracie' and there were special conspiracies to build her up. As Mr Kelly was often out for dinner, Mrs Kelly took over the family carving knife which she did even when he was home. Today Jack ('Kell') Kelly remembers vividly how his mother meticulously saved the bloody juice from the roast for Grace, a favouritism that he resented bitterly at the time. Grace was made to dunk her bread in it and was not always appreciative of its nourishing qualities. Another of Mrs Kelly's ruses to get Grace to eat up her bread and butter was to sprinkle it with white sugar.

In a household of such noisy extroverts Grace could have been stifled. That she was not is entirely due to her inborn tenacity and inner toughness. Years later she was to say to a group of fellow actors:

'Sometimes I have to wait a long time for things I want very much. I don't always get them, but something inside won't let me give up easily.'

These were no new thoughts. They were formed right back in those childhood days and she never wavered from them. Whatever she lacked in physical prowess Grace made up for in her imagination. She lived in her own dream world and peopled it with her own creations. Reality and fantasy were totally interchangeable.

As her husband was frequently away from home attending to his business or civic work Mrs Kelly was the mainstay of the family life. With her strict German upbringing she had a healthy respect for old-fashioned virtues and was determined that her children should be brought up with a social conscience and concern for others less fortunate than themselves. Today these principles are so much a part of Princess Grace that she in turn is now passing them on to her own children.

Religion has always figured prominently in the Kelly family life and before each meal the children were always asked to say grace. To this day all the children remember their mother's homespun grace said before each meal.

Peggy Bless us, Oh Lord, and these thy gifts we are about to receive from thy bounty through Christ our Lord.

'*Kell*' Do unto others as you would have others do unto you.

Grace Politeness is to do and say the kindest things in the kindest way.

Baby Lizanne Amen.

The family food was always nourishing and wholesome and the children were not allowed to leave the table until their plates were cleaned. They were constantly reminded of less fortunate children in the world— 'the starving Indians, the poor little black children in the South and the millions of Chinese orphans'.

Grace was the slowest and most fastidious eater of the children. There were those awful red cabbage days when her small face became sad and her mouth turned down. How she suffered. The family still remember the night she would not eat the nasty, grey, nourishing calves' liver, packed with its beastly minerals. Her anguish was immense as her mother made her sit for two hours at the dinner table as punishment.

Although the household always had domestic help the girls were made to keep their rooms tidy and make their own beds. If they failed to hang up their clothes they were fined a nickel from their twenty-five cents a week pocket money.

All the children had their own jobs to do and the girls were trained to be proper housewives. There was nothing sentimental about this operation. It was merely that Mrs Kelly had not found anything better to replace the same discipline and values that she was given as a child which had been handed down from her German antecedents.

During the long summer holidays the girls were taught to cook, sew, knit and crochet. While Peggy and Lizanne both loved to cook, Grace preferred knitting, but one of her specialities was making the good

German dish of curly cabbage and pork. She also knew the secret magic in how to make a white sauce 'real creamy'.

Those childhood habits persist today and in the library of the orange fairytale palace at Monaco or at the family *Mas* at Mont Agel, just above the hill-top in France, Princess Grace always has close at hand some knitting or embroidery on which she is working. Her greatest triumph was an embroidered waistcoat for Prince Rainier—a romantic flower design made in colourful *petit point*. Princess Grace always maintained that she would 'finish the vest in Heaven'. In fact, it only took her two years. When the family is alone in Paris or at their weekend house she often does the cooking. Her large collection of cookbooks go back to those early days of her first flat in New York and include not only traditional French and American books but Mexican, Chinese and Indian recipes.

The Kelly children's life was healthy and vigorous. Day dreaming and idleness were not encouraged. Saturday was a family day when Margaret and Jack Kelly took over the physical development of their children. In the winter the whole family used to go to the Penn Athletic Club at Rittenhouse Square where the Kelly seniors were active members. The children spent the morning taking athletic or swimming instruction which was followed by a 'treat' lunch. After this they usually all went to the movies or a circus if one was in town.

Once the whole family were invited to have lunch with the performers in their tents. While they goggled at the sight of bearded ladies and midgets and bare-thighed trapeze artists the least concerned was little Gracie. Later when the family asked her wasn't she impressed, she just shrugged her shoulders and gave away nothing. 'That's show business,' is all she said.

Although she did not have the stamina of her more athletic sisters, Grace put on a brave face keeping up with them.

During the summer months all the family went to the coast, where they had a summer house at Ocean City, New Jersey, and still do to this day. Ocean City, just below Atlantic City, where the respectable Philadelphian families brought their children, is just a great wide un-snobbish stretch of beach with a small footpath. The houses are sprawling, unpretentious and splendidly child-proof and the good-neighbour spirit flows from house to house.

To all the children at Ocean City Jack Kelly was a hero. Wasn't he the super man who brought the first surfboard back from Hawaii? Although the waves were not so dashing as those in Hawaii Jack Kelly used to perch Peggy and Grace on the board and coax them to ride in on the surf.

'Baby you sit right there and take whatever comes your way,' he would say to little Grace. 'There is nothing to be afraid of.'

And because his children felt that he was strong and totally reliable Big John instilled complete freedom from fear in all his children which has remained with them all through their lives. It is a kind of independence of spirit that only consistently loving parents can transfer into their children.

There were also acrobatics on the beach with Jack Kelly swinging little Grace round and round holding her firmly by the ankle and arm. Again, if she was afraid she never showed it. She knew that Jack Kelly would never let a child of his down, physically or mentally.

On family outings by boat in Atlantic City the Kelly clan often used to pass a nudist camp. 'Ma Kelly' was having none of that nonsense and used to order the children to the other side of the boat.

'And there we were on the other side of the boat . . . with binoculars', Grace Kelly recalled.

Early in their lives the Kelly sisters were made aware of the Women's Medical College. It was to haunt them throughout their teenage life and became one of Mrs Kelly's lifetime crusades. Raising funds for 'Women's Medical' was as normal to the Kelly children as Sunday Mass at St Bridget's Church. It was something they expected and accepted.

Peggy had her own personal schemes for raising funds. One of her favourites was to set up a flower stall at the front gate and inveigle passers-by to buy a bunch of flowers.

'When we didn't have enough of our own, I would tell my little sister Gracie to go and steal the flowers next door. She was very clever at it and would secretly pick bunches of violets in neighbours' gardens and sell them right back to them. I don't remember that we were ever found out once.'

Grace was particularly good at selling and few could resist her large innocent eyes and beguiling smile that lit up her whole face much as it can do today when she is happy.

To this day people in Germantown talk of the day the Kelly family put on a circus to raise funds for Women's Medical. Peggy was ten, 'Kell' just eight, Grace six and Lizanne a toddler. The tennis court was transformed into a circus arena and neighbours like the Levys were 'pressurised' into paying generously for the tickets.

'But we raised 250 dollars and were extremely proud of Gracie that day,' says Peggy.

Of course, everything was improvised and someone even made a movie of the day. Peggy was an authoritative, if somewhat bossy, circus master. 'Kell' did a strong man act, but it was 'Little Gracie' in a white tu-tu who stole the show. She was the tight-rope walker. It did not matter to anyone that in fact the 'rope' was a line drawn on the ground. With all the aplomb of an Olga Korbut she balanced her way along the 'rope', steadied, did a neat pirouette turn and tripped back.

The clapping was like music in her small ears.

When she was just eight years of age she was taken with her friend Alice Waters to see the movie *Madame Curie*. The two small girls returned home in a daze of romanticism and immediately decided to set up their own laboratory in the basement of the house belonging to Alice's parents. Carried away by the Curie saga, improvised tables became laboratory benches. They filled soda-pop bottles with coloured water and collected odd bits of junk that became make-believe laboratory equipment. Once the transformation was complete the two girls lured a neighbouring boy, Rusty Koelle, down into the cellar.

'We are about to blow you up,' Grace announced calmly as she fired a shot of soda water into a green concoction. A screaming Rusty escaped from his captors as the girls dissolved in giggles.

After school Friday was another favourite day for Grace and Alice. They were allowed into the Waters' kitchen where they would take out the *Boston Cook Book* looking for something to make. They would peer through and discuss all sorts of recipes, but the cooking usually ended up with plain old-fashioned vinegar toffee.

The two girls were relentless friends, as only small girls can be. They hated to be parted and could spend hours just talking. At this time Mr Kelly was running for mayor of Philadelphia and Alice's father was also in politics, but both fathers had a tough time to use the telephone in the evening. The girls just talked and talked.

When Grace was eight years old, her first hero entered her life. He was Douglas Fairbanks Junior who had been invited for a party by Mr and Mrs John B. Kelly.

Grace, with her friend Alice Waters, immediately fell in love with him and both girls blushed when he kissed them goodnight. Years later when she was a famous film star Grace mentioned the story to a newspaper reporter who wrote about it.

Friends of Douglas Fairbanks sent it to him and for years he carried the tattered snippet in his pocket wallet until it fell into shreds. It was to be many years later that he finally met Princess Grace again, who reminded him of her first kiss. He has since become a friend of both the Princess and Prince Rainier.

Another of Grace's friends at the Ravenhill Academy, a strict Philadelphian convent, was Dottie Langdon. Today she remembers Grace as 'painfully shy and often withdrawn. She was always quietly spoken, very feminine and sensitive to the point that she would cry at the drop of a hat.

'I don't mean that she was a crybaby. It was just that she felt things deeply. The Kellys had two huge boxers named Wrinkles and Siegfried. Once Siegfried was sick and had to be taken to the vet. When Grace described his sickness to her friends she bawled like a baby.'

As a schoolgirl Grace was above average but not very good at maths or the sciences. They were simply not in her line of vision. She preferred English, story writing and creative games, and sang French songs at parties in a small, sweet voice.

The Ravenhill girls were all taught to write in a squarish printing script which most of them never lost. Today Princess Grace has retained the same style of writing—elegant and feminine with clean bold outlines. Her notepaper carries the royal cipher in aquamarine, which is still one of her favourite colours.

Grace's elder sister Peggy, a lovable extrovert with beguiling Irish charm, was invariably the leader of the girls in the Kelly back yard. It was Peggy who decided to re-write *Cinderella* so that she and her friend Edie Godfrey could play with relish the main characters, the ugly sisters. Grace was given the role of 'Cinderella', who in Peggy's script had nothing to do except sit and look sad.

When she was twelve years of age Grace Kelly was allowed to become a 'pink girl', which was considered a very special privilege for a young American girl. It meant that she was a wartime hospital volunteer and that she was allowed to carry food trays to patients in hospital, thus saving the more senior staff.

Grace loved her hours of duty, not so much because of the work but that it gave her an outlet for her sense of theatre. On one occasion she was asked to take a meal to a man whose eyes were bandaged due to an operation. Grace was enthralled and not only offered to feed the patient but to brighten his life.

'You are now tasting rare green turtle soup imported directly from the king's palace in Barcelona,' she told the bewildered patient as she spooned out the thin watery soup. The gristly chop became venison from the king's private park, but it was when she came to the dessert that Grace was at her best.

'And now,' she exclaimed in a breathless voice, 'Two waiters are lighting the brandy on your crêpes suzette. My, how the flame burns. Can't you smell it? Now they are putting them on your plate from a gleaming silver dish. Gee, it smells divine.'

Thus tapioca pudding became a dish fit for a king and a war veteran gave his heart to the small voice at his side.

Four

It was in 1947 when she was just seventeen years of age that Grace Kelly made her first trip to Europe. In the previous year 'Kell' had been in London with his father and had gained a second in the Diamond Sculls. This year Mrs Kelly with Grace and Lizanne ('Lizzie') went along with 'Kell' and Mr Kelly. The girls had many new dresses for the trip, eight of which Mrs Kelly had made herself, and saucy straw hats. Mrs Kelly's stylish millinery could compete with any other hats at Henley that year.

The family all stayed at The Red Lion Hotel in Henley, which today boasts a plaque: 'Grace Kelly slept here'. With their exuberant good looks the Kellys were the best looking family at Henley—a Norman Rockwell cover from the *Saturday Evening Post* come to life.

In their luggage was a supply of meat as Britain was still on rationing. Mr Kelly was so concerned for 'Kell's' health that he even brought bottled water over in case the London water upset his son. Pictures appeared in the national newspapers of 'Kell' and his sister sitting round this modest supply of food. Like Jack Kramer, who had done exactly the same the year before when he was training for Wimbledon, the Kellys were to come in for some hurtful publicity about the meat.

'The only reason we did it was because we had heard that there was such a shortage of meat and we did not want to worsen the shortage,' Jack ('Kell') Kelly remembers.

Grace Kelly, with her pretty soft feminine looks, was like maple syrup to the contingent of boys from the Kent School in Connecticut and the Tabor Academy in New England.

'They pursued her with some vigour as Lizzie was a little too young,' recalls 'Kell'.

For middle-aged John B. Kelly his son's winning the Diamond Sculls was more than paternal pride. It was a vindication of his own humiliation when the Henley stewards had rejected his entry in the Diamond Sculls 27 years before. Twice national champion of America, he was advised by Russell Johnson, secretary of the American Rowing Association, that the rules had been changed in England and his entry would be honoured. He stepped up his training and was all set to go to England when he received a cable from the Henley Stewards rejecting his entry.

In John B. Kelly's own words to his mother: 'They won't let a man who has worked with his hands row against their *gentlemen*. They claim that a fellow who works with his muscles has an unfair advantage over an aristocrat.'

Even though he evened up the score some time later by beating the English Diamond Sculls champion at the Olympic Games, John B. Kelly never completely forgot the Henley snub. It would have been unreasonable to expect him to because of his liberal way of thinking. 'Sport is a great leveller,' he always said. This had been his first acquaintance with the rigidity of the English Establishment.

The family had been brought up on the Henley disaster and if they appeared more united than ever on the Diamond Sculls day there was certainly justification. John B. Kelly was fond of indoctrinating his children with grandmother Kelly's wisdom. That day he told 'Kell': 'A licking is not a failure. You are never done unless you let yourself stay licked.'

John B. Kelly told of his thoughts that day to a reporter:

'It's something like "Sorrell and Son", an old story, but true,' said Jack gravely. 'When it finally came to me today, there weren't any words that could do justice to my feelings, and there aren't any now. Now that it is all here I felt a tremendous feeling of pride for "Kell". He's the one that matters, not the thwarted ambition of an old guy who once got his fingers publicly slapped over here because he was born without a silver spoon in his mouth.'

The irony of the situation was that among young 'Kell's' titles was also Pennsylvania State Apprentice Bricklaying Champion.

Only the changing of the absurdly archaic rules at Henley had made

'Kell's' win possible. The family were elated and among the first to congratulate 'Kell' was his sister Grace, who had followed the race from the towpath.

While hundreds had jammed the New York dockside to greet John B. Kelly and his son 'Kell' on their triumphant return carrying the Diamond Cup chalice, Mrs Kelly had taken the girls on a holiday to Switzerland. It was to be a kind of compensation for Grace who felt she had let the family down when she had flunked the Benington entrance examination because of her poor maths.

Grace Kelly did not have a coming-out party nor did any of her sisters.

When John B. Kelly asked his daughter Peggy, 'I hear some of your school chums are coming out. Do you want to come out too?' she stormed back: 'I am out. Do you think I have to use those women who sell mailing lists of boys' names to parents of girls to get me a date?'

The result was that the question never came up for the other girls.

Five

Grace Kelly made her first stage debut when she was twelve years of age. It was at the Old Academy Players in East Falls where she had been given one of the lead roles in *Don't Feed the Animals*. The whole family were apprehensive and excited as they filed into their places in the front stalls. Jack Kelly's shining head was seen towering above the audience, but Mrs Kelly, so cool and confident outwardly, was inwardly nervous as a mouse for Grace.

In the middle of the performance Grace's stage-mother muffed her lines. The whole Kelly family stiffened as they watched her, with characteristic coolness, drop her handbag, turn her back on the audience and give her stage-mother her lines while she stopped to pick up the bag. It was the kind of instinctive stage 'business' and presence of mind that only a very experienced performer does automatically.

Quick to spot what had happened, Jack Kelly turned to his wife and said: 'We've got a trouper on our hands.'

The director of the play, Ruth Emmert, was not surprised. All through the rehearsals she had watched the tall girl and noted her poise and how completely in charge of herself she appeared to be. In fact, she had thought that Grace was fourteen and was amazed when she heard her real age. Grace swore her to secrecy in case her youth might prevent her from getting more grown-up parts in other productions. Her attention and complete absorption was also amazing in one so young. She was never late for rehearsals and could be relied upon to raid her mother's wardrobe and even furniture for props if she felt she could help.

After the opening night of another of her plays one of Phila-delphia's leading critics wrote next day:

'Grace Kelly, John B's pretty daughter, made her appearance last night in Uncle George Kelly's comedy hit *The Torchbearers*. For a young lady whose previous experience was slim, Miss Kelly came through this footlight baptism of fire splendidly. Although father and mother beamed at Grace from the front rows and other friends were scattered through the house, it was largely a theatrical crowd this girl faced on her break-in. From where I sat it appeared as if Grace Kelly should become the theatrical torch-bearer for her family.'

Grace should have made her stage debut some months earlier than she did. She had been chosen to play in *The Women* and no one in the entire cast had worked harder than 'the little Kelly girl', as she was called. Two days after the play opened Grace appeared at the dinner table flushed and with small red spots sprinkled all over her face. Mrs Kelly took one look and said:

'Gracie, what are those spots on your face?'

'Nothing, Mother, they are nothing,' Grace protested, trying to hide the light from her face.

But experienced mother that she was, Mrs Kelly took another look and announced firmly:

'Off to bed, young lady. You've got measles.'

Then turning to her elder daughter, Peggy, in her matter of fact voice said:

'Now, Peggy, you've got to take over Gracie's part.'

There was no use remonstrating. Tears were of no avail. When 'Ma Kelly' said something she meant it, and off to bed went Grace to have her measles in sheer misery while Peggy took over the script.

Word perfect, Peggy played Grace's role while the real heroine languished crossly in bed.

Because of her height, and her totally feminine approach to life compared with her tomboy sisters, at twelve years of age Grace Kelly had begun to take notice of her looks. It was a natural growing-up process in such a sensitive and introspective girl. She spent hours on the swing in the garden pushing her legs down and swinging with force. When her school girl friends asked why, she pertinently ex-plained:

'If you swing a lot it'll make your legs pretty.'

Fortunately the swinging left her with elegant tapering legs and not bulging muscles which could have happened. When she sat she was also careful not to cross her legs. 'It makes your calves look fat' was her matter-of-fact explanation.

During my stay in Hollywood talking to the directors and photographers who had worked with her, they all told me that it was uncanny how Grace Kelly knew what to do with her body. She was never known to be ungainly and always knew exactly how to place her legs and feet.

Besides teaching her children athletics and swimming, Mrs Kelly, who before her marriage had taught everything from athletics to dancing at the University of Pennsylvania, was determined that the girls should have well coordinated bodies. Since she was tiny, Grace had attended ballet classes and was far above average. Had she not grown so tall it is more than possible that she would have made ballet her career and not acting. The fantasia of the ballet world totally captivated her.

Unlike the rest of the family, Grace took no particular interest in competitive sports. She played them because it was part of the family's daily life, but showed no burning zeal like the rest of the children. At school she played hockey and basketball; at summer camp swimming and tennis. As an active member of the Girl Guides she worked hard and enjoyed collecting the various badges of achievement. During the war, when metal was short, the Guides of East Falls made a door-to-door collection for coat hangers. Grace got more than anybody. Whatever she chose to do as a child she did well, which runs true to her character today. She has a totally professional approach to everything, whether it is making dried flower collages as gifts for her friends or organising a Red Cross fête.

Just as the game of Consequences had been the fashion in Margaret Kelly's youth, the 'Slam Book' featured in Grace's crowd. She was just thirteen at the time. Jack Oechsle, one of 'Kell's' friends, made out a questionnaire which he called the 'Slam Book'. It was sealed and not opened until ten years later. Grace's entry read:

Favourite sport, swimming; *favourite actor*, Alan Ladd; *favourite actress*, Ingrid Bergman; *favourite colour*, purple; *favourite comedian*, Bob Hope; *favourite pet hate*, school. To the question *Do you want to be married?* she had written a firm 'yes'.

At thirteen when the metamorphosis usually occurs in girls and they first begin to indicate their final shape as women, Grace Kelly was no exception. She had all the traits that have carried her through her successful life. She also showed a glimmer of beauty—shining healthy good looks that begin with superb bone structure and end with an inner light, the misnomer now called sex appeal. As Peggy says:

'She never went through a gawky stage. Not too tall, nice and thin, no skin problems. She went from Girl Scout to belle of the ball without us noticing it. In her sweet and quiet way she had a million beaux.'

She already began to be aware of her limitations and her achievements, and suddenly she found that boys liked her.

They liked her for many reasons . . . the romantic, corn-coloured silky hair, the shy smile—punctuated with dimples at each end of the mouth which are still there today—that occasionally broke into a generous white grin: the berries and cream skin and the willowy body which, though on the skinny side, looked great in the flared skirted swimsuits of the period. There was also that enigmatic quality of self-preservation that was to take her through the Hollywood jungle unscathed.

But mostly they liked her because she could listen. As Howard Wikoff explained:

'Gracie had a pleasing way about her. She didn't talk too much, just listened. Instead of showing off and chattering all about herself like most teenagers she was attentive to her dates. She made each escort think he was King Bee. And you know some girls never learn that.'

She was popular because she made her man feel comfortable and a little bit of a hero. As Jack Oechsle remembered:

'If you wanted to sit, she'd sit; if you wanted to dance, she'd dance. And if you took her to a party she wouldn't float off with another fellow. She was your date and she remained your date.'

Even then Grace Kelly loved to dance barefooted. Whenever the Mills Brothers came on the gramophone with their *Paper Moon* Grace was off, living in a dream world of her own.

One of her first dates was with a boy called Harper Davis, a friend of her brother 'Kell'. Both boys went to the exclusive William Penn Charter School, and when Harper confided in 'Kell' that he did not have a girl to take to the school dance young Kelly suggested sister Grace. Peggy was a few years too old and Lizanne far too young.

At first Mrs Kelly hesitated. Grace was still young and vulnerable. Was she too young to begin the complicated business of dating with all its ramifications? She discussed it with her husband, who laconically answered:

'Well, she has to start some time. And she couldn't have a nicer boy.' Mrs Kelly agreed.

On the Friday of the dance Grace kept within ear distance of the front door. When the bell finally rang she dashed to the door to receive a box of orchids . . . her first corsage.

'Flowers for me? What a bore,' is how the family remembers this momentous occasion. But once the door was shut she rushed the box to the refrigerator. It was the beginning of a long line of corsages and after each subsequent dance she placed them in a Cellophane envelope and between the pages of an encyclopaedia. Each one was then pasted into an album and carefully labelled with the giver's name and the event. The albums still exist today.

This was the once-upon-a-time when school dances had a quixotic air about them. Grace set off wearing a sensible coat over her first long party dress as Harper Davis, handsome as a tailor's dummy in his first dinner jacket, called to collect her. It could have been a scene straight out of any of those pleasant, naïve family films that Hollywood was making at the time. It had the same quality of decency and prettiness about it.

Mrs Kelly was waiting up when her daughter came in. When Grace finally came home, she burst into the room positively glowing:

'Oh, Mother, I had a wonderful time.'

Within a few months, just nineteen years of age, Harper Davis was found to have multiple sclerosis and died seven years later. His death left a searing impression on Grace. It was her first real contact with death —someone of her own age and from her own world. She was desolate.

This was also the time of writing poetry, locked away from the boisterous Kelly world with her own private thoughts. They were fresh, charming verses—'some serious, some little gooney ones'—and they also had an unexpected pixieness which punctuates much of her conversation among friends today. This was written when she was fourteen years old.

> *I hate to see the sun go down*
> *And squeeze itself into the ground,*
> *Since some warm night it might get stuck*
> *And in the morning not get up.*

Grace's parents had hoped that she would continue her education at Benington College. They passionately wanted their children to have every possible advantage that education could give. Jack Kelly himself had had very little formal education, leaving school in his early teens to start first as a water boy and later as a bricklayer's apprentice in his older brother's business.

'It was a tough time to get a place in College as there were so many G.I.s wanting to enroll. Also Grace wasn't up to par because of her arithmetic,' Mrs Kelly truthfully recalls.

No one was less disappointed than Grace. In her own indomitable way she had decided that the only further schooling that she wanted was at the American Academy of Dramatic Arts in New York.

Hints had been dropped all round the family so that when Grace finally approached her father it came as no surprise. Mr Kelly listened patiently and explained that it was a dangerous profession, even if one was ever lucky enough to reach the top.

'You can't be halfway about it,' he said. 'While others play you will have to be getting your rest so that you will look nice the next day. And once you have reached the top you will become public property. There will be no privacy. The public will make demands on you. Are you ready to pay the price?'

They were words that she has never forgotten.

Grace Kelly set off for the audition at the Academy in New York with stars in her eyes. If she was nervous, none of the family was aware of it. Just as today she kept her emotions tightly locked inside.

In handwriting that has blurred with time her first appearance at the Academy, which was then housed in Carnegie Hall, is recorded in the audition book for 1947. It gives her name 'Grace Patricia Kelly' and her address as 'Philadelphia'. She weighed 126 pounds and stood 5 feet 6½ inches in her stocking feet. Her proportions were recorded as 'good'. It then jumps to her nationality 'American Irish' and her general education 'Stevens School'.

Grace played a scene from Uncle George's *The Torchbearers* and also a few lines of Portia from *The Merchant of Venice*. Mr Distell, her auditioner, noted in handwriting:

Voice   Not placed
Temperament   Sensitive
Spontaneity   Good youthfulness
Dramatic instinct   Expressive
Intelligence   Good
General remarks   Good, promising, youthful.

Grace Kelly was accepted and enrolled for every class that she was eligible for, including fencing. Years later, when she was to make the film *The Swan*, she asked for Sandor Nage, her fencing master from the Academy, to go to Hollywood to steer her through the fencing scenes. There was no need for a stand-in and they were stylishly executed.

The Academy gives no academic training of any kind. It is purely a school for actors. The boast of the Academy today is that Charles Jehlinger, who was its director for over fifty years, taught the Stanislavsky method before Stanislavsky did.

Shy Grace found the 'improvisation classes' a strain at first. Straight from a girls' school, she found it slightly odd to take part in classes emphasising 'freedom of the body' and frequently blushed. Recalling it years later she was to say:

'We would be assigned to go to the Bowery and observe a drunk and then come back and act out a drunk. One of the oddest assignments we had was to go to the zoo and watch a llama. I never quite figured out why because few of us have ever been called on to play the part of a llama. But I am sure it must have been helpful if the school thought so.'

It was the Academy, too, who cured Miss Kelly of her sway back. 'I was a sway back,' she confessed. 'When I was lying as flat as I could this teacher used to get down on the floor and would say "I can see air". This meant that I'd have to try and lie even flatter.'

The teacher's methods must have been effective because her carriage is one of the most arresting things about Princess Grace today. She not only stands straight and tall but there is not a hint of sway back.

For a girl as private as Grace Kelly the Academy was especially beneficial. She slowly began to shed her inhibitions like a flower opening its petals in the sunshine.

Among the list of distinguished actors who have all been trained at the Academy are Spencer Tracy, Robert Redford, David Hartman and John Cassavetes.

In the entrance hall of the Academy, now housed in a handsome red brick house designed by Stanford White at 120 Madison Avenue, midway between Broadway and the Forties, hang pictures of the Academy's most illustrious students. Among them is one of Grace Kelly at her first rehearsal. The same photo appears in the school's brochure with the words 'I am very grateful for the two years I spent at the American Academy and the knowledge I gained there as an actor and a person. Grace de Monaco.'

It is doubtful whether the blue-jeaned students of today ever bother to look at her photo, but ex-actress Frances Fuller, the present director, is overwhelmingly proud of this former pupil.

'Grace was always shy. She was almost humble. I am wondering if that part of her shyness might have been the aura of her Uncle George. The fact that he was someone that she looked up to and respected so. She was desperately determined to succeed too. We once found her rehearsing non-stop for 18 hours.'

It was Frances Fuller who finally suggested to her husband, Worthington Myler, that Grace Kelly was ready for professional work.

'I was handing on a lot of young talent to him as he was producing and directing in television and had several shows. One of the best known was called *Studio One* and I worked with him a lot on the scripts. He had asked my opinion about a part and as I had not spotted anyone else I thought was right I asked him to see Grace.

'I had an intuition even then that she would go a long way. I instinctively sensed ability and the perseverance necessary to make a good actress. Grace was not just a pretty face.

'I had the same reaction about Anne Bancroft and I recommended her to my husband. I stood in the back of the theatre and watched her all alone rehearsing and the intensity of her concentration hit me. Grace had the same dedication and spiritual toughness even then.

'It was my husband who tutored Grace in her first stage kiss. She had to be told how to kiss, she was so shy. She stood too far away and he had to teach her to lean forward. But she was lovely in the role.'

Frances Fuller follows all her girls through their professional life and had this to say about Grace Kelly.

'Didn't you feel that her development was extraordinary through the years? But not due to any particular effort on her part. She worked at what she was asked to do and did it well, and the rest of it was her good breeding and considered restraint within herself. It wasn't until *The Country Girl* that you really began to see the accumulation of her learning and maturity. I thought she was tremendous in it.

'Mr Jehlinger used to say "Give me 10 per cent talent and 90 per cent ambition and I'll go with it." In her quiet way Grace obviously had a great deal of determination and with enormous dignity set about building up what was to be her strength.

'Grace has always had an air of mystery about her and probably still has to this day. She holds back all the time.'

During her graduation party at the Academy John Cassavetes, himself then a fledgling actor and a year behind Grace Kelly, overheard someone comment: 'That Grace Kelly is such a pretty little thing. Isn't it a shame she's too shy ever to amount to anything.'

Six

Twenty-five years ago there was only one place suitable in New York for a young girl to live alone. To thousands of parents throughout America the Barbizon Hotel for Women at 63rd Street and Lexington Avenue—'the silk stocking district' as this fashionable part was called—was a fortress against the perils of that wicked city. It was not only a home-away-from-home, untouched by scandal, but no men were allowed into the private section. If a girl was ill and needed a doctor he had to practically produce his medical certificate before being admitted to her bedroom. A stethoscope hanging out of a young man's pocket was the oldest gag known at the Barbizon and never got past the lift door.

It was to this bastion of virtue that Mrs Kelly sent her daughter Grace during the period she studied at the Academy of Dramatic Arts. The Barbizon, a tawny twenty-two storied brick building was built in 1928 and is still 'home' to 700 women. In the days when Grace Kelly lived there every girl had to produce three character references before she was accepted and the waiting list was one hundred long.

Today the Barbizon is like a dowager duchess who has spilt the soup on her bosom. It is skimped, shabby, unloved. The once elegant duck-egg blue foyer, where girls in swirling New Look dresses met their beaux, is now bustling with an army of blue-jeaned girls with bossy, liberated bottoms.

The Barbizon has always been owned and operated by men and in the forties was managed by Hugh J. Connor, a cherubic man who learned the complicated art of hotel management at New York's Roosevelt and the Waldorf-Astoria. At the Barbizon he was as cosily concerned about his girls as an uncle with a favourite visiting niece. When they were sick he personally sent them flowers and if a girl ran short he acted as an unofficial paymaster until her next cheque arrived. Broken hearts were often mended in his small office behind the reception desk where he handed out advice like *petit fours* on a silver platter.

The Barbizon had style in those days and every afternoon waitresses in black, with starched white aprons, served tea in the lounge where the girls were allowed to bring their dates, only after they had been issued special passes. There was also a sun deck, gymnasium, swimming pool and library of 3,000 books as well as beauty, dress and book shops. It was the complete woman's world.

No one slotted into this camaraderie of the campus atmosphere better than Grace Kelly. It was her first time away from the family and her first taste of carefully controlled freedom. For a while she shared a suite with Jean Drouillard and Bettina Thompson, who also attended the American Academy of Dramatic Arts. The second year she roomed with Prudence ('Prudy') Wise, who later became her secretary. In her last year, when her modelling fees jumped from 7.50 dollars to 25 dollars an hour, she had a single room and bath. But so unobtrusive were her two years there that when I stayed there last year no one could remember what rooms she had lived in. I saw the shoe-box sized, chintzy rooms where Dorothy McGuire, Barbara Bel Geddes, Gene Tierney and Cathy O'Donnell had lived, but no one could remember Grace Kelly's. Nor do any of the present veterans, who have lived at the club for the last thirty-five years, ever remember her attending a 'clothes auction'. It was a custom when a girl left to get married that she sold off her wardrobe to the highest bidders. As many of the girls were models and had to have an extensive wardrobe, clothes swapping was another common occurrence. Grace Kelly never took part in this.

Many of the girls came from rich protective backgrounds like Grace Kelly but others had a hard time struggling along on student grants or meagre allowances from their parents. 'Money Talks' were another craze when girls would gather in a bedroom, sprawled over the bed and furniture, to gnaw pencils and make elaborate financial calculations which were never, of course, put into practice.

They were charming, beguiling grown-up children. Drugs and drink had no part in their lives. Mr Connor's safe was filled with curling tongs, electric kettles and electric rings, which the girls had smuggled in to use in their rooms for late-night snacks and hot chocolate, as these were forbidden due to fire hazards.

'Grace kept a great deal to herself. We always thought that she was very shy,' Mr Connors remembers today. 'I used to see her in the dining-room most nights sitting alone with her glasses on and reading a book through her dinner.'

When *Colliers* sent a photographer and writer to do a feature on the hotel the girls all dressed up in party dresses and brought their young men to be included in the pictures. In one photograph, looking down from the mezzanine floor over the wedding cake balustrade, quite alone, was an exceptionally pretty girl. Her name was Grace Kelly.

In those days at the Academy classes were split up into mornings, afternoons and evenings. Today the students work a four-hour shift to allow them to take a part-time job to help out their grants. With plenty of time to spare between her classes it was the most natural thing that Grace Kelly should drift into modelling to make some extra money. She was quite determined to pay her own way and not be dependent on her parents. Besides, she had the looks, the figure and was in the right ambiance among all the other models who lived at the Barbizon. It was fun and perhaps self-consciously it was a challenge to have to step out into real life. Once she began modelling she enjoyed making her own money and was clever at saving it, which she still is today. No matter what career she had chosen in life, Grace Kelly very early in childhood understood that hoary axiom 'a girl's best friend is money in the bank'.

Of her modelling career, years later in an interview in *Newsweek* she was quoted as saying, 'The money was very nice and that's what made it all worth while.'

Grace Kelly also did television commercials covering everything from Electrolux advertisements to 'the skin a fellow loves to touch'. About this phase in her career she was later to crack, 'I was terrible. Honestly, anyone watching me give the pitch for Old Golds would have switched to Camels.'

While the other girls spent their money on frilly 'New Look' petticoats and fashionable ankle-strap shoes, Grace Kelly chose the kind of clothes that were to become almost a uniform and even today are still her favourite way of dressing. She wore skirts and sweaters, rising from Botany wool to cashmere as her finances improved. She invariably wore sensible walking-shoes and mostly no hat.

After her marriage it was Prince Rainier who suggested to her that she would have to wear a hat on formal occasions now that she was a royal princess. She chooses simple knitted hats in winter and plain straw in summer, but mostly her hair is shining in the sun and wind.

Everything about Grace Kelly and Princess Grace of Monaco reeks of fastidiousness. In those Barbizon days there was always a look of freshness about her, the American finishing school lady-like look. From schooldays onwards she wore white cotton gloves that were to become almost a trade mark when she later went to Hollywood. Today she dislikes shaking hands without her gloves.

When she arrived at the photographic studios with her soft natural hair style, prim glasses and neat clothes, Grace Kelly looked more like an efficient secretary than a model. Once behind the cameras it was a different situation. She bloomed. She knew exactly what to do with her face and became known as 'the girl with a hundred faces'.

While the photographers admired her perfect white teeth and flawless complexion, which never needed retouching in candid colour shots, art editors of the leading magazines loved her wide-eyed, wholesome looks. She typified everything that was healthy and American. Doris Day and Grace Kelly have done more for publicising clean American womanhood than any other film stars. *Redbook, True Romance: True Story: Cosmopolitan* all used Grace Kelly's face week after week . . . smiling, radiating, glowing; the all-American image.

Whenever she could, Grace Kelly went to the theatre. She preferred its intimacy to the movies and it is more than probable that she both absorbed and inherited this interest from her two uncles, George and Walter Kelly.

In her second year at the Academy she invited one of her acting friends for a weekend. It was a risky thing to do in a family of teasers, but he meant sufficient to her at that time to brave a family ribbing.

Mrs Kelly took one look at the effete young man at her daughter's side and decided to ask 'Kell' to do her a favour.

Remembering the story recently, as we had breakfast together in the kitchen of his luxurious penthouse in Philadelphia, Jack Kelly said:

'She asked me to bring over on the Friday night three of my bigger and better looking friends. One was the Olympic Butterfly champion and looked a bit like Kirk Douglas and the other was a big looking guy, a weight-lifting type, who was my partner in rowing races and was also in the life guards at Ocean City. There was another chap also a big, tall, swimming type.

'I gave them the word that this fellow was a bit of a creep, which I had deduced from my mother's description. When they came into the room they gave Grace's guy the grip and in a second had him on the floor.

'My sister was so mad at me for bringing these animals home and embarrassing her that she was quiet for a month. At the time she was commuting to New York every day, leaving by the 7 a.m. train in the morning and returning about 7 p.m. at night. I did rowing practice every evening and would just be getting in when she returned, so we sat down together to have our dinner alone. For a month we ate in silence with the very occasional "yes" or "no" to any question I asked her. It took a long time before she forgave the rest of the family too.'

Grace Kelly in her young days was never as close to her athletic brother as were her sisters. They simply had different ideas about life and its values. 'Kell' also had the unnerving habit of seldom approving of the more aesthetic type of boy friends that his sister Grace continued to bring home.

All her life she has developed a round, if somewhat fastidious, taste in her friends. In men she likes intellectuals and creative thinkers— directors, writers, designers, musicians, artists, actors, politicians.

'I considered one of these actor guys she brought home as a wee bit effeminate and not my type,' 'Kell' Kelly explained. 'At a family dinner we had one Saturday night at the Philadelphia Country Club my parents asked me to join them. I explained that I had a date and they said, "Bring your girl along", which I did. She was a former beauty queen and had an outstanding figure to say the least and liked to show it. She also wore a lot of make-up, which none of my family did.

'She was about two years older than I was, had been divorced and had a six-year-old child, which of course my parents were not aware of. Nevertheless I walked her straight through this crowded dining-room at the Country Club and every man snapped his head around. As I arrived at our family table my father and Peggy's husband gave me the eye and looked approvingly. All the women in the family scowled and sulked.

'Next day when we were going to St Bridget's church as usual on Sunday, Grace got on my back. "You insulted your mother by bringing that woman to the club," she said.

' "All I can say," I replied, "is that every man in the room thought she was great, which is more than could be said of your escort."

'We had quite an argument about that particular incident.

'Don't let Grace's frosty beauty fool you,' 'Kell' Kelly told me. 'She can be physically tough, too. I remember one of my Marine friends showed Grace some ju-jitsu holds. She was pretty quick learning them. Once years later she went up to photographer Howell Conant, a friend of hers, put her arm round his neck and before he could say a word had tossed him on his back. That was our Gracie for you.'

In recent years 'Kell' has separated from his wife, the former Mary Freeman Kelly, national swimming champion of America, which is an unhappy situation in any Catholic family; they have a family of five children.

'I would say that we have been closer almost in recent years than we were when we were young. I can't say that any one of my sisters was particularly closer than another to me but because of some personal problems I think my sister Grace has been a little more understanding of my situation and we have become closer over the last few years.'

Compassion and loyalty have always been an integral part of Princess Grace's character.

Seven

Two years away from the all-enveloping aura of the Kelly clan and Grace was even more convinced in what she wanted to do. It was not that she did not enjoy the family enclave, which at times could be smothering, but she knew instinctively that there was also a world outside of Philadelphia where she belonged.

From modelling she was soon making 400 dollars a month at the rate of 25 dollars an hour, which was enough in those days to keep any girl happy. Even at the prime of her career as a top cover girl in 1919 Mrs Kelly, the former Margaret Majer, had never earned more than five dollars an hour. Grace also did fashion shorts for newsreels which took her to Paris and Bermuda, and were highly profitable. During her second year she refused any financial help from her family and paid her own way. Like her Uncle George Kelly, she was wildly independent about money matters, and still is.

Later in life Grace was to say that she made as much money out of modelling as in pictures. This may be true simply because unlike the big stars of today—Elizabeth Taylor, Sophia Loren and Brigitte Bardot—she had never been given a cut on the profits from the highly successful films she made.

Photographer Ruzzie Green remembers her at that time as 'what we called "nice, clean stuff" in our business. She was not a top model and never would be. She was the girl next door. No glamour, no oomph, no cheesecake. She had lovely shoulders but no chest. Grace was like

Bergman in the "clean way". She could do the smush stuff in movies like in *Rear Window*—and get away with it.'

Others remember her at this period as 'terribly lady-like, almost sedate with her tweed suits, sensible shoes, small hats with veils and white gloves'.

When Grace Kelly finished her two-year course at the Academy she was ready to test her acting wings. Each year two students from the Academy, a girl and boy, were chosen by Theron Bamberger to appear at his Bucks County Playhouse in New Hope, Pennsylvania. In the spring of 1949 Grace Kelly was chosen and as coincidence it was Uncle George Kelly's hilarious comedy *The Torchbearers* in which she was to play.

Such is the fragmentation of time that when I visited the picturesque Bucks County Playhouse last year no one clearly remembered Grace Kelly. There are those who remind you of 'the pretty girl who taught one of the stage hands to swim' and others 'a charming shy girl who cried a lot'. Her performance was not a sensation but neither was she slammed.

Back in New York, Grace Kelly made the rounds of the casting offices. She read for thirty-eight parts, which even included the role of the ingénue in *The Country Girl* which was later left out of the movie. She read for almost everything that was being cast. Remembering this period she was to say later: 'People were confused about my type but they agreed on one thing. I was in the "too" category— "too" tall, "too" leggy, "too" chinny.'

When I discussed this recently with Frances Fuller of the American Academy she was not incredulous. 'I can quite believe that. Grace was just one of a number of girls trying to break into the theatre or television. The difference between her and many others is that she never gave up. She went for interview after interview, always arriving on time, impeccably turned out. Of course, she must have been disappointed time after time but she never let it make her bitter. She just plugged on.'

Grace Kelly was lucky in that unlike other girls she knew she could pay her rent and there was money over for daily ballet lessons and even voice production at the New School, under its director Sanford Meisner.

It was during the period that she was taking lessons with Sanford Meisner at the Neighbourhood Playhouse that the New York office of Fox Studios telephoned her agent and asked if she could meet the director Gregory Ratoff immediately. This volatile Hungarian was then an impressive name in Hollywood and did not like to be kept waiting.

Grace Kelly was in her usual working uniform, a shirt and skirt with sensible flat shoes, but hurried over. Years later she was to retell the incident to *The Saturday Evening Post*.

'All the other girls looked cute and sweet in high heels. I looked so terrible, my agent was embarrassed. But when Mr Ratoff saw me, he said "Perfect." This was a switch. My whole life people had been telling me I was imperfect.

' "What I like about this girl is that she is not pretty," Mr Ratoff said. My agent insisted, "But Mr Ratoff she is pretty." Mr Ratoff would not be talked out of it. "No, no, no, she is not," he said . . . "Take off your coat."

'When I took it off and he saw my old skirt and shirt he was in ecstasy. "Magnificent," he said. "Cannot you spik with the Irish accent?" '

Although she had never spoken with an Irish accent she replied, 'Yes, I will try.' She then went home and worked on it conscientiously. She did in fact test for the film which was to be called *Taxi:* but the director did not like her.

It was quite evident that Gregory Ratoff wanted Grace Kelly for the part of the Irish immigrant girl. Just as Alfred Hitchcock was to later, he obviously sensed the untouched sensual potential behind the icing-sugar looks, but his producer thought differently. Grace Kelly lost the part to Constance Smith, who on the surface with her blue black hair and Celtic eyes probably looked the part better and may have handled the accent more naturally. In those early days an accent did not come easily to Grace Kelly's finishing-school voice.

Years later this self-same test was seen by John Ford who was looking for a quiet English lady type for his film *Mogambo*. The shirt and skirt and her English style secured her the part that was to be a milestone in her life—in every way.

There were also the exciting times when work came in a rush and within a fortnight she played anything as diverse as a schoolgirl to the saucy music-hall singer in black mesh stockings in *Lights Out*.

Her theatre break finally came when she was asked to read the grim daughter's part in Strindberg's *The Father*.

It was Wednesday evening, 16 November 1949, at the Cort Theatre when Grace Kelly made her Broadway debut.

In the cast of *The Father* were two distinguished actors, the late Mady Christians whose work Grace Kelly admired, and Raymond Massey. She was later to say that she only got the part because both Raymond Massey and Mady Christians were tall and flat shoes suited her role anyway. She revered their professionalism and spent many hours in Mady Christians' dressing-room listening, and learning, while the older woman talked. They in turn enjoyed her fresh and unspoiled good manners, so rare in the acting profession.

On the opening night of *The Father* there was a party for the cast afterwards, as was the custom on Broadway in those days. Grace Kelly brought along her parents, who were distinguishable among the guests by their debonair looks. On seeing them Raymond Massey was intrigued. Why was his old friend Jack Kelly from rowing days there? He went over to greet them and was astonished to know that in fact Grace was their daughter.

She had told no one in the cast about her parents or background. This is a classical example of the very private person that Grace Kelly is and why today she is still tremendously reticent about her family life.

Even though the show closed, as a budding actress Grace Kelly felt that she had now outgrown the Barbizon. She wanted her own place where she could invite the small circle of friends that she had by now collected. She moved into a smart two-roomed apartment, Number 9A, in Manhattan House at 66 and 3rd Avenue—a shiny white house for which 'Kelly for Bricks' had supplied the building material.

Intensely feminine about the atmosphere in which she likes to relax—it can best be described as 'organised chaos'—she moved all her treasures from Philadelphia to the new apartment and 'Kelly's place' was created. On a gleeful shopping spree, she not only bought everything for the kitchen but like most American women created her own individual and pretty bathroom. She chose deep pile, shocking pink towels and had them embroidered with her own monogram—GPK. In America when a bachelor girl buys her own initialled towels it is a sign that her bank account is in a healthy state and that she has arrived.

To complete her apartment Grace Kelly acquired a parakeet called Henry. He could not be farmed out easily to friends when she went to the Coast to make a picture. On one occasion John Foreman moved in with his cat to keep Henry company. When he heard that Mrs Kelly was calling at the apartment he popped the cat in a cupboard. But 'Ma Kelly' was not to be fooled. The moment she entered the door she sniffed:

'There is a cat in this place.'

She walked from room to room but fortunately did not open any cupboards. When she left Henry, John and the cat resumed their carefree chaotic, bachelor existence.

Friends who went to Grace Kelly's apartment at that time remember the large circular table of ebony Formica which operated on a spiral and served as both a coffee table and dining table. No one remembers her cooking especially, but if she did it was probably the beginning of her *Bœuf Stroganoff* days.

Word games became a favourite at Grace Kelly's place. It was a game devised by Alfred Hitchcock for Lizabeth Scott. The idea was to drop the first letter of a name—Ickey Rooney, Reer Garson, Rank Sinatra, Ary Grant, Ing Crosby, Ette Davis, Orgie Raft—and see what you got!

It was also at this period in her life that Grace took up photography. Everyone and everything was photographed. She was so delighted with this new interest that she even developed her own negatives, sloshing round in a dark bathroom.

Though Prince Rainier was originally the family photographer his place has now been taken over by Princess Grace, who has recorded every age, every nuance of her children's life.

It was a fizzy time in New York. Everybody was young and hopeful. The theatre was thriving and television was the exciting new medium. There was a constant party atmosphere in those days and Grace Kelly, actress and potential film star, was very much part of it. Most of her friends were less well off than her so everyone wanted to go to 'Grace's place' where there was always food and champagne 'splits' in the refrigerator.

On nights when she was alone Grace was perfectly happy to sit reading, sewing chiffon scarves or other frillies to jazz up her wardrobe or even to get on with her crochet. She was, and still is, perfectly self-sufficient in her own company.

During these formative acting years another woman came into Grace Kelly's life who was to guide her destiny over the next few years. It was a short but formidable period. She was Edith van Cleve from the powerful Music Corporation of America. Today this bright sprightly woman lives in semi-retirement in New York with the knowledge that she guided at least two remarkable names in cinema history—Grace Kelly and Marlon Brando.

'Grace was still at the Academy when I first saw her. A man I think called Richardson telephoned me that he had a lovely looking girl whom he thought had great potential for pictures,' she recalled, 'and he thought that I ought to see her. She was going to play that afternoon in *The Philadelphia Story*. I went to see her and I agreed with him one hundred per cent. She was lovely looking, dressed beautifully, moved well, spoke well and everything that I thought would eventually be right for pictures.'

It has been one of Princess Grace's greatest assets that no matter what people eventually think of her, for good or for bad, her first impression is quietly impressive. Her own special propulsive and incandescent good looks are enigmatic and beguiling.

'I don't remember what she wore the first day she came to the office. I am sure that it was something very simple and in exquisite taste. She always had that,' says Miss van Cleve, 'but she did have a model's hat box with her.

'We discussed her future and she agreed with me that she was not ready to go to Hollywood. In fact I had the distinct impression that she would have preferred a stage career and I don't think her family were very keen on Hollywood either. She certainly had no wish to take up a long contract. She was never an eager-beaver girl, if you know what I mean.'

Shortly after Christmas in 1950 Grace landed a part in a play called *Alexander*, by Lexford Richards, in Albany New York. With her fine bones and chiselled good looks it was a tailor-made part for her—that of a society-girl turned singer appearing in a smart New York night club. It gave a glimpse of the extrovert that she was to play so memorably in the film *High Society* just a few years later. The play went into rehearsal for two weeks followed by a two-week run. Grace Kelly was already a favourite with the cast but had always kept slightly distant simply because this was her way of communicating. At the closing night party when one of the actors played an electric guitar she suddenly threw off her high heeled pumps and danced barefoot. As she twirled with her full skirt sweeping the air she ran her hands through her chignon and a cascade of butterscotch coloured silky hair fell round her shoulders.

Ernestine Perrie, the production stage manager, is said to have exclaimed loud enough for the whole party to hear:

'There it is! I've said all along there was fire beneath that surface of ice! That Kelly has stardust in her hair. You'll see!'

John Foreman also has vivid memories of a Kelly flamenco.

As we talked in his Los Angeles home late one night he described it.

'Grace Kelly never did anything that she wasn't qualified or capable of doing. One night at a party I saw her turn different music on and dance a flamenco as well as Ava Gardner in *The Barefoot Contessa*. It was a kind of surprising thing coming from Grace. At what point had she rehearsed this so that she knew it would work? The fact is that it did work and we all applauded her.'

The fact that Grace Kelly danced an impromptu flamenco on two occasions is as unimportant as if she had tucked a rose in her hair taken in the context of her exciting life. But it does add credence to my belief that she never makes a spontaneous move without first having thought it through thoroughly. She had surely practised in private.

Warm, generous, but never impetuous. Her every gesture and thought is a controlled reflex. She knows all the time exactly what she is doing and this I believe to be the key to her character.

John Foreman also has his own clear memory of the Kelly impact. 'I had just become an agent at M.C.A. in the television department. I went to meet this girl and we had lunch at the Plaza Hotel. Even in those days it was surprising to see a girl come to lunch with a hat and gloves on. I remember the hat had a little veil. I thought at the time "This is a strange dead arsed girl" but by the time that the lunch was over I decided that she wasn't strange or mousey at all. She was somebody who had her act together. She was—and is—a very special lady.'

When the definitive story of New York television is made the name of Grace Kelly will be synonymous with the early fifties period along with Maria Riva, Mary Sinclair and Felicia Monteleagre. They were the stars.

One of her most significant early shows was in 1950 when she won her first TV acting job. Fred Coe, then producing the original *TV Playhouse*, was seeking an unknown but talented actress for his production of *Bethel Merriday* by Sinclair Lewis. He spotted Grace in her small part in *The Father* and immediately sent word that he wanted to see her.

Fred Coe believes that as an actress Grace Kelly was lazy. He is quoted as saying in an interview at the time of her wedding:

'Perhaps it is because she is such a beautiful woman and things come to her relatively easily. But I think that she has never fully shown her real talent.

'I remember she was always a little removed—not a snob, but she had her eyes set on a very high goal very early in her career. There was a feeling of security and great determination about her. It's easy to say this now but I thought even then she had a queenly quality about her.'

Grace Kelly subsequently did other 'Playhouse' shows and went on to appear in most of the live dramatic series.

Sandwiched in with her theatre and television roles Grace Kelly accepted her first role in a film to be made in New York called *Fourteen Hours*. In this film she had a short but tantalising part as the lady negotiating a divorce across the street from a man on a ledge. There was nothing spectacular in it at all except for two things. With the money she earned she bought her first mink stole and as a result of the film some high-school girls in Oregon formed the first Grace Kelly fan club. She was totally bewildered when she heard the news of the club and characteristically commented:

'Why would anyone want to choose me for a fan club?'

Grace Kelly was never over-concerned about money even when she became a star. Edith van Cleve remembers when she was arguing about money for her during the time she played in Philadelphia.

'I was having a little trouble getting it,' she said.

' " Don't worry, please," Grace said, "because the Playhouse in the Park is one of my father's projects. I want to do whatever is best for the theatre." '

The night that Grace Kelly played at the Playhouse in the Park in Philadelphia, John B. Kelly was spellbound with pride and all the family were in the audience.

'For a short period Grace joined the Elitches Garden Theatre in Denver, which at the time was one of America's most important stock companies. She was interviewed in New York by the Gertlers, who ran the theatre. I had already had a film offer for her from the Coast to play in an experimental Western *High Noon* but I did not tell them,' says Edith van Cleve, 'I then had a further telephone call to say that Grace was wanted for two pictures. By now the Gertlers were getting slightly pressing as they always liked to have their contracts signed up before leaving New York to go back to Denver.

'I telephoned Grace and said, "Now we have to decide between these two things. The salary on the movie will be 750 dollars a week and all the Gertlers pay for an ingénue is 125 dollars a week. In spite of this I want you to go to Denver because you will play big roles and it will be great training for you. You are still so young and when you do go into movies the technique that you have learned there, and knowing what you are doing, will be invaluable."

'Without hesitation Grace replied that she would do whatever I wanted her to. So I told the people in Denver that she would go there even if she had to leave the company earlier than September. I was perfectly honest and said that she had another offer which might come up but I believed that the movie wouldn't go on time. The picture was supposed to start early in the summer and the Gertlers began in June and went through till September and the company was supposed to stay intact.

'I gambled on the movie's delay, of course, because I thought it was more important for her that summer to get big roles in a good company.

'The picture did not go on time, which is exactly what I had hoped. This gave her all the summer in Denver, where she opened in *For Love of Money*—a great role for an ingénue.

'I knew Grace would succeed because very few people had her distinction and beauty. This distinction she has is very rare—a lovely, cool, dignified young woman and very unactressy. She is nothing like other people. It is a very special quality.'

Edith van Cleve is a tough, forthright woman and has been around the film world a long time. When I spoke with her I felt that had she wanted to she would not have minced her words. Her final summing up of Grace Kelly, Princess Grace of Monaco was this:

'She was loyal, direct, simple, straightforward and honest. I never saw her complain about anything. I never saw her have a tantrum. And I never remember hearing her talk about money. She always remembered everything. When she went abroad she always returned with a small gift and even today every Christmas she sends me a card with pictures of the children. I keep them each year so I can compare how they are growing up. I never had anyone I enjoyed working with more than I did her.'

Eight

Grace Kelly's first film on the Coast was *High Noon*. It was a superb choice to launch her in for three obvious reasons. Gary Cooper was at his peak—strong, reliable, top box office draw. The script was stringent, believable and heroine-stuff. Stanley Kramer was the producer and Fred Zinnemann was the director, the man who knew exactly how to handle cool ladies and get the best out of them. He was later to crack that Grace Kelly was the only actress ever to have applied to him for a job wearing white gloves.

It was the strangest trio of human oysters. Gary Cooper, the original quiet American whose sum total of conversation was to look down from his golden heights and mumble 'yep' or 'nope'. Fred Zinnemann, a strangely withdrawn man, and Grace Kelly as shy as a mountain violet.

It was no less hilarious when Zinnemann on noticing Grace's almost painful shyness took her to one side and counselled:

'You ought to learn how to speak to people and what to say to them when you meet them.'

High Noon is the story of one man, Sheriff Kane, who had the moral, mental and physical courage to stand alone against the lawless. Around him in this shabby little Western town the people had vowed to stand close to their sheriff, but as the moment of confrontation came they faded away like lizards in the desert. They left him to face it alone.

Then came the great action shots as quick thinking, quick shooting, the sheriff disposes of three of the outlaws who had come to kill him.

Grace Kelly, his pretty wife in the film, whose Quaker upbringing made her abhor killing, picks up the gun and kills the fourth. It was a moment of subtle under-acting but also one of the most illustrious ones ever caught on the screen.

As the film fades Sheriff Kane, tall as a Redwood pine, slowly puts his protective arm round his wife as they walk to the wagon and ride off. Superb cinema. Superb performances.

High Noon gained Gary Cooper his second Academy Award and for Grace Kelly further proof that she was not just a pretty face but really could act.

The part suited her in every way. She could identify with it. Grace Kelly never was an instinctive actress. She had to really think herself into her parts and only when she came to the conclusion that it was right for her did she feel comfortable. Besides, she looked the part of the chaste Quaker wife yet with enough undercurrent to keep the box office interested. As one Hollywood surveyor put it, 'a face which reminds me of a cool, fast stream in a mountain hideaway'.

Out on the Coast M.C.A.'s bright boy Jay Kanter regularly covered the various studios as a routine part of his job and in doing so included the Stanley Kramer Company. He told me how Grace Kelly came to get the part.

'I knew Fred Zinnemann and Carl Foreman were doing a Western called *High Noon* and we talked about the various people for the different roles. It was a breakthrough in Westerns as it had a moral and intellectual appeal and the cast had to be absolutely right. They told me what sort of actress they wanted for the part of the sheriff's wife. It was a smallish role but extremely important to the climax of the picture. As a matter of fact Gary Cooper had not been cast in the picture at that time.

'I had already had a letter from Edith van Cleve about this new girl. We all had a very high regard for Edie's ability as an agent and knew that she wouldn't be recommending anybody who wasn't a good actress. If I remember, in addition to her glowing account, Edie also sent a couple of pictures.'

At that particular moment in Hollywood it was difficult for any young actress or actor to get an important role in the film business without granting the studio some sort of an exclusive arrangement for their future services. It was to prove a nightmare for many budding stars who found themselves at loggerheads with their studios and could not get released. Today it is quite different simply because the structure of the major studios is not the same.

'Grace was absolutely firm that she did not want to be tied down to a seven-year contract, so this was the first hurdle, but somehow we got round it so that the way was open for her to come out.

'I remember picking her up at Denver airport where she had been playing with a stock company (the Elitches Garden Theatre). She said, "Hullo". Just meeting her for the first time was quite an experience. She seemed to have it there in one look.'

On the way to the hotel Grace Kelly and Jay Kanter stopped off to meet a friend of Jay's . . . on hindsight a carefully planned ruse I suspect. The result was that the late Arthur Jacobs handled Grace's publicity for many years and it was during this time that she also met Rupert Allen who has been taking care of her personal publicity, including her wedding, ever since. Any special occasion in Monaco involving Princess Grace or her children and Rupert Allen is to be found immaculately behind the scenes.

Jay Kanter and I were talking in the flower-filled 'den' of his Beverly Hills home. Outside by the pool the children were preparing a barbecue. It was a typical Los Angeles film set. He walked round and round while he was speaking. It was as if he was groping for the exact words in which to describe something special. He did not want to make a mistake.

'It's not that you suddenly look at somebody and you go religious or anything like that kind. I don't know what it is. There was this girl and she was as attractive as one could be. From the film business's point of view she had a freshness about her but she also looked as if she knew where she was going and there was no turning it off. She went about it in her own way. I don't know what it is about people. They begin to affect you and you start to talk about them. Yes, I think that is what Grace had more than anyone.'

The word I feel that Jay Kanter was searching for is *charisma*. This melodious Greek word has a special meaning for each person. To me it means the kind of personal magnetism, or aura, that some people have and which draws others to them.

It is mental rather than physical; spiritual more than fleshy; people are born with it and seldom acquire it.

The most extraordinary example of all time was Jesus Christ. Others to a lesser degree and within the fabric of our lifetime are

Ghandi, Aneurin Bevan, Lady Edwina Mountbatten, President John Kennedy, Billy Graham, Queen Elizabeth the Queen Mother, Gertrude Lawrence, Edith Piaf and Bob Dylan.

To the outside world Grace Kelly, film star, or Princess Grace of Monaco may appear cool, introverted, remote, but to her close friends who have been permitted to penetrate behind her shy façade her charisma is bewitching . . . enslaving.

All her leading men, including such mature spoilt stars as Clark Gable, Bing Crosby, Ray Milland, James Stewart and William Holden, were to fall in love—a little more, a little less—with Grace Kelly. But no one could have foreseen the remotest possibility of this happening the day she stepped off the plane on to the Los Angeles airport.

During the making of *High Noon* Mr and Mrs Kelly insisted that Lizanne and Peggy went to Hollywood to be with Grace. It was a pattern that was to prove successful and be repeated in all her early films. At no time did she ever live alone. When her sisters could not go Prudence Wise, a friend from Barbizon days who became her secretary, accompanied her.

The three Kelly sisters—and any one of them could have been in films—stayed at the Château Marmont for the three weeks in which Grace was filming.

Today the Château Marmont sits on Sunset Boulevard like a flamboyant cabouchon ruby in a Woolworth necklace. It too is shabby and living on glorious memories of the past. In the days when the Kelly sisters lived there and the whole world could hear the heartbeat of Hollywood, it was bustling with stars. Bette Davis always stayed there and still does today. Myrna Loy and Boris Karloff are names revered by the few remaining original staff. Today it is the Los Angeles home of Lynn Redgrave and her family.

The huge entrance hall with its grand piano, fake baroque furniture and overwhelming vase of artificial flowers looks as if it is part of a derelict film set. Even the swimming pool which once gurgled with lovely young stars is seldom used. The Château Marmont is part of the living death of Hollywood today.

Grace, Peggy and Lizanne had a suite which meant that they could 'fix' their own meals if necessary. Each morning as the alarm clock went off at 6 o'clock there was a scurry to get up in time to drive out to the M.G.M. studios. And punctually the sisters would be there in late afternoon to collect her.

In the evenings they would collect up some of the boys who had been with Grace Kelly at the American Academy of Dramatic Arts and all go on to small restaurants.

'We knew that the boys did not have much money and we girls did have a dollar or two,' relates Peggy. 'So we had a game. We had a lovely old friend from San Francisco down and we pretended that she was a very wealthy old aunt—which she wasn't—and we said it was she who paid the bill.

'Grace was never late home at nights as she had to learn her lines for next day. We used to hear her and she always set off in the morning word perfect. She was very particular about that.'

At the weekends they played tennis with the same dinner-date boys, many of whom later became very fine actors.

Grace Kelly herself was never entirely happy with the film *High Noon*. She has always been disarmingly honest with herself and was to say:

'Everything is so clear working with Gary Cooper. When I look into his face I can see everything he is thinking. But when I look into my own face I see absolutely nothing. I know what I am thinking, but it just doesn't show. I wonder if I am ever going to be any good. Maybe I had better go back to New York and make my face show.'

Director Fred Zinnemann was to think much the same. The talent was there but like a diamond the facets needed to be polished. Edith van Cleve was later to meet him at a party at Bette Davis's. He went straight up to her and spoke about her protégée.

'She is going to be a star—no doubt about that. But she ought to have a little longer in the theatre.'

Even though the critics noted Grace Kelly's performance kindly in the accolades they wrote about *High Noon* she herself was disappointed and still unsure that she would finally make the top grade. Her character is an intriguing mixture of humility and compulsive drive.

No one was more delighted to get back to her beloved New York than she was. And once more 'Grace's place' was open.

Nine

By now M.G.M. had offered Grace Kelly a seven-year contract starting at 750 dollars a week, which seemed the right step to take in her career at this stage. She was just twenty-two years of age, had very little actual film experience and was virtually unknown to the movie public round the world. Despite all this she was quite determined in her demands and in her contract specified that she was to have a year off every two years to go back to the theatre; that she could live in New York instead of hanging around Hollywood as most of the stars were required to do. Astonishingly, M.G.M. agreed to her demands.

When the film *High Noon* was finally released Grace Kelly was invited to the gala opening at Lee Theatre in Fort Lee, New Jersey. It was her first public performance as a screen personality and she carefully chose a dress of black taffeta and aquamarine net which she bought from Bonwit Teller, that refined New York store for stylish shoppers.

As always she looked incredibly pretty as she cut a cake and made her first professional speech. Also included in the programme was a mannequin show, and to everyone's horror out tripped a model wearing the identical dress as worn by the film star. Heads immediately turned to Grace Kelly to see what she would do. With the utmost charm, her eyes twinkling with fun, she made a deep curtsey to the model. Everyone sighed with relief as what could have been an embarrassing situation was turned into a complete victory for the young film star.

At least once more in her lifetime Princess Grace was to have a similar situation and again showed an adroit way of handling it.

A few years after her marriage Princess Grace used to slip down to the beach at Monte Carlo and swim in the early morning, several hours ahead of the time the international set stirred their heads for their first orange juice. The sea was usually empty except for the other occasional early bird. On such a morning the Princess was happily swimming around when a wave took her close to another woman swimmer. They bobbed to the surface together and found that they had on the same swimsuit. Simultaneously Princess Grace and Countess Mannerheim, formerly of Sweden and now of Monaco who told me the story, burst out laughing and nodded to each other before another wave swept them apart.

There is a similar story of the Duchess of Windsor, who arrived at a party in Paris only to find another guest wearing an identical dress. The other woman tactfully went home and changed.

When director John Ford was looking for an English type for the secondary role in *Mogambo* he thought of Grace Kelly and saw the test she had made for *Taxi*.

'She's no mere beauty,' he said, 'that girl can also act.'

Mogambo was to be a remake of that successful chestnut *Red Dust* in which Clark Gable was to play his original role of the White Hunter. Veteran writer John Lee Mahin had completely up-dated the original script which had been set in Malaya with Jean Harlow playing 'Honey Bear', the brash chorus girl, and Mary Astor the 'good woman'.

For the second time round Mahin set the scene in Africa and Honey Bear's lines were revitalised to suit Ava Gardner. To Grace Kelly fell the role of the lily-cool English lady, Linda Norley, who had a passionate love affair with Vic Marshall (Clark Gable). Her opening lines were nothing short of banal as she stepped off the river boat and met Mr Gable. 'How do you do, Mr Marshall! I find Africa so exciting and thrilling.'

In Mervyn LeRoy's office in Beverly Hills, tall, gangling, skinny John Lee Mahin—his sun-withered face that looks as if it had been hacked from the Grand Canyon crowned by a baseball hat—talked to me of the part he wrote for Ava.

'Ava got the good lines. Grace just had to look the part, but she did it so convincingly that she almost stole the picture from Ava.'

Oddly *Mogambo* (which means passion in Swahili) was to be a catalystic experience for all its main characters. For Ava Gardner it meant playing the role with which she had been obsessed for twenty years—since she had seen *Red Dust* as a girl; for husband Frank Sinatra it was the realisation that their self-destroying marriage could never be repaired; for Grace Kelly it meant an awakening as a woman and the self-assuring knowledge that she was now really on her way to stardom, and for Clark Gable it was proof that age does not wither a man's virility.

Before leaving for Africa Grace Kelly explained in an interview that she wanted *Mogambo* for three reasons—to work with the legendary director John Ford, to act with Clark Gable and a free trip to Africa. She got all three.

The dramas began almost before the airplane took off. In his biography *Ava* Charles Higham (W. H. Allen) places the scene.

'On October 21 she (Ava Gardner) gave a weekend house party at Frank's house inviting Bappie (her sister), Ben Cole, Ava's business manager, and Lana Turner, another client of Cole's and an old friend of Ava's. One night all but Ava and Lana left the house to go to another party. Frank came home unexpectedly.

'There are many versions of what happened next. Whatever the reason, Frank flew into a rage and demanded the two women leave the house. The quarrel became so violent that neighbours complained and called in Police Chief Gus Kettman to settle the matter.'

Ava Gardner, the press officer of the film, and other minor members of the vast company set off to Africa by plane. At Zurich, where they changed planes, they were to pick up Grace Kelly. As the publicist Morgan Hudgins describes:

'We found her, lovely, blonde and composed, reading quietly in the airport terminal lobby. The book, as I recall, was one dealing with the experiences of an African white hunter.

'The local photographers fell all over themselves trying to get pictures of Miss Gardner. No one paid any attention to the other young lady. How were they to know that before very long she would become probably the most celebrated, and certainly one of the most photographed, girls in the world.'

For the film, which was to be shot in Kenya, Tanganyika and Uganda, M.G.M. had mounted what was to be remembered in Nairobi as the greatest camera safari of all time. The cast consisted of 8 white hunters, 175 whites and 300 blacks. There was everything from a mobile hospital to thirteen dining-tents, a travelling movie theatre and massive kitchens. Food and supplies were flown in daily to a special airstrip that had been cleared out of the jungle. Robert Surtees, the cameraman, had special refrigerated trucks to keep his film in.

People in Nairobi today still talk with a mixture of amusement and derision at the *Mogambo* safari and over drinks in the bar of the Stanley Hotel they retell the story of how Ava Gardner bathed naked in her canvas bath in front of the native boys assigned to her quarters.

Much more amusing is the apparently real version as told by Bob Surtees to Charles Higham.

'I'll never forget Ava's reaction when she got word of this. She roared with laughter, and immediately flung her clothes off, running bare-assed through the camp to the shower in front of everyone.'

Grace Kelly is remembered as 'the pretty girl at Gable's side who liked to go off with the chaps hunting'.

In her usual professional way Grace Kelly, who was then merely a contract player, settled in with her knitting, her camera and her own very special brand of naïveness.

'Don't worry about the Mau Mau,' she wrote home to her parents, 'M.G.M. have promised to take care of me.'

British actor Donald Sinden, who was also in *Mogambo*, has remained on friendly terms with the Princess ever since.

Remembering back to the film he says:

'I think Grace is the only person in the world who would have done this. She arrived in Nairobi ready for the three months' location having already acquired a working knowledge of Swahili!

'On my second evening at the New Stanley Hotel, she, Clark Gable and I had dinner together and Grace amazed us both by ordering the entire meal in Swahili. At the close of the meal she called after a departing native waiter, "*Lati ndisi*" (or it sounded like that). Clark Gable sharply enquired. "What's an *ndisi*?" We had already gathered that *lati* meant "bring" and the waiter replied in perfect English but with an American accent: "It is a banana."'

In the beginning of the film Ava Gardner had some difficulties with John Ford, who was known more for his brusque handling of gunmen in Westerns than for his tact with the ladies. I was also told by a member of the crew that there was a certain coolness as the two leading ladies 'circled each other like tabby cats waiting for the first one to scratch'.

Ava Gardner always claimed years later that she hated making this film and hated Africa. Grace Kelly was to say that she loved every minute of it.

Ava was joined by a fretting Frank Sinatra, her husband of less than a year. For the irascible Sinatra it was a time of nervous tension. He loathed the heat, flies and constant quarrels with Ava. Added to all this he was urgently waiting to hear if he had got the part of Maggio in James Jones's best-seller *From Here to Eternity*. This was more than just another film role . . . it was the chance to make the comeback he desperately needed at that time to prove himself as an actor and perhaps save the marriage.

Film locations are strange places where human egos and emotions are exaggerated. It is as though time itself stops. There is no past, no future. Just today with all its inbred passions and jealousies. Romances have the same ephemeral importance as those on ships. They seldom endure back in the harsher reality of daily living.

Ava and Frank spent much of their time together . . . loving, brooding, arguing, drinking, quarrelling. Clark Gable and Grace Kelly found their own satisfactory relationship. While the rest of the camp slept safely in their tents, Gable and Kelly were often up at dawn to go big game hunting with Frank ('Bunny') Allen, the renowned white hunter who specialised in safaris for the movie industry.

Grace Kelly enjoyed the personalities of both these men and the bewildering vastness of Africa intrigued her. The space, high skies, animals and dawn sunrises were something she had never before experienced.

During the making of the film she was once fifteen minutes late and Clark Gable, the complete professional himself, blew her up so much that she was terrified of being late from then on.

'She was an absolute darling,' one anonymous member of the crew told me. 'Ava was all temperament and drama, but Grace just behaved quietly like the lady she is. If in fact anything went on between Gable and herself it was all done with great circumspection and dignity.

'Quite obviously Gable liked her. Who wouldn't? She was always quietly there and never got in the way. It was probably the first time in his life that he had ever met a woman like Grace. He was obviously fascinated and seeing her in that setting cast a kind of spell over them both.'

One day when Clark Gable had a scene to shoot out in the bush and Grace Kelly did not, she asked if she could come along with him. It was going to be a very rough ride simply because there were no roads, just jungle trails. The Land-rover also had no springs and it would be a decidedly bumpy and uncomfortable ride.

Gable turned to her and said: 'Oh Grace! What do you come out here for every day? Why didn't you take it easy and go for a swim today?'

Grace Kelly turned those big blue eyes on him and quietly said: 'I wouldn't have missed this for anything. I love to work on locations because I get to learn something everywhere I go.'

'But you could read all about this,' he bantered.

'Oh no. I want to get my own impressions so that some day I can tell all these stories to my grandchildren.'

Gable never forgot that story and loved to tell it to his friends when she became Princess of Monaco.

That the immense African scene had a profound and even lasting effect on Grace Kelly is illustrated in this other Gable story. When he returned from filming one day he asked in the camp where she was and was told that she had gone out in the afternoon, taking a book with her.

Gable was perturbed that she was alone with so many wild animals around and went to find her, taking a favourite path she had to go to the beach to watch the sun set. He found her sitting on some rocks with the book open quietly crying.

'Grace. What's wrong with you? Why are you crying?' he asked.

'I can't tell you. It was too beautiful. I was just reading about a panther in the snow and I look up and here is a lion coming walking along the beach to the water. He was out of his element too but he just walked along the water as far as I could see,' she told him.

Clark Gable also admired her sporting side, a necessary equipment for survival in the Kelly family. When a herd of elephant came within 40 yards of her one day when she was out hunting with him, Grace Kelly remained still and composed. The shooting of some of the sequences had to be done under a special armed guard in case of Mau Mau terrorists. The film was not without its own dramas such as when the twenty-six-year-old assistant director, John Hancock, was killed when his jeep overturned.

But there were also celebrations, plenty of them. Ava and Frank turned their first wedding anniversary into quite a party. 'I have been married twice before but never for a whole year,' Ava was to crack.

Both Ava Gardner and Clark Gable had birthdays on location. For Ava's on Christmas Eve Frank Sinatra arrived back triumphant at having secured the role of Maggio. In his luggage were packets of spaghetti, tomato sauce, a mink stole and a diamond ring. He also brought his own little Christmas tree which he set up complete with lights outside Ava's tent.

Grace Kelly had been knitting in secret a pair of socks for Clark Gable. But like much of her knitting they were never finished. Shops were non-existent so each day the week before Christmas she would steal something from him until she had enough for a large sock which she hung up at the end of his bed.

Rumours of the Kelly-Gable romance were reaching London so good and strong that ultimately one London columnist cabled Gable: 'Rumours sweeping England about your romance with Grace Kelly. Please cable confirmation or denial.'

When he received the cable Gable showed it to everyone within earshot and said loud and clear: 'This is the greatest compliment I've ever had. I'm old enough to be her father.' No one was fooled.

Producer John Foreman recalled to me his reaction to the gossip. 'We were all jealous of the men that Grace saw. This used to amuse her heartily because we were very critical of who it happened to be. I remember being vitally pissed off when the stories came back from Africa that an affair was occurring between Grace and Clark Gable. It took me some years to decide if indeed it happened.'

Hollywood is never kind to its favourite children. The laws of libel are lax and it constantly weaves near-truths round its stars. That Gable and Kelly liked each other was evident. The rest is pure speculation.

When Earl Wilson in his pertinent column asked her on her return how many times she had been out with Gable she parried.

'Oh, I never counted. I wasn't the only girl he dated and he wasn't the only guy I went out with.'

Wilson: 'He must be more than twice your age.'

Grace Kelly: 'He is 52. I know because he celebrated his birthday in Africa.'

Wilson: 'Do his ears stick out so much now?'

Grace Kelly: 'They don't stick out at all as far as I could see. Maybe he fixes them some way. I had a girl friend who had protruding ears. She put something on them to make them stick closer to her head and once when she was having a date with a boy she wanted to impress very much the glue came unglued with a loud crack. She went right to the ladies' room to fix her ears.'

To an even more persistent interviewer she tossed off: 'Clark liked my silences.' Even the toughest of Hollywood columnists were to find that when Grace Kelly made up her mind not to discuss her personal life she meant it.

Gable was capable of being just as discreet. When tackled point blank about the romance he answered: 'Such a sweet well-brought-up girl.'

When it was inaccurately reported that Gable had given her a diamond bracelet, the friendship was on such easy grounds that she promptly telephoned him and asked: 'Well . . . where is it?'

Like every other tourist to Africa Grace Kelly came back with a bracelet made from the hair of an elephant's tail. Again when the ever inquisitive Earl Wilson asked her about it she said: 'It's supposed to bring good luck and good health. I never take it off.'

'Not even in your bath?' he queried.

'The elephant didn't take it off when he took a bath,' she replied sweetly.

To pin down any accuracy even with Princess Grace's family is difficult. One does not want to intrude on what was obviously a personal family matter. But marriage to the much-married Gable would not have been in keeping with Grace Kelly's own religious beliefs nor the family's wish, and it is doubtful whether in fact it would have lasted. Her family met Gable—Mrs Kelly had long been a fan of his—but the romance cooled off when they were both back on their own home territory.

Though so completely opposite in every way—the one living out her lush life in public, the other so intensely private—Ava Gardner and Grace Kelly ended the best of friends and remain so to this day.

One incident that probably brought them closer together than anything else was when, just before Christmas, Ava was secretly flown to London where in hospital she lost the baby she had been expecting. Even though her marriage to Frank Sinatra was unpredictable, she wanted his child.

No one could have been more understanding when she returned to the heat and forced gaiety of Africa than Grace Kelly. She keeps her compassion for such special occasions as this, but once given it is warm and strong and lasting.

When Grace Kelly married Prince Rainier, Ava Gardner was among the select *coterie* of Hollywood friends asked to the wedding and was one of the most arresting looking women at that fashionable event.

An odd sidelight to *Mogambo* was the heavy bill the studio received for Miss Kelly's luggage when she arrived back from Africa. Everyone was curious as to what could possibly be in the suitcases until Grace explained: 'They are my rocks.'

Jay Kanter describes the rocks' home-coming to Los Angeles.

'I got this call from our man in California who is in charge of looking after the M.G.M. people. He called me up and said: "Listen, the studio isn't one to complain and we know about these things on location but for God's sake. We have just got a bill for overweight for your friend Grace Kelly that amounts to just a horrendous amount of money." (I can't remember now, but they were really shocked.)

'They just didn't know if it was a mistake because Grace wasn't the sort of person to travel around with 40 pieces of luggage. She wasn't a star of that calibre at the moment anyway. So I called her up and I said: "Grace, gee this is a terrible complaint and I don't think they really mean it but they are damned upset about it."

'There was a pause and then she laughed: "Oh I know what it was. I sent back a couple of small trunks, I suppose they were like foot lockers, and they did weigh a lot, but do you mean to say that they sent them back by air. They were only rocks that I was collecting."

'She was totally ignorant and surprised that all her luggage would naturally be sent back by air.'

All during the filming she had been gathering the peculiar amethyst-veined rocks that one picks up in Africa in the fields. These and other rocks became the foundation of a collection of stones that she was to collect for several years.

At the time she was sharing an apartment in Sweetzer Street, off Sunset Boulevard, with actress Rita Gam. They had been friends since modelling days in New York. The one was as fair as the other was dark. While Grace Kelly was in Africa collecting her rocks Rita Gam was in North Africa on location with *Saadia* and making her own collection. Unbeknown to each other they both landed home with suitcases of rocks.

While Grace Kelly enjoyed 'African sessions' with Rita Gam, she rarely spoke about it to other people as she was shy that friends might expect her to deliver a travelogue. Even her family found it difficult to chisel anything out of her. Mr Kelly was to say at the time:

'You know the girl must have had a lot of fascinating experiences but she won't talk.'

It could have been the fact that no woman had ever looked more beguiling in a solar topee; that Bill Tuttle (make-up) and Sidney Guilaroff (hair) both of M.G.M. had turned Grace Kelly into a shining beauty; that Clark Gable had given her a new assurance. But one thing was certain. She was a much more glamorous woman after her return from *Mogambo* than before.

Grace Kelly had also picked up a lot of film technique from veteran Ford as well as developing a 'crush' on Clark Gable. Ford, the taciturn Irishman, usually so short on words about his leading ladies, was publicly predicting that Grace Kelly would soon be a star.

For her performance as the cool English wife stirred to frustrated passion for White Hunter Gable, Grace Kelly won a 'best supporting role' nomination for the Academy Award.

Grace Kelly had begun the final climb to the top.

Ten

Beautiful women seldom have an interest in or compassion for other women. It is a fact as old as Cleopatra. But in speaking with the dozens of people—men and women—while collecting material for this book I found that all were unanimous in their appraisal—and even love—for Princess Grace and the film star Grace Kelly.

They spoke in platitudes which were often difficult to break down. I refuse to believe that the aura that surrounds any member of a European Royal Family—however minor—is responsible for this loyalty. The answer lies deeper . . . in the very structure of the woman. In her appreciation and reaction to all human beings and most of all to her friends.

Back in Los Angeles from the heady all-male scene of Africa after completing *Mogambo* she stepped easily into her modest, light-hearted girlie life, the two-bedroom apartment in Sweetzer Street which she shared with actress Rita Gam.

Sweetzer Street may have changed over the last twenty years, but I doubt it. The apartment blocks are square, modern, functional and unimpressive.

Rita Gam now lives in Park Avenue, New York, with her two children from her marriage to publisher Tom Guinzburg. At the time of sharing an apartment with Grace Kelly she was married to Sidney Lumet the producer. Now she is on her own again and looking very like those giggly days twenty years ago. She is still incredibly beautiful and does selective acting.

'We met on a Saturday in California. I was living at the Beverly Hills Hotel and she had an apartment in Sweetzer Street, a street that was full of call girls. Grace was living with her secretary "Prudy" Wise,' she told me.

'Grace said, "Wouldn't you like to join me in sharing this flat? 'Prudy' can sleep in the living-room and we can all go to the movies together."

'I said, "Why not" and moved in straight away. It was cheaper than a hotel and as we were both working we had the same hours.'

There was a zany 'My Sister Eileen' quality about life at Sweetzer Street. There was the time they all went on the prune diet—'a mad diet of prunes, steak, eggs and more prunes. Our housekeeping tended to be chaotic and once when we found we had a pruneless larder we trailed all over Hollywood in the dead of night to find a prune shop open.

'Of course we cheated all the time, excusing ourselves as we ate a fat piece of pie or hunk of cake. Breakfast in the morning was a shamble. I guess we'd throw an egg in the pan or boil one with a piece of toast. I would drink hot water and Grace coffee. We'd be off to the studios by 6.30 or 7, just when the other Sweetzer ladies were coming home.'

There were nights when they both slipped round the corner to get a hamburger or cheeseburger and have an early night. The refrigerator was always stacked with 'splits' of champagne which was drunk consistently even with 'burgers.

Today champagne is still Princess Grace's favourite drink as she rarely drinks spirits.

Sundays the three girls usually slept right through since they all liked and needed a lot of sleep. If they had not been asked out for dinner, Grace and Rita took it in turns to cook.

'Grace would do her spaghetti bit with green salad or if she was in a cooking mood her *Bœuf Stroganoff*. The next time I would do my *Duck à l'Orange* with wild rice.'

When the bulges became eminent . . . or the girls thought they were . . . there would be crazy fits of turtle racing, a form of slithering along from side to side on the bottom.

There was no television, so if they were home the trio sat around talking about men, books, film gossip or designing clothes which they had made up by a dressmaker. Since Grace by now had a stream of Hollywood bachelors telephoning, Rita or 'Prudy' would sift the calls while she listened in. Even today there is a hot line in telephone numbers, especially ex-directory ones, among undesirable men or cranks. Sometimes they went for walks, but this was not entirely satisfactory owing to the friendly prostitutes who were also out walking.

There was a kind of protective attitude about Grace and Rita who were amazingly unspoilt for two such beautiful girls. Rita was more emotional but Grace had the cool, calm common sense as this story from Rita illustrates.

'One night we were invited to a party by an agent called Charlie Feldman and a friend of his from South America. Prudy had not been invited. We told him that we were going on to a party by Sam Goldwyn and he said, "That's fine I'll send a car over and take you both on".

'Grace told me to tell him we were driving ourselves, and how smart she was. At the dinner party when the big seduction scene started I began talking more and more because that's what I do when I get nervous and Grace started getting colder and colder. Then the lights got dimmer. The dinner was nearly over and the hands were on my knees. I became hysterical and whispered, "Let's go, let's go."

'Grace just said, "We'll go in a minute. Let's wait for dessert because it might be good." So we did wait and we had our dessert and then Charlie said, 'Now you leave your car here and I'll take you over." "In no way," Grace answered firmly. "We'll drive ourselves." So off we popped and had a super time at the Goldwyns and left those two standing.

'Grace was amusing to live with. She was never mean or cross but always generous and fun to be with. We both kept falling in love with all the wrong men, the married ones, so the only ones we could go out with usually turned out to be the tacky ones. No, I don't remember talking about our love life intimately to each other. Remember we were both well-brought-up girls.'

Prudence Wise continued to live with and be Grace Kelly's secretary for several years but was to die of leukaemia, another death which Princess Grace was to feel deeply.

All through her days in Hollywood, even after she became a star name, Grace Kelly was in fact extremely careful to take an extra girl friend or sister along with her on dates. The old-fashioned word is 'chaperone', but it is my deduction that it was Grace Kelly's way of combating the kind of vitriolic gossip that Hollywood is noted for. She was taking no chances. Later when her name was linked with

Bing Crosby her sister Peggy was with them on their one public date.

When I later confronted Edith Head, chief of Paramount's designing unit, with what she had once said in an interview in *The Saturday Evening Post*: 'There is a lot of solid jaw under that quiet face of hers,' she smiled in her quick bird-like manner, 'And I was dead right. Grace always had amazing horse sense.'

Eleven

Grace Kelly was soon back in her beloved New York. She had never settled happily in sprawling, inhuman Los Angeles and probably felt far more at home in Africa and Europe. She also missed that peculiar immediacy of New York where you meet friends walking on the street or can telephone them and they are there within a few minutes. Manhattan has an intimacy as well as immense style that is unlike anywhere else. At least the Manhattan that this sheltered girl would know.

There are the stylish apartments on the East Side with gay striped canopies, smiling white-gloved doormen; the robust bawdiness of Broadway; the exclusiveness of the small theatres tucked away in side streets; the tall sky towers like melting ice cubes in the summer sun; the drifting magical mists through the early morning in Central Park; that Aladdin's cave called Bloomingdales up the street from the Barbizon where she still loves to shop today.

Like all short-sighted people even the glare of the Hollywood sun distressed her. She preferred walking in the rain in New York.

Despite having made two successful films—*Mogambo* and *High Noon*—Grace Kelly was far from being an international star. Directors were not crowding for her work as they were to be only three years hence, and outside America she was still virtually unknown.

Back in the East with no film work in view she was delighted to be offered the leading role in *The Moon is Blue*, a play to be staged in Philadelphia's Playhouse in the Park. Any of her initial shyness in playing in her home town had now been overcome and in fact she enjoyed the challenge of this highly professional drama centre.

It was while dining at Philadelphia's smart country club that she was to receive a long-distance telephone call from Jay Kanter telling her that a deal was being set up for her to co-star with Ray Milland in *Dial M for Murder* at Warner Brothers, but even more important, to be directed by Alfred Hitchcock. It was a proven point that any unknown Hitchcock had discovered had every chance of being a star overnight.

Mr Hitchcock had in fact already met Miss Kelly after he had seen the test she did for *Taxi*. Grace Kelly later described her meeting with him at Warners: 'I could not think of anything to say to him. In a horrible way it seemed funny to have my brain turn to stone.'

In his study within his bungalow on the Universal set Alfred Hitchcock talked to me about that first important meeting. It was the kind of leather and oak room that fits into dozens of English country houses and looked ill at ease in Hollywood. Shutters were drawn to keep out the harsh Los Angeles sun. The atmosphere was sombre and serious. The benign Mr Hitchcock looked like a Buddha in a Savile Row suit. He did not smile. He scarcely blinked. I could not even see him breathe. His words were strangely without animation as he talked, in the flat English voice he has retained all those years, about his favourite film star.

'She is a very handsome woman, extremely intelligent, extremely sensitive with a tremendous sense of humour and natural qualities that have made her what she is.

'I once had a writer who when I said at the end of the script, "These people don't have enough character," he answered, "Well, you know for some people to have character they also have to have faults." She belies that particular comment. She has character without faults.'

There were long pauses as we sat looking at each other. I had read that he freezes at the word anecdotes so I mumbled something about human interest stories. The Buddha clasped his hands over that great expanse of stomach and looked slightly reproving.

'I was looking for a lady for the part and there are not many ladies around who can also act. Grace was a phenomenon at that time in the film industry. I am not a believer in the sexy type. I think it should be discovered in a woman. If you take the English woman, North German or Nordic types you know they all look like school teachers, but I gather that they are murder in bed. The English woman is the most promiscuous type.

'In *Dial M for Murder* we needed an English type and Grace fitted that particular requirement and was the most suitable of the actresses I interviewed. An actress like her gives the director certain advantages. He can afford to be more colourful with a love scene when it is played by a lady than when it is played by a hussy. Using one actress, the scene can be vulgar, but if you put a lady in the same circumstances she can be exciting and glamorous. And that is exactly what I did with Grace. Maybe she has fire and ice and great passion but she does not flaunt it.

'You could see Grace's potential for restraint. I always tell actors, "Don't use the face for nothing. Don't start scribbling over the sheet of paper until we have something to write. We may need it later." Grace has this control. It's a rare thing for a girl at such an age.'

When I reminded Mr Hitchcock of a former saying of his, 'the perfect actors or actresses can do nothing well but they still do nothing better than anyone else', he permitted himself a very tiny smile. 'What I meant is that their personality and presence is such that it attracts attention. It's like the famous actor Sir Gerald du Maurier, who could walk on the stage and light a cigarette and yet make it interesting.'

This is what he found in Grace Kelly. 'Grace Kelly has a presence . . . a charisma. She also has reason . . . she is a reasonable person. I will place Grace by far the most amenable and co-operative and untroublesome actress that I have worked with. What is it that Gertrude Stein said . . . "a rose, is a rose, is a rose". What else can you say about her?'

Another Hollywood observer said: 'Most of these dames just suggest Kinsey statistics. But if a guy in a movie theatre starts mooning about Grace there could be nothing squalid about it; his wife would have to be made to understand that it was something fine—and bigger than all of them. Her peculiar talent, you might say, is that she inspires licit passion.'

Hitchcock's genius was that his timing was right. The public during the late forties and early fifties had had a surfeit of bosoms and bottoms and bulges pushed into its face and was now ready and eager for someone with distinction, someone who looked well-bred, someone unobtainable. Twelve years before it had been Greer Garson, followed six years later by Deborah Kerr. And now it was to be Grace Kelly— the still centre of the whirlpool.

As Van Johnson quaintly summed it up: 'Hollywood went for Kelly in rebellion against a broadside of broads.'

Each film in that comparatively short but memorable career added an extra dimension to her acting. She wanted to learn and her capacity for listening was endless. It was Alfred Hitchcock who lowered her voice. Although she had taken voice production lessons ever since she went to the American Academy of Dramatic Arts, and had no trace of that indigenous Philadelphian accent, it was Alfred Hitchcock who finally coached her in how to pitch her voice lower.

'The reason was,' he explained to me, 'that in any emotional scene the lower the voice the more range you have to go. But if you already have a high pitch as most English women then in the higher notes you tend to become shrill.'

Grace Kelly's *Dial M for Murder* voice was the beginning of the enchanting transatlantic voice that millions of television viewers have come to know all round the world. When last year Princess Grace on two occasions read extracts from the Bible on the immensely popular English television programme *Stars on Sunday* it was her voice, soft and sweet as a ripe apricot, that people remembered. No one had expected it to sound so low and rich and anglicised.

Returning to New York, Grace Kelly was determined to have another try in a play, but although she twice read for the role of Roxanne in *Cyrano de Bergerac* to play opposite Jose Ferrer she did not get the role. Of course she was disappointed, as she had been many times before, but of her eternal optimism she said simply: 'I've often thought to myself that if I ever let go at times like that I'd never come up again.' Self-pity has no place in her make-up.

On the same day when she heard that she had lost Roxanne she went to the Radio City Music Hall to see *Mogambo* but hurried home to take a long-distance call from her mentor Alfred Hitchcock saying that he wanted her to star in his new thriller *Rear Window* opposite James Stewart.

'The whole point was that when I cast her in *Rear Window* there was an opportunity in that particular character (a fashion magazine editor) to dress her and make her extremely sophisticated and all done without any of the horrible unpleasantness that you see today,' Mr Hitchcock explained to me.

I was discussing *Rear Window* with a former Fleet Street journalistic colleague and quite suddenly this timid little man had a strange glint in his eye. It was almost as if I was not present as he talked aloud: 'I remember that scene in *Rear Window* when she walks across and sits on Stewart's lap. It is one of the most sensual scenes that I have ever seen on the screen.' Almost punch drunk, he shook himself out of the trance.

Under Hitchcock's manipulation Grace Kelly bloomed in *Rear Window*. As a sleek career girl she distilled what Hitchcock calls 'sexual elegance'. It was all there from the stunning wardrobe that Edith Head designed for her to the way she spoke, walked and even combed her hair. No other woman I know of could have produced a nightgown from her handbag with such innocent and mischievous delight. You could have cuddled her the way she did it.

The film was also notable for the scene where she places a kiss on James Stewart's forehead. Hitchcock made twenty-seven takes of that scene and had it been any other actor I would swear he had bribed the director. But James Stewart, who adored her, remains one of the few actors she worked with who did not fall head over heels in love with her.

When asked if he thought Grace Kelly was cold he answered, 'Grace is anything but cold. She has those big warm eyes—and . . . well if you ever have played a love scene with her, you'd know she's not cold.'

James Stewart has his own idiosyncratic way of speaking. It is like a long, lazy summer afternoon and you hope that each sentence will never come to an end. He was to say at the end of the film:

'The public is like an old setter dog in smelling out anything good, and Grace is good. She has class. Not just the class of being a lady—I don't think that has anything to do with it—but she'll always have the class you find in a really great race horse.'

His was a protective, fatherly devotion. Years later when he heard of her intended marriage to Prince Rainier he remarked: 'I'd have split my throat if Grace ever did anything that was not like herself. If she had married one of these phoney Hollywood characters I'd have formed a committee of vigilantes.'

Over a period of eighteen months James Stewart has been disinclined to talk to me about his days working with Grace Kelly in *Rear Window*. Maybe now he is tired, bored, or old, but there was a time when it was rumoured that he used to arrive on the set with a bunch of flowers for her, pretending that they had been picked from his own garden.

And when he told a magazine, which was indeed an original thought, that Grace Kelly could have played all the Garbo roles—Camille, Ninotchka and Queen Christina—this was professional devotion indeed.

Rear Window was also the beginning of a working association that developed into a deep friendship between Grace Kelly and Edith Head. Edith Head is a bird-like lady who has remained constant to her own inimitable image much the way Anita Loos has. They are Hollywood originals.

I visited her to talk about Grace Kelly at her white dolls' house bungalow at Universal City; just round the corner from Alfred Hitchcock.

Everything about her reminds me of a witty little bird, from her neat, black, satin-smooth head to button bright eyes that never miss a trick. Her movements are quick, decisive, and words explode out of her. Despite all the Hollywood razzmatazz I felt she could still be teaching Spanish and French at Bishop School in La Jolla where she went after gaining her Master of Arts degree from Stanford. Edith Head is a whip of a woman and totally refreshing.

We talked about Grace Kelly the woman: 'I think that Grace accepts her work of any kind for what it is. She is the total professional in whatever she does, whether it is as a model, actress or princess. She is also such a feminine looking person that you have the feeling that she could easily be pushed about. On the contrary I have never worked with anybody who had a more intelligent grasp of what we were doing. Under that very sweet and demure face there is great will power.'

And now Grace Kelly the actress: 'You see, working with actors and actresses everyone has a different language. So many people ask me that same repetitious question, "Who is your favourite actor or actress?" I say "Grace Kelly" every time. Not because I am fond of her, not because she looks so superb in anything I design but designing for her is an extraordinary experience because you don't actually work *for* her you work *with* her. I don't think people realise that there is a very analytical brain behind that beautiful face. I have never made sketches until I have worked them out with her. In other words we sit down. She is one of the few women who is completely objective. In other words you show her fabrics and she discusses them like a professional. She knows the difference between a hoop skirt and a crinoline. She is a very well-informed person.

'Practically no woman in the world over the age of five doesn't have a preconceived idea of what she likes. Unfortunately little girls with blue eyes have been told by their mothers "you are so lovely with your baby blue eyes in baby blue dresses". And so it goes all through. They instinctively say "I would rather have a square neck than a round one." I run into that all the time with women, but the extraordinary thing not with men.

'There is practically no other woman besides Grace Kelly who does in no way project her personal likes and dislikes into a character.

'You see, she came into the industry with a head start and a lot of advantages. She had culture, breeding, money, education, fully equipped with practically every weapon with which to fight. It was an extraordinary background for an actress. Very few people come with that.'

Already Grace Kelly had begun to collect her own élite fan club of fastidious actors and actresses who genuinely admired her work as opposed to being blinded by her professional beauty. One such was Douglas Fairbanks Junior. He told me of this period.

'Many years before Princess Grace was married some magazine interviewer asked her if she had ever been in love. As I recall the story—no doubt embellished by wishful thinking—she answered "Yes" but she didn't really know the man.

'He was only a photograph, or a figure on the screen. On being pressed as to who it was she replied it was *me*!

'When a dozen friends, at least, sent me copies of the interview I naturally ballooned with pleasure and kept one copy in my bill clip until time and overuse wore it out. As we had many friends in common, particularly David Niven, I kept hoping to make an effort to correct this oversight of Fate, and although it took some time, we did at last meet and she and Prince Rainier have since become close, valued and honoured friends.'

Twelve

With the completion of *Rear Window* Grace Kelly began one of the most extraordinary careers of any movie star in history. By now not only the fans but the exhibitors were solidly behind her and she was given star billing for the first time. One advertisement simply announced 'Grace Kelly in *Rear Window*'. This was all the more amazing as she was batting against the formidable favourite James Stewart.

Even more astonishing is the fact that within the next year she was to make five pictures that all became box office successes. It is titillating to speculate how much longer she could have gone on at that pace and how much time would pass before she would have been toppled from her pinnacle by a satiated public looking for a new celluloid heroine to fill their fantasy world.

One of the highest accolades that any citizen of America can have is to be chosen for the cover of *Life* magazine. It is a privilege reserved for presidents, peacemakers, warmongers and names that have been splashed across the world's newspapers.

When Grace Kelly was invited to sit for her portrait for the magazine a young photographer named Howell Conant was assigned to her. Again like so many of those early contacts it was to become a lifetime friendship and many of the finest pictures taken of her over the last years were made by Conant, who lives in New York. His pet name for her was 'Queenie', an irreverence he still retains to this day.

As one of Princess Grace's friends explained to me: 'It takes a long time to be accepted as a friend of Grace's. But once you are there she never lets you down. She has a consistency of character, temperament and behaviour, both in private and public life, which is the testimony of someone who really knows what loyalty is all about.'

Grace incidentally was not the only Kelly girl to make a *Life* cover. 'Kell's' wife, the fomer Mary Freeman, a pert caramel blonde, became one of America's top women swimmers and as a result became a *Life* cover. Specialising in back stroke and medley, she established three national American Athletic Union records, won the National Senior Indoor 200-yard back stroke and 300-yard medley championships, competed in the Olympic Games at Helsinki and accumulated enough cups to fill a room.

After Grace Kelly's *Life* cover, a deluge of reporters descended on her, much to her amazement. Magazines and newspapers chose their most experienced writers to gain 'in depth' interviews. Instead they came away totally baffled with a notebook full of slender quotes and the memory of those pregnant silences. After their interviews they knew no more about her private life than when they first met her.

It was not that she did not want to answer their questions. From the minute of her conception Grace Kelly had beautiful manners! It was just that she was an enigma and viewed the reporter with suspicion and quiet amusement from behind her private Iron Curtain.

Elizabeth Taylor has spent a lifetime baring her bones across eight continents. Ava Gardner ripped open her heart with monotonous regularity until she escaped to Europe and oblivion. Every year Marilyn Monroe exposed her tiny soul like a child with a chronic heat rash. But Grace Kelly always remained true to herself and no one was allowed to penetrate behind her calm blue eyes. I wonder that she has ever looked there herself.

She had, and still does have, a genuine horror of talking about herself. She flatly refused to discuss with reporters what made up her 115 pounds and would not allow the studio to release the usual data on bust, waist and hips.

It has been suggested that her aloofness and complete contempt for publicity stunts was in fact a clever ruse and an up-dated version of Garbo's 'I want to be alone'.

Nothing could have been farther from the truth. She just could not genuinely understand why other people would be interested in reading about her other than an appraisal of her acting performance in a film. As a serious-minded actress this seemed to be the only important thing.

When Marilyn Monroe was asked what she wore in bed she cooed breathlessly 'Chanel No. 5' and this much tooled remark passed into Hollywood folk-lore. The Hollywood columnist who dared to ask Grace Kelly whether she wore nightgowns or pyjamas got a laser beam reply: 'I think it is nobody's business what I wear in bed. A person has to keep something to herself or your life is just a layout in a magazine.'

When another brash reporter was foolish enough to ask if she wore 'falsies', she blushed and looked genuinely terrified. It was as if someone had deliberately trodden on a kitten.

Once when she was being particularly harassed working in the film *Green Fire* during the day and appearing on the *Bob Hope Show* in the evening she exploded to Edith Head:

'If I don't feel like talking that's my business. I'm not employed to give monologues. I'm hired to be an actress.'

Rita Gam, who was to see how she suffered during these early interviews, says: 'Grace was gentle. She was a gentlewoman. She was something so totally new to Hollywood. I am sure that Grace didn't ever consciously say to herself, "I won't give any of myself to this interviewer." She just wanted to get away from the lush self-indulgence, extravagance and vulgarity of Hollywood in the early fifties. Grace didn't have to go in for any exhibitionism of any kind. She has always been a mature human being.

'People might have called it temperament but it was really her way of taking what she wanted from life instead of letting life take her over. She is one of the few women I know who has real clarity and purpose and has taken real deep and sturdy roots in her life.'

During those early Hollywood days Grace Kelly was constantly heard to remark:

'Why do they want my picture? I don't think I am very interesting.' And she really meant it. She was not just being coy.

Though she had an attractive pair of legs and wore a swimsuit well, she did not think that she was the leg art type and would do anything to get out of posing in clothes that hit her above the knees. She stubbornly refused to have anything to do with the traditional cheese-cake publicity stills.

In her favourite publicity still from Hollywood days she wears a pale green chiffon pleated evening dress and is perched archly between a pair of Grecian columns.

'This was probably the real Grace Kelly,' photographer Franker was to say years later, 'soft, graceful, elegant—a sort of diluted crème de menthe.' He was equally sincere when he said, 'She is the type of girl that you put on a pedestal then you turn around and walk out of the museum.'

The paradox is that while the publicity departments of the various studios worked day and night to think of suitable quotes to super-impose on the public image of their stars no one dared try that trick on Grace Kelly. Even then she had an unmistakable royal presence. Her dignity wrapped her like a protective cocoon.

There are few thoughts of Grace Kelly that are irresistibly quotable lifted out of context. Gimmicks of any kind did not fit into her way of life. But there was one occasion in the South of France when a journa-list asked her: 'What is the secret of your fatal charm for men?'

'I really don't know why men like me. I guess it is because I am a girl,' she answered.

The combination of Alfred Hitchcock and Grace Kelly is indeed a strange one. Of all the directors who could have worked with her at that time he seemed the most improbable. Elia Kazan might have appealed to her intelligence and brought out another dimension in her just as he did with Vivien Leigh in *A Streetcar Named Desire*. George Cukor was an obvious choice with his ability to get inside the feminine mind. Katherine Hepburn, Garbo and Elizabeth Taylor all produced a new kind of magic under his intuitive direction. Vincente Minnelli, William Wyler and Daniel Mann were all possibles to extract the distilled essence of Kelly. But it was Alfred Hitchcock, the rank out-sider, who took the long chance that paid off. He wanted the kind of inner brilliance that could ignite a screen and Grace Kelly in return needed firm handling, the hallmark of Hitchcock direction.

Grace Kelly was always factual about herself as an actress. It was one of her most appealing traits. Neither vain nor suffering false modesty, she was also aware of all her faults, including the fact that she disliked the left side of her face.

But most of all she was willing to listen. As a director Alfred Hitch-cock liked her level-headedness, her reserve, her mystique. Though too wholesome looking to be mysterious, she settled instead for a fragile tantalising perfection that occasionally irritated women but never men. And this is just what appealed to Hitchcock.

He also enjoyed her inspired ability to get to the studio on time, seldom fluff a line and her consideration to everyone on the set from producer to the lowliest clapper boy. Henry James has called this quality 'the deeper sense'—something Princess Grace has always understood.

Thirteen

Without one day's rest Grace Kelly went straight from *Rear Window* back to Paramount for the making of *The Bridges of the Toko-Ri*, a sugary war film.

The part of navy pilot William Holden's wife in *Toko-Ri* was not big enough to attract an important star but it was a cameo that required exactly the right actress to play it. The director-producer team of George Seaton and Bill Perlberg wanted an unknown with a fresh, untarnished face. It was the kind of quality role that Deborah Kerr, Audrey Hepburn or Vivien Leigh could have played, and as it proved, so could Grace Kelly.

Many girls were auditioned for the role, including one who turned up in a black dress and six-inch crucifix. Grace Kelly wore her usual 'uniform'—a shirt and skirt, flat-heeled shoes and glasses. Her plain-Jane impact was not exactly devastating but, as with everyone else during her life, Seaton and Perlberg warmed to her. They saw in her the exact ingredient necessary for the part—a cool exterior with inner passion.

Everything in the jigsaw puzzle fell quickly into shape. M.G.M. were willing to lend her out to Paramount for 25,000 dollars, and as her salary was only 10,000 dollars this meant a clear profit of 15,000 for M.G.M.

By today's figures, and the kind of money that revolves round Sophia Loren and Elizabeth Taylor, this was an insignificant deal. But money, as such, has never been Grace Kelly's criterion for work.

On hindsight *Toko-Ri* did little to enhance her acting career and did not require her to stretch herself, which is when she gave her best performances. The only thing remarkable about it is that she consented to appear in a swimsuit in the Japanese bathhouse scenes and it brought William Holden into her life. They have remained firm friends ever since and he was to again star with her in *The Country Girl* which changed her whole professional status.

One of the most extraordinary and endearing qualities about Grace Kelly is that all the men who have been involved with her in an 'affaire de cœur' have remained totally loyal and devoted ever since. Strangely it is through their eyes that one gets a clearer picture of this woman rather than from her women friends.

The men are like a bunch of copy writers in the fifties with the assignment to promote English cotton dresses. 'Good taste, freshness, dignity, charm, honesty, integrity, refined' . . . and so the words flow on.

'Bill' Holden is no exception. During the two pictures he made with Grace Kelly they spent a great deal of time together on and off the set and he knows her better than many other people. I caught him on the wing in the Beverly Hills Hotel where he was staying, en route from his Palm Springs home to somewhere.

Though twenty-odd years have gone by there was a lilt in his voice and the platitudes fell like autumn leaves. But these were 'for real' and therefore none the less attractive.

'I have such respect for her talent and ability,' he told me. 'She is such a conscientious hard-working human being. Very often beauty negates ability and talent. But this is not the case with Grace.' (Hitchcock was to say something similar.) 'She was so sensitive to other people's problems.'

One strange remark he made which could only come from a naïve all-male who really understands the workings of women very little was this: 'Every woman who saw her and could identify with her thought that they were beautiful too.'

Most of us are positively covetous that anyone could have so much beauty . . . and manage her life so well.

William Holden continued: 'In that period in Hollywood she became a symbol of dignity. Women like Grace Kelly and Audrey Hepburn help us to believe in the innate dignity of man—and today that is what we desperately need to believe in. She is an exceptional human being. She not only had good judgment and good taste but a tremendous ability to concentrate and was an absolute delight to work with.'

On the Hollywood grape-vine there was much talk about the next film that William Perlberg and George Seaton were to make for Paramount.

David Selznick had bought it as a vehicle for his wife Jennifer Jones, and Bing Crosby and William Holden were lined up as co-stars. Selznick had the same kind of determination to consolidate Jennifer Jones as a major star as Randolph Hearst had for Marion Davies. With Jennifer Jones the results were more laudable. When Perlberg and Seaton got word that Jennifer Jones was pregnant, the flap that was expected did not in fact arise. Because of the dowdy clothes that were required for the part of the mousey wife Selznick thought that the picture could be finished with Jennifer Jones in the part.

Perlberg and Seaton had other plans. They just looked at each other and said simultaneously, 'Grace'. They became so entranced with the idea that they quietly let Grace Kelly in on their conspiracy. A copy of the script was 'leaked' to her and she knew that this part was right for her.

So did at least a dozen other Hollywood stars. It was a similar situation to *Gone With the Wind* and every actress longing for the part knew it could get her a coveted Oscar. The 'rooting' took place at dinner parties, through the powerful columnists and at the Sunday pool parties; wherever there were people gathered together. Mrs Seaton and Mrs Perlberg had never been so popular as a possible shortcut to their husbands.

Though Mr Seaton and Mr Perlberg were strongly in favour of Grace Kelly there was one obstacle—and a formidable one at that. Bing Crosby was against it. He made it quite clear that he could not see the golden good looks of Grace Kelly in the part. Nor did he think she had the acting stamina.

This was the final straw that Grace needed. The Kellys have always been fighters and Grace is no exception. She contacted her agent Lew Wasserman and goaded him with the facts. 'You have got to let Metro release me to play this part. If you don't I'm going to quit the picture business and go back to the theatre in New York.'

M.G.M. made a deal. They upped her price from 20,000 dollars to 50,000 and insisted that after *The Country Girl* was finished she return to the M.G.M. fold and make two films for them.

With the help of Edith Head, Grace Kelly completely transformed herself. She not only changed the obvious things like making her hair dull, coarsening the set of her jowl by sticking out her bottom lip, wearing her glasses on top of her head and playing some of her biggest scenes in a sloppy cardigan, but she visibly changed. She added years to her age by slouching and gave her soft shining eyes a despairing glaze.

After one week's shooting Bing Crosby was gallant enough to remark to Seaton: 'Never let me open my big mouth again. This girl can really act.'

It was only natural that Mr Crosby, who was then in between marriages, took his leading lady out to dinner. It was common knowledge at the time that Bing Crosby was quietly looking around for a new wife and Grace Kelly could conceivably have been in his mind. When Mrs Kelly was asked about the 'romance' by a punishing reporter, she retaliated: 'My Gracie with Bing. I don't blame her. Bing and Clark have always been favourites of mine.'

William Holden remembers the fun they had on the set making *The Country Girl* . . . the kind of rapport when three people feel superbly comfortable in each other's presence. The threesome hardly ever left the set and usually had tea together. Bing used to bring his bird books to show Grace, who invariably had her head in a book.

'Grace and I were involved in a scene where Bing was just out of jail. It culminated in my grabbing her and kissing her. I forced my mouth on her mouth and my teeth clicked like a billiard ball off her teeth.

' "Would you mind not doing that. I'm terribly afraid we'll crack each other's teeth. I'll try to hold the passion down," she replied.

'She was always ready for a laugh. "Listen, you have just kissed me," she continued. I replied puzzled, "Yes." "Well, don't let it go to your head," she quipped.'

It was a tremendously happy film in that everyone gave of their best. As the ageing alcoholic matinée idol Crosby settled down to his own pace with that streak of brilliant professionalism. William Holden gave his usual competent performance and was delighted to be working with Grace again. But it was Grace Kelly who lifted the film up into astonishing heights. She brought to the role of the slatternly wife a compulsive and moving tenderness. Clearly she had added a new dimension to her acting.

When she first arrived on the set the technicians and electricians scarcely gave her a second glance. To them she was just another blonde, another job.

At the end of the film Grace Kelly was their girl. There was not a man on that set who would not have done anything for her. On the final day they presented her with a plaque on which was engraved 'To Grace Kelly. This will hold you until you get next year's Academy Award.'

The winning of an Academy Award is not only a financial bonanza for any actress or actor, which can multiply their studio value overnight, but it is an emotional triumph.

It is the justification of years of disappointments, hard work and belief. An emotional experience that can transform a life, catapulting it up into the rarefied world of being an international star.

For weeks Hollywood had been buzzing with conjecture.

Grace Kelly was quite sure, despite the studio rumours, that she would not win an award for her part in *The Country Girl*. She herself thought it would go to Judy Garland for her diamond-brilliant comeback role in *A Star is Born*.

Grace lunched at the restaurant at Paramount Studios on the day the awards were to be announced. Tensions ran high as people kept coming over to her table to wish her luck. Bing Crosby was one of the first: 'Good luck, Gracie. We're keeping our fingers crossed for you.'

William Perlberg and George Seaton were sure that their star would win and assured her, 'Everybody's rooting for you.'

As the lunch progressed the tension increased. The only one who remained calm—or appeared to—was Grace Kelly. She just kept eating her salad. Mr and Mrs Kelly had remained in Philadelphia anxiously awaiting news.

The evening had been planned that Edith Head would join Grace, French actress Zizi Jeanmaire and Don Hartman, head of Paramount Studios before going on to the Award ceremony. She had made Grace's dress, which was to be the only personal one that she ever created for her. It was an aquamarine slipper satin with shoe-string shoulder straps and matching cloak. Her only accessories were a pair of long white gloves—naturally—and a hand-made petit-point evening bag.

Edith Head recalled: 'A lock of her hair had fallen down from her chignon. We were standing by a vase of flowers and as she tucked the lock in Grace picked up a little yellow rose and pinned it into the chignon. It was a gesture that she thought nothing of. Next day it was picked up by the fashion writers everywhere who probably thought it had all been planned. You see, she does these things so spontaneously, so naturally. Everything she does I think has her individual stamp.'

Hollywood's Pantages Theatre was packed for the occasion with that special kind of electricity that a competition of this importance inspires. Grace watched her friend William Holden as he took the envelope to read the name. In a clear resonant voice, looking straight at her seated in the audience he announced: 'Actress of the year—Grace Kelly.'

Every head turned as she slowly walked up the aisle amid the clapping and congratulations to take her award. Some actresses bounce up. Others almost trip, but Grace seemed to float down the great aisle and up on to the stage.

No one was more delighted than 'Bill' Holden to hand her the shiny bronze statuette. The audience was hushed as she began to say in almost a whisper, 'I will never forget this moment. All I can say is thank you.'

TV technicians were so sure that Judy Garland would be chosen that they had wired her up in bed at the Cedars of Lebanon Hospital following the birth of her baby son, so that the cameras could switch over there. When Grace Kelly was announced instead, Judy's husband Sid Luft said: 'Baby, * * * * the Academy Awards, you've got yours in the incubator.'

Besieged by reporters and photographers waiting to photograph the new award winners, Grace was asked to pose with Marlon Brando, best actor of the year for his role in *On the Waterfront*.

'Why don't you kiss Marlon?' one of the photographers asked her.

'Well, I think he should kiss me,' Grace replied. It is typical that even in this volatile moment no one could upset her public equilibrium. It was only after she had returned to the privacy of her own apartment after the party at Romanoffs that she allowed herself to cry. She cried for an hour.

Jack Kelly's proud moment that night was when he received a Western Union telegram from friends which read 'The Country Girl has become the girl of the country.'

It was this night too that brash Jack Kelly was to make one of his most fatuous and teasing remarks. He had asked some friends to the Kelly home in East Falls to watch the Oscar ceremony on television. When Grace's name was announced he remarked: 'I can't believe it. I simply can't believe Grace won. Of the four children she's the last one I'd expected to support me in my old age.'

It was a remark that was to be quoted in and out of context for the rest of his life. It was also the observation of a father who had so little patience for anyone who was not totally obsessed by sport as he was. Peggy and Lizanne had fulfilled his hopes, but Grace with her mediocrity of sports talent, her super-sensitiveness and reserve was the only one of his children that he could not communicate with mentally. Although he was to become absurdly proud of her, she always remained an enigma to him.

The bronze Oscar statuette which she won that night now stands on a shelf in the salon of the private apartment in the Palace of Monaco.

Now that she had finally proved herself to be an actress of star quality, M.G.M. viewed their protégée with new interest. Their big plans for their meteoric star turned out to be *Green Fire*, a piece of Hollywood trivia about emerald hunting in Colombia. No one was happy on that film, including both the stars, Grace Kelly and Stewart Granger. But at least it gave Grace a chance on location to collect some more rocks to bring home.

When the film made its début in the Broadway Theatre Grace was furious. On the outsize poster was the figure of a woman . . . it was Grace Kelly's head but pinned on to a bosomy, lascivious body suggestively draped in green, that was certainly not hers.

'It makes me mad and the dress isn't even in the picture,' she said.

Other actresses, including Elizabeth Taylor, who have had the same despicable treatment by their studios, have created such a fuss that the hoardings had to be replaced. Grace Kelly had her own private way of retaliation. She just stayed away from that side of town.

By now Grace Kelly was more than ever determined to find the right film for her. She was professional enough to realise her worth and anxious to avoid something as worthless as *Green Fire*.

M.G.M. now offered her Sir Walter Scott's classic *Quentin Durward*. She read the script carefully—she never makes up her mind about important things in a hurry—and decided to refuse it.

Her reason was quite simple. 'All the men are jousting but all I have to do is to wear thirty-five changes of costume, look pretty and frightened clutching a box of jewels. I'd be so bored.'

With her self-protective intuition she was right. The enchanting Kay Kendall took over the role which added nothing at all to her film career.

Grace Kelly was next offered a Western called *Tribute to a Bad Man* in which Spencer Tracy was to star. She went out to Hollywood from

New York to discuss the proposition. After two days of talk, in that quiet voice of hers she announced that she would delay giving her decision until a final script had been prepared.

This must have been a big decision for a young actress as working with Spencer Tracy was considered one of the great 'plums' of Hollywood. Apart from Marlon Brando he was probably the greatest film actor Hollywood has ever produced and was also one of the most generous spirits in the history of films.

With her uncanny determination Grace Kelly once more turned M.G.M. down and hiked back to the composure of New York. This was exasperating for M.G.M., who promptly sent her a telegram suspending her until further notice.

Grace Kelly was 'bewildered and disappointed' but with her characteristic coolness was to tell the Press: 'It's my first experience with a thing like this, and I guess that there is nothing that I can do but sit here and wait till they want me back. I feel very strange not getting a salary any more.'

With typical Kelly candour and no bitchery she added: 'I felt I had to turn down the roles because they're just parts that I couldn't see myself playing. I hope that they are not too mad at me. Perhaps I was spoilt by my loan-out pictures. Now Metro say that they won't lend me to other studios any more. They feel it is time that I made one for them and of course they have a good talking point.'

There had been in fact several roles at M.G.M. that Grace Kelly would have been interested in but the studio were not in agreement.

Over in Hollywood Dore Schary, head of M.G.M., was more explicit: 'We feel that Miss Kelly has certain obligations to us. After all we were the first to give her a chance. All her offers came after she appeared in *Mogambo* . . . Maybe she has a few complaints but we are all willing to discuss whatever is wrong.'

Fourteen

Two charming Europeans were to play a significant part in Grace Kelly's life before she met Prince Rainier. They were Jean Pierre Aumont and Oleg Cassini.

Taken in the span of Princess Grace's life and her ultimate choice in Prince Rainier, these two romances may not be important but they do illustrate the kind of worldly man that she was attracted to. They were the complete opposite to the all-American image that she had been brought up with and the two men who had dominated her childhood, her father and her brother.

It was in 1955 during the time that she was friends of both of them that she did in fact meet Prince Rainier.

Oleg Loiewski-Cassini was born in Paris, the son of the late Countess Marguerite Cassini, daughter of Czar Nicholas II's ambassador to the United States and Alexander Loiewski, a Russian diplomatic attaché.

He and his brother were brought up in the rarefied cultural world of Florence, where his mother opened a dress salon after the Russian revolution. Though Oleg Cassini himself would have preferred the more gregarious world of the diplomat or professional soldier, the family's finances made it more expedient to follow in his mother's footsteps. He opened his own dressmaking salon in Rome so as not to be in competition with Mama. On the sporting side he played tennis for Italy in the Davis Cup when tennis was still a glamorous pastime for gentlemen.

Four years later, with very little except absurd optimism, he and his brother Igor set out for America to seek their fortune. They had all the urbane charm, wit and international charisma to titillate New York Society.

Oleg immediately set up his own dressmaking salon and Igor became the piquant society columnist under the pseudonym *Cholly Knickerbocker*. They were both adored and feared as they sprinkled New York parties with their *double entendres* with the same exuberance as Zsa Zsa Gabor employs to dissect her husbands.

When Oleg was chosen by President John Kennedy's wife, Jacqueline, to make many of her clothes, his social *cachet* and financial success were secured.

Both brothers were to become American citizens and as well as serving in the cavalry in World War II Oleg married two very controversial American women. First the cough-drop heiress Merry ('Madcap') Fahrney—he was the fourth in what was to finally be a series of eight husbands—and the second was the beautiful film actress Gene Tierney who, by coincidence, had also lived at the Barbizon Hotel with that other young budding star, Grace Kelly.

Oleg loved—and still does—to be seen with beautiful women. To a girl reared on the stuff that American men are made of he was like a draught of glacier cool, Dom Perignon. Pure, undiluted sophistication.

This then was the man who set out to attract Grace Kelly with predatory intensity, the such she had never known before.

They met in a droll way. He had gone to the cinema with a friend to see the film *Mogambo* and nudging his companion in the dark as a beautiful cool blonde swished her way through the jungle, he said: 'This is the girl for me.'

'You are not lacking in modesty, are you?' his friend snapped.

'No, I am not lacking in modesty. I just think she is the type of girl that I would like,' Cassini replied.

Continuing the story to me in his New York office, he recounted: 'I had always liked actresses. They had a special fascination. Not because of the publicity or anything but because of the character they needed to succeed. I had already been married to Gene Tierney with whom I had two daughters and was now heart free again.'

After the movie the two men went to dinner in a small French restaurant and as they prepared to sit down Cassini turned round automatically to his right and saw seated next to him Grace Kelly, who was dining with the French actor Jean Pierre Aumont.

'I had some kind of resentment for him because when I was in the Army during the war he kept calling my wife, Gene Tierney, all the time to take her out, but I suppose all is fair in love and war.

'I managed to get myself introduced to Grace, who was polite but not particularly encouraging. But her smile was warm. I went home that night saying, "Well, this is destiny . . . how could it be otherwise? I'm going to work on this thing." Although I did not know her character, she invited all the things that I think are attractive in women —clean-cut good looks and a coolness of appearance.'

Within the next few days, having secured Grace's address, Cassini began to bombard her with flowers. Vast amounts of flowers delivered daily. After one week of this floral barrage he telephoned the apartment on 63rd Street and with his characteristic ebullience said:

'I'd like to speak to Miss Kelly.'

'Who's speaking?' came the cautious reply.

'This is your friendly florist,' Cassini quipped.

There was a silence and then a small peremptory voice replied, 'Who are you?'

'I would like to tell you who I am but do me the favour, as long as I promise that we have already been introduced, to meet me for lunch or dinner.'

Grace Kelly said that she would think about it and then made the suggestion that as she was lunching with her sister that day would *the voice* like to join them. Sisterly solidarity in such matters was typical of the Kelly girls.

'I managed to get her aside for a while and she told me that she was going back to California. "Well, I would like very much to get to know you better," I persisted, "I go there often as I have many friends there and would you mind if I called you?" '

At the time Grace Kelly was finishing a short-lived romance and Oleg Cassini's arrival hit her at the right time emotionally.

During the early part of their friendship Grace and Oleg had such rapport that they disliked being apart for any length of time. After a heavy day's filming she enjoyed being with him and dining in the small restaurants he had a genius for finding.

Other women who have known Cassini have told me that he had that incomparably rare talent: when you were within his orbit he made you feel all-woman and unique. He knew every nuance of how to make a woman bloom although he could be an awesome sight when he became jealous.

When Grace was filming *The Country Girl*, a most exacting role, she telephoned Cassini one evening at 7 p.m. at his Long Island home which he shared with his mother and brother. She was staying at the Bel Air Hotel and wondered if he would come out and cheer her up.

'She said she needed my company. We had a field outside the house with a swimming pool at the end. I was so overjoyed at the thought of seeing her that I rushed out and took one dive in the pool. There was no water. I landed flat on my face and broke my nose, which immediately became gigantic.

'It did not bleed, so I did not bother to go to a doctor. Instead I went straight on the night flight to California. I had told Grace on the telephone that I had had a little accident.

'When I knocked on the door of her apartment in the Bel Air she opened it, took one look and closed it again. She was certainly not devoid of a sense of humour.

'We had a couple of fights at that time because several important guys, like Frank Sinatra, now wanted to be seen with her. I have a very violent temper and while I was quite willing to go back to New York I did not feel like sitting around while she went out with someone else.

'I began to discern something I did not like in myself at that time. I felt that my enemies were obliging me to make this a challenge and not a natural love affair.'

Grace Kelly met Jean Pierre Aumont during her early acting days in New York and their friendship was to span over a period of two years. They were to meet intermittently, but it was not until 1955 that her family and friends considered him a serious contender in marriage.

Aumont had been married to the beautiful film actress Maria Montez who had died leaving a small daughter, Marie-Christine, but though his home was in the countryside outside Paris he was frequently in America with his acting commitments. Just as Yves Montand was to enchant Marilyn Monroe, so Jean Pierre Aumont fascinated Grace.

He had a kind of wanton charm superimposed on golden good looks that defied age . . . 'a wonderful man whom everyone loves', as Grace herself was to say.

His friends were legion, including many among the British theatre. During his period in the 1939-45 war when he was serving with the Free French Forces in England he frequently stayed with Vivien Leigh and Laurence Olivier at their mini stately home Notley Abbey. He and Vivien were later to enthrall New York in 1963 in the musical *Tovarich*.

The Kelly-Aumont romance did not in fact reach its crescendo until the Film Festival of 1955. Newsmen hungry for gossip soon latched on to the possibility of a romance between Grace and Jean Pierre and doggedly trailed them.

When first queried about marriage, Grace was her usual reticent self, but when one newsman informed her that Jean Pierre was telling everyone of his love for her she blushed and answered:

'We live in a terrible world. You can't have secrets from anyone. A man kisses your hand and it is screamed out from the headlines. He can't even tell you he loves you without the whole world knowing it.'

As for Jean Pierre, he proclaimed for all the world to hear:

'I adore Grace. Any man would be proud to marry her. She is a wonderful woman.'

Just before she left Cannes, after bewitching everyone at the festival, Grace was handed a copy of *Life* and blushed furiously—with anger.

There in black and white was a picture sequence that might have been taken straight out of one of her films. The sun was shining, the mimosa drenching the hillsides and the champagne cool and crisp. The hero and heroine held hands. They kissed. They snuggled. There was even one picture showing Grace kissing Jean Pierre's hand. It was all perfectly innocent, joyous fun that belonged to two people.

Unbeknown to them a hidden camera had recorded every moment of this lunchtime love story.

In reporting the matter to its readers in America a few weeks later *Motion Picture* wrote: 'Rumours were flying through Cannes that Aumont was less surprised than Grace at the magazine's disclosures. Also, stories which had originated in Cannes were seeping back to America that the romance was nothing but a publicity stunt.

'Grace may or may not have heard these rumours, and the timing could have been just a coincidence but the night she left Cannes she told a reporter, "Jean Pierre and I are just good friends. There is no truth to the rumours about a romance, but there would have been two years ago."'

Grace Kelly herself was deeply shocked. Anything more likely to chill a romance with this shy girl was the public exposure of her private feelings. It was the first time her well-kept privacy had been invaded.

But all this did not deter Grace from leaving Cannes and staying over in Paris for six days when she and Jean Pierre were inseparable. Grace stayed for a few days in the discreet Raphael Hotel where Garbo and Ingrid Bergman like to hole out when they are in Paris.

During this weekend she accepted the invitation to go riding of

Gordon White, a rich young English film star addict who had once been the frequent escort of Audrey Hepburn.

In the evenings Grace and Jean Pierre took in several of the current plays . . . *Intermezzo* at the Marigny Theatre, after which they went backstage to meet the stars Jean Louis Barrault and Madeleine Renaud. They followed this up with Patachou's opening at the Olympia Theatre.

After this word seeped through Paris that they had eloped and were already married. This of course was impossible, simply because it is not so simple for an American girl in France to marry a Frenchman at a minute's notice. Also anyone knowing Grace would realise that she would never have married without at least some members of the family being present.

The pressure grew so intense that on the Friday Grace asked her studio M.G.M. to issue an official denial of marriage plans. But when questioned further by a persistent reporter she would only add obliquely: 'I see no obstacles to marrying a Frenchman. Love is not a question of nationality . . . I love France and the way Frenchmen's minds work.'

The greater part of the following weekend was spent at Jean Pierre's country home *Les Rochers* at Rueil-Malmaison. Here she had been quietly getting to know his daughter and his closest relatives, including those of Maria Montez. It was a simple family gathering.

In London the *Daily Herald* printed a story that Aumont had announced that he would marry Miss Kelly and that the marriage would take place in America.

What happened privately that weekend is pure speculation. Even to her family and closest friends Grace Kelly never opened her heart about such personal matters. But the facts are that she did leave the following day as planned and went back to America.

It is too easy to speculate about other people's personal affairs, but on the surface this romance had lasted two years and looked as if it would last forever. The fact that Jean Pierre was seventeen years older made it all the more tenable since Grace had always enjoyed the company of older men. He was of the Catholic faith and his nationality obviously had not deterred her nor the presence of his delightful daughter.

Perhaps Jean Pierre supplied the real answer when he told a reporter: 'I like her very much but things are too fast. We are being pushed by all this publicity.'

Much of what happened in her own pre-marriage days may have coloured Princess Grace's decision today that her own children must be able to have a private life of their own. To select, develop and discard friendships without the continual blaze of publicity which surrounded her own early romances once Grace Kelly had become a name that belonged to the world.

Fifteen

All through her personal life and film career it was not a question of luck that Grace Kelly had but an ability to bend people's wills towards her advantage. She inspired everyone to throw out their protective nets and shield her from the harsh realities of life.

A case in point was the spring of 1954. It seemed certain to everyone that after her suspension by M.G.M. she would not be allowed to work for anyone until it had been irrevocably settled . . . in the studio's favour.

Both Louella Parsons and Hedda Hopper blazed away in their columns that they did not think it was feasible that M.G.M. would lend out their hottest property for the fourth time to Paramount for a stylish new Hitchcock thriller to be called *To Catch a Thief* which was to be made on the Riviera. They reasoned, with some accuracy, that if Grace Kelly was that good, a property could be found by M.G.M. in which to star her.

Batting against M.G.M. was a formidable team indeed. The threesome consisted of Grace Kelly and her two knights in shining armour, Alfred Hitchcock and Cary Grant.

Grace was so convinced that they would win that she persuaded Edith Head to begin designing her clothes for the film. 'No matter what anyone says,' Grace told Edith in her turtle-dove voice, 'keep right on making the clothes. You'll see I'll be in it.'

The 'heavies' went into action and Grace was kept informed on the end of the telephone. Paramount in the end did get their way, but it may well have been on the premise that M.G.M. wanted William Holden badly enough for a picture they were scheduling. Also Grace's cash price had once again gone up steeply.

There was a story at the time ricocheting round Hollywood that the Kelly family could have bought out M.G.M. had they wished. This, of course, is far from the truth, but it does give some indication of Grace's public image: of a determined young woman who was now in the position to make the kind of films that she wanted and not accept anything thrust upon her.

Grace and Edith Head had a fine time choosing the glamorous clothes that the part called for . . . a wardrobe fit for a successful fashion editor. This was their third film together and no actress and designer worked more in harmony.

They both stopped over in Paris for the final accessory shopping. Edith still remembers with immense affection their shopping sprees. Alfred Hitchcock was generous in that he recognised two perfectionists and appreciated the need for quality of detail in any picture that he directed. It was part of his stock in trade.

'Grace had just heard about Hermès and one afternoon she said to me, "Let's go and buy some gloves. I know where we can get the nicest gloves in the world."

'Like two girls in an ice-cream shop, once inside we fell in love with everything we saw. We chose gloves with little roses embroidered on them, gloves with open-work trim, all kinds of gloves. Grace got more and more excited as she got the same kind of joy collecting gloves as other women did diamonds. Finally they presented her with a package and an astronomical bill. Gloves and shoes are the only things where Grace loses count of money.

'For a moment she looked confused and said: "I haven't got that much on me."

'We pooled our resources and it still wasn't enough. In the end they let us go back to the hotel and the gloves were delivered later which, of course, wouldn't happen today. She would have walked out with them.

'The story illustrates that in spite of all her intelligence and business ability about contracts in those days she still had this rather charming childish exuberance about her when it came to shopping.

'Two years ago I was again shopping in Paris for a Hitchcock film and picking out shoes for the star. Guess whom I met? Grace was there at it again, buying shoes. Our eyes met and we both laughed. The lovely thing about Grace is that she never changes with her old friends.'

The film was a dream to make simply because it was such a happy crew. By now Alfred Hitchcock knew better than anyone every nuance of his new star and how to use her to the best advantage. The script about an elegant cat burglar had the right touch of fantasy and escapism, and her old friend Cary Grant was to play opposite her.

Cary Grant has threaded his friendship all through Princess Grace's life in a very special kind of way. Theirs has never been a Hollywood affair in the accepted sense, but their enjoyment of each other has endured the years. Both he and his wife then, the former Betsey Drake, have today remained along with David Niven as her closest friends from her former Hollywood days. When Henry, the parakeet, died, they replaced him with the gift of Oliver, a 6-weeks-old poodle which accompanied Grace Kelly to Monaco.

By the time Grace left for the Riviera for the outdoor shots of the film she was so exhausted that friends close to her feared a possible breakdown. The cumulative effect of five films in a year had begun to affect her health. She could not sleep, was apt to burst into tears and was desperate for much-needed rest. Any spare time she spent alone trying to catch up on her ebbing strength.

On the stopover in New York she was besieged with the Press at the airport, and although surrounded by her agent Jay Kanter and Paramount officials she just avoided one of those pitfalls that many an actress has been tripped into.

Someone in the publicity department of Paramount had collected a gendarme's cap and cape from the costume department and suggested to Grace that she wear them as she came down the steps. It was to be a news gimmick for the film which involved the French police chasing a cat burglar.

Tired and exhausted as she was Grace could sniff out a cheap publicity trick and turn it to her advantage with all the charm of royal blood. 'I don't think Mr Hitchcock would like it,' she faltered in her soft voice. 'I would prefer not to do that.' And the miracle is that no one dared suggest it again. They had received the message loud and strong that no one pushed Grace Kelly about.

It was the delicacy of the way in which she handled the whole situation that was to amaze Jay Kanter. Once more an awkward situation had been adroitly turned into a minor Kelly triumph, an attribute that has stood during several maladroit moments over the last twenty years in her exacting career as a royal princess.

On arrival in Paris Grace contacted Hitchcock and begged to be allowed to sleep a couple of days before making the trip south. The film by now had already run into minor troubles due to bad weather and she was asked to proceed immediately to Cannes. Which, of course, she did.

Harry Ray, who was the make-up man of the film remembers the first telephone call he had from the star.

' "Have you any Kleenex? Could you bring me a couple of boxes up to my room?" she asked.

' "Sure," I replied, as I suspected immediately why she wanted Kleenex as French toilet paper is so harsh. She also asked me if it was all right if she got a little tan. Wally Westmore had advised her against it and, typical of Grace, she just wanted to check that it was all right with me.

' "Go right ahead. Don't get too much but just take it easy so that you don't get sunburnt," I told her. The part called for an American girl vacationing with her mother on the Riviera so it seemed to me quite natural that she should pick up a little tan for the part. Besides, she looked pale and tired and some sunbathing would do her good, I felt. She turned the softest apricot colour which was fine for the Technicolor the film was being made in. Her skin was just gorgeous . . . beautiful. All I had to do every day was to add a little cheek rouge, a soft pink lipstick and a little mascara. It took me seven minutes flat. She was the first woman I have ever worked with that I didn't have to put foundation on.

'I have never met anyone with a skin as lovely as Grace. Arlene Dahl has a nice skin but not as good as Grace's. I must say this truthfully. She is the most charming, nicest girl I have ever worked with in the business.'

It was once again a matter of days before the whole camera crew had 'fallen a little in love' with Grace. 'You couldn't help yourself,' Harry Ray confirmed.

Alfred Hitchcock is known to be a meticulous master, but he prefers a more civilised working schedule to many other Hollywood directors. He never begins shooting in the morning before 9 a.m. and lets his stars have as much time off as possible for sightseeing. There is never any talk of keeping them hanging around. The man is much too professional to waste anyone's time unnecessarily.

One day when they had finished shooting at noon Grace Kelly asked Harry Ray if he would like to come with her in her car and do some sight-seeing. He agreed as he knew it would be fun.

'She then asked the driver if it was permissible to go up in the palace grounds and drive around.

'He replied that she could even go into the palace if she wanted.

' "No—we don't want to go in," she replied. "All we want to do is to go into the grounds."

'So he drives up this winding road to the palace. It was beautiful up there. Just beautiful. Beautiful view and the soldiers on guard there with their beautiful uniforms. I remember they were blue with some red in them and they looked just lovely,' Harry Ray recalls today.

'I turned to Grace and said, "Now isn't this just beautiful. You know there is a Prince who lives here all alone. It seems a pretty dull life to me living up here on top of a hill."

'She turned to me and said, "Why?"

'I said, "For instance, Grace, if he wants to take a swim he's got to get into his trunks and a robe and get a car and driver and go all the way down that road to the beach."

'She kind of laughed and said, "Don't you think he might have some sort of a beach house, Harry?" And that was the end of the conversation.'

One of the first major changes Princess Grace persuaded Prince Rainier to make at the palace after their marriage was the installation of a large swimming pool in the private part of the grounds where they could swim without going down the hill. It was also Princess Grace's idea in 1957 that a heated indoor swimming pool be built on the waterfront for the use of tourists and local people.

The following year after she had been photographed with Prince Rainier at his palace for *Paris Match* during the Cannes Film Festival she was to meet Harry Ray on a set in Hollywood. They talked nostalgically of their days on the set of *To Catch a Thief*.

'You know, Harry, I finally did meet that Prince,' she said. 'He was a very nice guy.'

We had been talking on a sound stage at the Studios at Universal City. Harry Ray, with his jazzy shirt and pale marmalade hair, still makes up the stars although he does a lot of television work these days. 'I miss the glamour of the fifties—those were the days,' he sighed.

'Wonder if she would remember me,' he mused. 'Could you get a little message to her if I wrote on a card?' I assured him that I could. He went away quietly by himself for some time and then came back to me.

'What shall I call her? Do I have to write that Princess stuff or what is it, Your Serene Highness? No . . . to me she was Grace and Grace it will be.' There and then perched on the arm of an overturned chair he wrote his little message which I duly sent to the Princess in the palace at Monte Carlo.

When asked later about his part in the film, Cary Grant was to tell Margaret Panton: 'It was a delight the whole film. From an actor's point of view she knew her business. She learnt quickly if there was something new to learn and she didn't slow things down by temper fits. She saved the studio money.

'We had a scene in the film where I had to grab her arms hard, while she was fighting me, and push her against a wall. We went through that scene eight or nine times, but Hitchcock still wanted it again. Grace went back behind the door where the scene took place and just by chance I happened to catch a glimpse of her massaging her wrists and grimacing in pain. But a moment later she came out and did the scene again—she never complained to me or to "Hitch" about how much her arms were hurting.

'She isn't one of those girls who wastes time by being angry. She was always patient on the set, even when hairdressers and make-up men were fussing over her between takes of a difficult scene. If a dress didn't fit, well it just didn't fit, and that was that, with no hysterics. So, of course, they got the dress fixed faster for her than for a girl who was screaming about it. No wonder she was popular with the wardrobe and make-up people, even if she didn't go around slapping them on the back.'

Sharing Grace's evenings after the day's filming was Oleg Cassini, who stayed two months with her during the making of the film. They lived in the same hotel, the Carlton at Cannes, and their evenings together had a subliminal domestic air about them.

The complete disciplinarian that she is, Grace divided her day into two parts. There was the professional life on the set and her evening private world with Oleg Cassini. Each night after a hard day's shooting he planned a new gastronomic adventure.

An endearing thing about this then waif of a girl was that she was the born *fourchette*, which translated from the French means a *good fork*.

She was willing to try anything, and though she was still an inexperienced gourmet with method and determination she set about to rectify this.

Every evening, sometimes alone, or with the Hitchcocks or Cary Grants, these two friends would try out a new restaurant. Oleg Cassini knew every inch of the Riviera from Saint Tropez to Portofino, and wherever they went from five-star restaurants to small bistros he was known. It was a period of good food, superb wines and lots of laughter. Just what the overworked, overwrought Grace Kelly needed. They would hear that the *mousse des poissons* was good at a certain restaurant or the *bouillabaisse* sensational a little farther along the coast. Hitchcock was a renowned gourmand and Cassini was not only an amusing raconteur but also had a cosmopolitan knowledge of good living. The dinners were leisurely and gay as only the evening hours can be on the fun-seeking Mediterranean coastline.

Some nights they went to the Casino, where invariably the Kelly luck held, others were spent dancing at the Palm Beach Casino or Maxims in Juan les Pins. Some were even spent driving in the hills overlooking Monaco to watch the Principality in the pinkish haze of the setting sun and as the night lights turned it into a gigantic jewel casket.

To everyone who saw Grace Kelly and Oleg Cassini they behaved like two people very much in love, totally isolated in a world of their own. In an unreal atmosphere guaranteed to nurture any romantic feelings.

One evening after dinner at a small harbour restaurant in Cannes they went on to the Casino and later to dance. In her direct way Grace asked Cassini what were his plans for the future and for her.

He explained that his plans for her included anything that would make her happy, including marriage. They had now known each other for over a year and undoubtedly were fond of each other. But if there were doubts in Grace's head she carefully stacked them away that night and let her heart rule her head. They ordered a bottle of champagne and drank to the new life ahead of them. The family's possible protests and Cassini's two marriages, a formidable obstacle for any conscientious Catholic girl to overcome, were all carefully blocked off that night. They were just two people caught up in the euphoric glamour of the Riviera.

Next morning at church, where she went every Sunday, if Grace had any further doubts these she conveniently forgot. From the religious point of view the differences were not so insurmountable. Born of Russian parents, Cassini was a Greek Orthodox by religion and therefore not too distant from the theories of Roman Catholicism.

Where the heart has a reason Grace was even able to convince herself that his two previous marriages—to Merry Fahrney and the film star Gene Tierney—would not present a very serious problem simply because as he had not been married in church, through Catholic eyes these marriages were not legal.

Her main concern, and a very deep one, was presenting her family with the facts. Even with the Atlantic and Mediterranean between them the influence of the Kelly parents was unmistakably there.

With all this in mind Grace Kelly and Oleg Cassini agreed that the engagement was to be kept a secret until she had had time to discuss it with her family. In any case it would never have entered her head to have had her engagement announced anywhere except from the Kelly home.

If there were any doubts about Mr Kelly, Grace felt that her mother would understand her choice and condone it. She had always made it perfectly clear that she did not want her daughter to marry into the film industry.

'When I thought of her getting married at all I hoped that she would not choose someone from her own profession because it seemed to me that two stars in the family could put a real strain on family happiness,' Mrs Kelly was to say. 'For those reasons I had hoped that she would marry someone of real distinction—not an actor, but perhaps a fine surgeon, a painter or a successful industrialist.'

To keep up the deception and so that nothing could leak to the press they agreed that Grace would return to the States with the Cary Grants and the Hitchcocks on a boat as planned and that Oleg Cassini would fly ahead to wait their arrival.

She arrived back in New York for a twenty-four-hour stopover before proceeding to Hollywood for the interior shots of the film. Already the pressures of fame had begun to catch up on her. Her family wanted to repossess her, her agents and the Press were clamouring for interviews, the studio had things to discuss with her. Added to this Cassini, her new fiancé, was standing waiting for her outside her apartment house.

I asked him in New York about the fatal meeting with Mrs Kelly which was perhaps the crux of the whole short-lived romance.

'It was all very difficult because of the pressures that were taking place, but Grace telephoned her mother and arranged that we would meet for lunch. I attempted some sort of humorous quips but I immediately sensed that Mrs Kelly was in no mood. It was a cold almost bitter reception, possibly because she had been totally unprepared for the fact that we wanted to marry.'

Mrs Kelly in fact came straight to the point: 'Look here, Oleg. You're a charming escort, but in my opinion you are a very poor risk for a marriage,' she told him.

'I tried to tell her that time had elapsed between the two involved people and in the decision-making process alone on the Riviera we had made up our minds. The essence of the matter was either Grace loved me or she didn't love me.'

It was not a very cheering lunch and for Grace it must have been a distinctly chilling time. She had always thought her mother would support her in the engagement.

From then on it was open war. The Kellys brought in their friends and supporters, who all painted a lurid picture of Cassini the womaniser.

'I don't know or ever have considered myself to be a womaniser. I certainly have always liked the company of beautiful women. I never denied it. I tried to explain to Grace, and I think she believed me, that if you are a perfectionist you go out and look until you find the right person. I sincerely believed that for me at least that time had come.'

By now Cassini had been a constant companion of Grace's for nearly four months, a long enough period for two people to come to a decision simply because it had been so concentrated.

The Press had begun to fan up the whole situation and the atmosphere with the family deteriorated. After a while Cassini put a kind of ultimatum on a time limit telling Grace, 'I am not marrying your family, I am marrying you. I want a final answer.'

In looking back over the whole period Cassini has this to say today: 'It became a contest between me, the prize being Grace, and all the organised resistance that the family could bring to bear. It shouldn't have been like that.'

Hedda Hopper pitched in with the family and wrote an article in which she said: 'With all the attractive men around town I do not understand what Grace Kelly sees in Oleg Cassini. It must be his moustache.'

With Grace in his conspiracy Cassini answered with the following telegram: 'Dear Hedda, I give up. I'll shave mine if you shave yours.'

At one point in his courtship Cassini had sought the advice of an old friend of his, Mr John Kennedy, father of the President. As a senior citizen of some standing and himself a staunch Catholic, Cassini thought it would weigh in heavily to have the President's father on his side.

Kennedy suggested that Cassini bring Grace over for lunch and he would have a good talk to her.

'Don't worry, don't worry at all. Leave it all to me. I'll have a good talk to her,' he had promised.

'We all went to a little French restaurant,' Cassini remembers, 'and no sooner had we sat down than old Kennedy started in on Grace. I sat spellbound as I listened.

' "Now listen, Grace, you are a good Catholic girl," he said. "You represent a good Catholic family and you must not get involved with Oleg. He's a wonderful guy but it wouldn't work."

'I looked in amazement. I said to him, "What are you double crossing me about in this way when your own daughter Pat married an actor [Peter Lawford]?"

'I called him a dirty monkey but he stuck to his guns. We did remain friends despite all this for many years afterwards. But Grace and I were completely taken aback. This is not what we had expected to hear.'

Although their clandestine engagement had never been publicly confirmed, Grace Kelly and Oleg Cassini continued to see each other all through the following year.

Their friendship was to finish dramatically in December 1955 when Grace telephoned him from New York to Florida, where he was then living.

'I want you to be the first to know because I don't want you to read it in the papers, but I have accepted to become the bride of Prince Rainier,' she told him.

They agreed to meet two days later in New York. These two extraordinarily different people went for a boat ride on the Hudson so that they could talk in privacy and end their romance.

She explained that though she had cared a great deal for him during their time together that there were too many pressures against the marriage and for this reason it would never have worked out.

'That's how it ended,' Oleg Cassini said quietly. 'I was absolutely desolate because what could have been a very beautiful love story between two people had become some kind of international situation.

'I am a competitive person and I was bitter—very bitter. I have never done anything towards her that I can reproach myself. Maybe she has something to reproach herself towards me. I am not analysing the thing properly—after all she was the big star and I was just an expendable toy is the way I look at it.

'It took me a long time to get over it. I would wake up in the morning and say "Well, today I am going to see Grace" and then realise that she was not part of my life. It was not easy because apart from naturally being in love with her, I was sincerely fond of her and I really thought we could have made a life together.'

Even today it is patently obvious that Oleg Cassini still has tender, poignant memories of Grace Kelly.

'It is a nice feeling and in the final analysis I think she made a good choice. I honestly, truthfully say that she did the right thing and I think in the long run the life she has now is probably more enjoyable for her.'

When Grace Kelly's engagement to Prince Rainier was announced, Cholly Knickerbocker, loyal to his brother and in a rash moment of anger, wrote two stinging items in his gossip columns which would certainly have been better left unwritten.

Oleg Cassini last saw Princess Grace several years ago in Cannes. He was in a bathing suit rushing to catch a boat and she was accompanied by her close friend Vera Maxwell, the dress designer from New York.

'Hello Grace.'

'Hello Oleg.'

Only four words were spoken.

Today Oleg Cassini is a distinguished, silver-haired sixty-two-year-old charmer. He has remained a bachelor ever since and I suspect that his romance with Grace Kelly was the highlight of his life. In a small gilt-edged frame he keeps in his house is a photograph of them both taken at a fancy dress ball. She is dressed as an Olympian maiden and he as a suntanned gladiator. He lent it to be included in this book.

They both look incredibly happy.

Sixteen

In 1955 the one star from Hollywood that the French Government wanted at the Cannes Film Festival was Grace Kelly. Although she had not been seen in Europe in *The Country Girl*, she had made an astonishing impact both there and in Europe for her role in *Mogambo*. The cinema audiences liked what they saw. Her classical beauty and elegance were just as intriguing outside America as within. Rumours of her personal charisma had also seeped through from her stay on the Riviera the previous summer where she filmed *To Catch a Thief* for Alfred Hitchcock.

Now once more she had gone back to New York and in her quiet tenacious way had left her lawyers and agent to sort out the question of her suspension by M.G.M. She had intended to fill her time changing apartments, always a traumatic experience for her, and in looking for a replacement for her secretary-companion who was leaving New York to live elsewhere.

Then came one of those absurd anomalies that could only happen in Hollywood. Even though she was considered one of M.G.M.'s most prestigious assets technically they could not ask her to go to Cannes simply because she was under suspension.

A telephone call was made to Rupert Allen, a former feature writer for *Look* who had carved himself a niche as liaison man every year at the festival between the Hollywood contingent and the French Government.

Rupert Allen was not only educated at the University of Toulouse but is a man of culture and engaging charm that was just what was required for such a delicate operation. For instance, one American star and her husband decided that they had had enough of the festival after two days and quietly took off with their driver and car, laid on by the festival, for a trip to Italy. The French Government found such Hollywood behaviour irritating and irrational. Rupert Allen is the password to tact. He solved it.

Recalling the problem of the Grace Kelly impasse Rupert Allen said of the incident:

'I telephoned her and said something like "It is very easy for you to go and it's spring. You'll get a free trip to Europe and all your expenses paid in Cannes and you can stay as long as you like in Europe afterwards.

' "Go and enjoy yourself over there instead of sitting round here and fretting about everything else. Your new secretary can wait. The festival people will also be happy if you want to bring a chaperone."

'Grace said that she would think about it. She does not make snap decisions. But she did call back and said that it was a marvellous idea and would I tell them that she wanted to bring with her Baroness Gladys de Segonzec, who had become a close friend during the filming of *To Catch a Thief*. They would arrive together from Paris.'

She had earlier agreed to a request from Pierre Galante, one of the editors of *Paris Match*, and husband of Olivia de Havilland, that if she visited the Film Festival she would be willing to take part in a picture story for his magazine based on the not too original idea of Celluloid Princess meets Flesh and Blood Prince.

To the Prince it was just another day's job to publicise the Principality and attract tourists. Added to this he had always been agreeably amused with people from the entertainment world.

For Grace Kelly it was part of a busy schedule but also a point of honour in obliging a friend. She did not even know for certain that she would meet the Prince.

On arrival at Cannes from Paris she was slightly perturbed. The visit to the palace had been planned for her busiest day. Part of her amazing strength and ability in the management of her life and emotions is that she likes everything to be properly organised and does not enjoy being caught off-guard.

When Pierre Galante explained to her that the audience was in fact with Prince Rainier and that it could not be cancelled she immediately agreed. But there were several practical problems still to be overcome.

The morning schedule included a Press conference with swarms of gesticulating French and Italian journalists and photographers all shouting at her: 'Thees way Gracee, that way Gracee.' She had chosen from her luggage a black glazed chintz dress heavily patterned with stylised flowers. A dominant dress, but also one that did not need pressing. With her eye for professionalism she was the first to realise that it was too 'busy' for a picture story and would overpower the faces of the principals.

As there was no time for a hairdressing appointment she washed it herself and dried it in the wind en route to Monte Carlo.

It is a two hours' drive from Cannes to Monte Carlo. Elias Lapinere of M.G.M. publicity department who was designated chauffeur for the day decided that there was only one way to get there and that was fast. He put his foot down on the accelerator and set off at Grand Prix speed. Following behind in a car were two *Paris Match* photographers.

For somebody like Grace who does not like driving in cars, and positively loathes speed, the next half-hour must have been traumatic. When Lapinere put the brakes down to avoid crashing into a lorry in front, the *Paris Match* team behind concertina-ed into the back of the car in which Grace was travelling, smashing the rear end.

There was no time for remonstrances so with a caved-in front and rear the cavalcade sped on. Near Nice they passed an Italian contingent of festival stars, including Gina Lollobrigida. The photographers wanted to stop to take a picture of the two stars together, but Pierre Galante hustled them on.

The cars pulled into Monte Carlo at 2.50 and since Grace Kelly had not eaten all day they all went to the Hotel de Paris for a quick sandwich. Ham sandwich still in hand, she was driven across the city to the royal palace bathed in sunshine and the royal standard floating in the breeze.

The standard which normally indicated that the Prince was in residence was, in fact, a false alarm.

The Prince was still lunching at his villa at Beaulieu, where for six years he had shared much of his time with French film actress Gisèle Pascal. He sent his apologies and instructed an aide to show Miss Kelly and her party his palace, and he would arrive as soon as possible.

To fill in time the *Paris Match* photographers took pictures of Grace wandering all over the palace. Just as she was about to leave to catch up with her minute-by-minute schedule at the festival, the Prince arrived.

If she was nervous, Grace Kelly certainly did not show it. 'She looked lovely, just lovely,' commented Pierre Galante.

When they met, the American girl offered her hand elegantly to the Prince, who bowed. It was a moment of history.

The Prince turned on his incredible charm and took her round his private zoo, explaining how his animals all loved him and would not hurt him. He is known personally to each animal who can almost sense his arrival before it sees him.

This acute affinity with animals has been inherited by Princess Caroline, much to the Prince's delight.

The Prince showed her his chimpanzee, but what impressed her the most was when he put his arm into the lion's cage.

Together Prince Rainier and Grace Kelly made a decorative couple as they strolled round the grounds and posed for photographs inside and outside the palace.

Before agreeing to the picture session the Prince had already talked the matter over with Father Tucker, rector of St Charles' Church in Monte Carlo and his personal chaplain, spiritual adviser . . . and confidant. They both agreed that there could be nothing harmful in the pictures.

Later the Prince was to say to Father Tucker: 'I granted permission for the visit, but I did not include in it that I would meet Miss Kelly.'

Hand over heart the loquacious Father Tucker, for evermore to be called the Cupid Priest, wrote his own unofficial viewpoint in the *Philadelphia Bulletin* after the event:

'I sensed that the Prince was being half apologetic, fearing that I might have some objection to his meeting a screen actress. I said to him:

' "My Lord Prince, please get me straight on this. Grace Kelly is exactly the type of Catholic girl I want you to meet." '

The same evening the Prince went over to the Rectory to talk to Father Tucker about the day's events. Quite obviously that meeting had made a lasting impression.

'I found the palace all aglow,' is how Father Tucker was to describe the next few days. 'The Prince couldn't wait to talk to me about Grace. There would be all these little exuberances every time I met him and it seemed that on every possible occasion he would drop me a note always mentioning something about Grace.

'I noticed too (over the next week) that the Prince betrayed signs of seriousness whenever a new item appeared about Grace Kelly, especially if she had been seen in the company of someone else.'

For Grace Kelly, meeting Prince Rainier was a pleasant interlude in the day. When the last photographs had been taken there was a frantic dash back to Cannes, where the American representatives to the film festival were holding a party and she was to be in the receiving line shaking hands with 1,500 guests. She herself was giving a dinner party for ten of her friends to be followed by the screening of Paramount's entry *The Country Girl*. This was topped off by an evening party given by the studio which finished at 4 a.m.

There was little time to speculate about the attractive man she had met that morning. On hindsight it is interesting to recall that she did not mention the Prince to either M. Galante or the photographer on the drive back.

Father Tucker, who had not been present at the meeting, with a twinkle in his Irish eyes, quickly followed up his hunch that this was to be a significant event by sending Grace Kelly a letter which read:

'I want to thank you for showing the Prince what an American Catholic girl can be and for the very deep impression this has left on him.'

One can sense the delicacy and deliberation the puckish little friar spent before couching such a letter.

Grace Kelly replied in a conventional little note saying that she was sorry to have missed Father Tucker but that she hoped that she would return to France soon and that they could meet then.

There was no exchange of any correspondence between the Prince and Grace Kelly nor any meeting until he arrived on the evening of Christmas Day of the same year for dinner at her parents' house.

The link between was 'Aunt' Eddie and 'Uncle' Russie Austin, from Margate, New Jersey. The Austins had been friends of Margaret and John Kelly for many years, spending many summers together at Ocean City.

When they arrived for the summer season at Monte Carlo Russell Austin was told that there was not a table available at the Sporting Club where one of the season's most colourful galas was taking place.

Impetuously he placed a call to the palace and asked to speak to Prince Rainier, saying that he was a friend of Grace Kelly. It is most unlikely that the Prince would in the normal way take such a call, but he not only did and sent the Austins ring-side seats for the gala that night but also invited them to tea at the palace next day.

They talked about America and the Kelly family in general.

'If ever you come to our country,' 'Russ' Austin said when saying goodbye to the Prince, 'do be sure and let us know ahead of time so that you can visit with us.'

The Prince assured him that he had no intentions at the moment of visiting the States. But just three months later this was exactly what he did.

Father Tucker claimed that he was the match-maker. 'Perfect matches are made in heaven but safety matches are made by men' was one of his favourite axioms.

Russell Austin also takes the credit. 'I was the Dan Cupid and directly responsible for the initial match-making between Grace and the Prince,' he told friends.

But it is a pleasing thought that, on that spring afternoon in Monaco in 1955 when Grace Kelly curtsied to Prince Rainier, there was a little magic in the air.

Seventeen

Since early in her film career Princess Grace has always been interested in the occult. She herself is an intelligent amateur graphologist, reads the *tarot* cards but prefers to cast horoscopes for people she has just met and then compare afterwards whether she was right or not, rather than of her friends.

Prince Rainier sometimes gives her a piece of writing from one of his official letters to hear her comments. Invariably she hits the nail on the head with her quizzical appraisal.

She herself has had her own writing analysed by Britain's former televison personality Jeanne Heal, who has written a book on graphology and for which Princess Grace wrote the Foreword.

In all her homes in New York and on the West Coast stacks of horoscope magazines and the latest books on astrology were scattered round. Two books she consulted frequently were *The Pursuit of Destiny* and *Astrology for Everyone*.

At her parties she was at her happiest sitting on the floor with her feet tucked up under her giving a guest a reading. She herself is a Scorpio. As I mentioned in the Foreword, Vivien Leigh, who was born under this zodiacal sign, said of Scorpions: 'Scorpions burn themselves out and eat themselves up and they are careless about themselves—like me.'

This appears to be patently untrue of Princess Grace. She prefers to waft through life at her own procrastinating pace, but there is one similarity. Like Vivien Leigh she also revels in that enchanting occupation of *serendipity*. The Concise Oxford Dictionary describes serendipity as 'the faculty of making happy and unexpected discoveries by accident'. It was coined by Horace Walpole after *The Three Princes of Serendip:* a Ceylonese fairy story.

Most of Princess Grace's friends are born under Leo—John Foreman, Carolyn Reybold, Bettina Gray, Maree Rambo, Gant Gaither and Alfred Hitchcock, Paul Gallico and Anita Colby. Both Princess Caroline and Princess Stephanie are Aquarians and Prince Albert is a Pisces. The rank outsiders, the exact opposite in character to Scorpions, are the Geminis, with their double-sided character of dark and sunshine moods.

Prince Rainier is a true Gemini which together with his Mediterranean culture and nature added the surprise element in their first years of marriage. Before her marriage Princess Grace told friends that in her marriage she wanted to be dominated by a man in the important issues and not just in the choice of a restaurant.

Being married to an interesting and complicated man like Prince Rainier cannot always have been easy, but life with a Gemini is never dull. And he is no exception.

Through the years her interest in the occult has diminished although she is still fascinated by astrology. She has been interested in Dr J. B. Rhine's theories of extra-sensory perception, in Buddhist theories of reincarnation (of which she believes that the Bridie Murphy experiments were interesting evidence), in table rapping, the *Ouija* board and spiritualism. In her Hollywood days she enjoyed a good séance with a gifted medium and when she was in New York often consulted her favourite gypsy fortune-teller at the Russian Tea Shop.

In August of 1955, before returning to Hollywood to begin work on a new film, she gave a Leo party for all her friends. The large cake was decorated with a Lion.

When she herself became forty years of age in 1969 she resurrected the idea in Monaco and gave a party for all of her Scorpion friends who could make the journey.

In September 1955 Grace Kelly flew to California to begin work on *The Swan*, the screen adaptation of the Ferenc Molnar play. It is a beguiling story of a girl who rejects the love of her young tutor to marry the crown prince. The cast was a formidable one and included Alec Guinness on his first visit to Hollywood, the French actor Louis Jourdan and it was to be directed by that veteran Charles Vidor.

It was a part made for Grace, romantic, enchanting, beautifully dressed and needing an extra dimension of acting to turn it from candy floss into charming sophistication. The trip out was hazardous as the plane was twice struck by lightning, which is probably a contributing factor to why the Princess dislikes flying even today.

She settled into a house which she rented from the food reformer Gaylord Hauser. It was a small charming white Regency-style house with a garden and pint-sized swimming pool for Oliver. By now Oliver had become so much part of her life that he was accepted by her friends as a personality in the Kelly household. Where Grace went, Oliver went, travelling curled up on her lap whenever she flew from East to West Coast and vice versa.

Helen Rose, who was later to design Grace's wedding dress, came up with some enchanting designs for the clothes for the film. Fragile, beguilingly feminine, they suited Grace Kelly's porcelain beauty.

Two weeks after her arrival in California the entire cast and crew took off in two DC-7s hired by M.G.M. for the trip. Their destination was Asheville, North Carolina, for location shots at Biltmore where they had leased the Renaissance-style château which George Vanderbilt had created.

Everyone was slightly overwhelmed by its grandeur, but not Grace. She told Jay Kanter: 'It's like a beautiful palace. I love it.'

Grace Kelly's public face was a hodgepodge of fact, fantasy and circumstances. Round her had grown a whole world of clichés—white gloves, frosty beauty, steel insides.

She herself laughed at it, and though it upset her at the beginning she was to say later:

'I thought that I had dispelled that cool business after *Rear Window*, but I guess it's something I'm stuck with.'

The truth is that she is far from cool in her life among her friends. She is a fun-loving, warm-hearted woman who takes a delight in playing practical jokes on her friends. It is in fact one of the minor delights of her marriage to Prince Rainier that she totally understands and joins in his often schoolboy humour.

In the script the prince tells his future princess:

'Remember what it means to be a swan . . . to glide like a dream . . . silent, white, majestic . . . there you must stay, Alexandra, head high, cool, indifferent to the staring crowds.'

Out of camera range it was a completely different Grace. 'I found her delightful and fun to work with, very professional and also full of giggles,' Alec Guinness told me when recalling the film.

Jessie Royce Landis, who had played Grace's mother in *To Catch a*

'She was such a happy baby,' said Mrs Kelly about her second daughter Grace.

Princess Grace looking relaxed, amused and contented.
Photo:
Gianni Bozzacchi

(Below) The all-American beautiful family. From left: 'Kell', Peggy, Grace, Lizanne and handsome John B. Kelly.

(Above) Every brother needs a sister some-time in his life. Grace was always at the dockside to wish sculling champion 'Kell' luck before he pushed off.

'There's hills in them thar gold,' cracked Alfred Hitchcock when he saw Grace Kelly in the spectacular dress Edith Head designed for her in To Catch a Thief.

The Country Girl *was the film that changed Grace Kelly from just another pretty film star into an Academy Award winner. She is pictured here with Bing Crosby.*
Photo: The Kobal Collection

*Two people in love: Princess Grace and Prince Rainier
exchange a tender moment during their second wedding
service in the Cathedral of St Nicholas.*

*The proud family gather at Princess Grace's bedside to admire
the new arrival, Princess Stephanie.*
Photo: John Hillelson Agency Ltd.

The growing Grimaldi Family in their first formal photograph in the gold salon. It carries Princess Grace's signature.
Photo: Collection Archives du Palais Princier

Growing up...The family relaxes with the new poodle who has replaced Oliver. Photo: René Maestri

Princess Grace and Prince Rainier escort Princess Caroline
at her first Red Cross Gala. Father and daughter had the first
waltz alone on the ballroom floor.
Photo: John Hillelson Agency Ltd

A moment of ecstasy for a sick old lady as Princess Grace hands her an Easter Egg.
Photo: Lukomski

A small citizen of Monaco receives his Christmas parcel from Princess Grace at the annual party at the palace.
Photo: Detaille

Thief, was once again playing her mother and aiding and abetting her in Grace's pranks.

When they heard that Alec Guinness had received one of those fatuous star-struck letters from a fan signed 'Alice', they laid their plans. They had him constantly paged in his hotel by 'Alice' (no one can remember the lady's other name in the process of time). It was done with great consistency every few hours. When they heard that he was dining at Antoine's, he was paged again. They plagued him with loving telegrams all signed 'Alice'.

Alec Guinness was almost hysterical wondering in fact whether this mad woman did exist and became fearful in case he should bump into her. It was a long time before he finally tumbled to the joke. When he told Grace about his Alice nightmares she laughed so much that she fell off the sofa she was sitting on.

'Roycee', as Jessie Royce Landis was called by her friends, also had a delicious sense of fun.

Film units on location, living and working together in a confined space, tend to make their own fun. It is a strange world with no past, no future. Just the present celluloid world cut off from reality. The clever practical joker who can lighten the off-set moments becomes like the queen in a beehive. Indispensable.

New York is a city that evokes passion in people. For Grace Kelly it was home . . . the city she loved most in the world. Often when she would finish filming in Hollywood on a Friday evening she would get on a plane for New York just to spend the weekend there.

Sitting around one evening after a day's shooting in the octagonal grey stone pump room at Asheville's Manor Hotel, where the cast of *The Swan* were staying, the conversation turned to New York and the fun began.

'It's awful! Just like a bombed city these days,' cried Jessie Royce Landis.

'I'm told they're tearing down Carnegie Hall next year,' put in Louis Jourdan.

'The Plaza Hotel is going one day soon,' Jay Kanter added, 'and you know they are even going to tear down the Met.' (Metropolitan Opera House.)

All this time Grace had been sitting very quietly with her hands crossed becoming sadder and sadder. Finally she burst out:

'I can't stand it! I'm going to quit the movies, go back to New York, run for Mayor and stop all this destruction!'

The film was finally completed on 23 December. Grace packed her bags and set off for New York and a Christmas party at the Jay Kanters.

Next day, still tired from jet lag, the completion of the film and the Kanter party, she left for Philadelphia and a typical Kelly family reunion.

Only this year there was one difference.

Eighteen

For some time the question of Prince Rainier marrying and producing an heir had become a matter of urgency in his Principality. Should he have failed to do this, on his death Monaco would have been taken over by France once again . . . a thought totally abhorrent to its 30,000 tax-free citizens!

To understand the immediacy of the problem it is necessary to search back into the Grimaldi family history which dates back to the twelfth century. This powerful family, wishing to expand their territory, set up a trading post at the foot of the Maritime Alps. They have been called merchant adventurers by some, brigands by others.

They flew their flag over Monaco for nearly five centuries until 1793 when the French revolutionaries annexed the area to France. This was short-lived, as when Napoleon was defeated the victorious allies restored the Grimaldis to Monaco.

It was not until the end of World War I that the French concluded an astonishing treaty with Prince Rainier's great-grandfather Prince Albert. Because of a mysterious claim to Monaco by a truculent German family called the d'Urach's—a hideous thought—the French granted Prince Albert a treaty recognising Monaco as an independent Principality whose sovereignty could not be ceded to any foreign power except France.

There was a clause in the treaty that if the throne of Monaco ever became vacant for one day it would immediately be returned to the protectorate of France.

Prince Rainier had succeeded to the throne from his grandfather Prince Louis II in a complicated way.

In 1869 Prince Rainier's great grandfather, Prince Albert I, in a bid to curry favour with Great Britain, took an English bride—Lady Mary Douglas-Hamilton, daughter of the eleventh Duke of Hamilton and Brandon.

Shortly after giving birth to a son, Prince Louis II, Lady Mary was so unhappy in the vast palace that she decided to flee the country, taking the boy with her. It took eight years of litigation before the marriage was declared void.

As a second bride Prince Albert I looked to the New World and took an American girl, New Orleans born Alice Heine. This marriage lasted several years and it is through this first American Princess of Monaco that Monte Carlo became a cultural centre.

After his disastrous marriages Prince Albert returned to his constant love, the sea. When he served in the Spanish Navy he was known as *Albert the Navigator*, and it is due to his efforts that the Oceanographic Museum in Monaco was founded at the turn of the century.

Lady Mary was the chief influence in Prince Louis' life as he spent much of his youth with her before joining the French Army. Here he fell in love with Juliette Louvet who, it is said, was an enchanting laundress.

One faction of Monegasques stoutly defend that he did in fact marry the girl, but the more conservative historians say that, though it was an *affaire de cœur*, it was never officially acknowledged.

From this romantic union in 1898 was born a girl named Charlotte Louise Juliette, the mother of Prince Rainier.

The child was brought up in Paris until her teens, when her grandfather summoned her back to Monaco to be instructed in court procedure and in the role that she was destined to play as heiress to the throne.

Just one year later she married the dashing Duke Pierre de Polignac and bore him two children, Prince Rainier and Princess Antoinette. He was created Prince Pierre upon their marriage.

Even this marriage, which began so hopefully, fell apart a few years later and ended in divorce in 1933. Prince Pierre was banished from Monaco and it was not until after the war that he returned to live in Monte Carlo. He is extremely fond of his American daughter-in-law and was to become one of Princess Grace's leading champions during the first perplexing years of her marriage.

After the break-up of her marriage Princess Charlotte renounced her rights to the throne and took herself off to live in a large country house outside Paris. Princess Charlotte has never returned to the Monaco she loved so much since her son's wedding.

Prince Rainier, a handsome and virile twenty-six-year-old, was crowned Son Altesse Serenissime (His Serene Highness) in 1949.

The title of *His Serene Highness* perhaps needs explaining. In a kingdom such as Great Britain, Holland, Denmark, Sweden or Belgium where the king or queen is ruler, he or she is known as *Your Majesty*. In a principality such as Monaco, which is ruled by a prince—a title created for themselves by the Grimaldis in the fourteenth century—the sovereign is known as *Your Serene Highness* despite the fact that he is an absolute monarch.

For the early years of his reign Prince Rainier showed no signs of settling down, much to the consternation of his subjects. There had been his four-year friendship with Gisèle Pascal. As Head of State marriage to a divorced woman would not have been acceptable.

As the King of Sweden and Prince Charles know only too well, it is almost impossible for a prominent male member of any leading royal family to court a girl without the whole world looking over his shoulder. Prince Rainier was no exception. As he was to say in an interview in *Collier's Magazine* to David Schoenbrun, before his fate-sealing trip to America:

'You see, my greatest difficulty is knowing a girl long enough and intimately enough to find out if we are really soul mates as well as lovers.

'I consider it a duty to my people to get married, but there is a higher duty above politics, the duty of a man to be true to himself, to fulfil himself as a human being, by taking a wife he loves and consummating that love. I will not marry except for love. I will not agree to a loveless marriage of convenience.'

It is for this reason also that he refused to take part in the Adriatic matchmaking cruise organised by Queen Frederica of Greece in anticipation of finding suitable partners for her own children.

Just before he left for his Philadelphian rendezvous Prince Rainier was asked to describe his ideal woman. It is no coincidence that in fact it was a blueprint of Grace Kelly.

'I'd like a girl who is fair haired, the sort of subtle beauty that grows on you. She has long flowing hair and her eyes are blue or hazel flicked with gold.'

He also said that she must be charitable and unspoilt as he particularly disliked the glossy smart-set type of international beauty.

'I want my wife to be a normal human being with her own personal likes and dislikes.

'I want an intelligent girl but not an intellectual. There is nothing more disagreeable to a man than to have a wife who knows more than he does on every subject. It is even worse than being beaten at tennis.

'I cannot bear intellectual snobs, or snobs of any kind.

'I must be the boss, or else I am not a man but, at the same time, I am not a dictator. It takes two to start a fight and two to make a marriage.'

Financially, too, Grace Kelly slotted into the description of the Prince's ideal bride. He neither wanted to marry a woman who might covet not only prestige but also his money, nor did he wish to be embarrassed with a capricious heiress as a bride.

Through her film earnings, and later an inheritance from her father, Princess Grace has her own private income which helps her to maintain the financial independence she is accustomed to.

Meantime the citizens of Monaco sat and waited . . . and prayed.

It was against this intricate background that the news of the Prince's engagement was hailed with sheer delight in Monaco. It is difficult to assess how much the head ruled the heart among its tax-free subjects, but the outward burst of excitement—and relief—was real enough. They were soon to have their own princess—and a possible heir.

During the autumn of 1955 when Prince Rainier was quietly planning a trip to America, the puckish Father Tucker was positively bursting with conspiracy. While Grace Kelly was to be seen every morning walking her poodle, Oliver, along 63rd Street, three of the world's astute, middle-aged male brains had been conspiring a most eccentric plot. So bizarre, so daring and so improbable it would have stunned the world.

Had it come to fruition the entire history of Monaco might have been altered and a love story as provocative as that of King Edward VIII and Wallis Simpson been enacted.

I had first heard fragments of the story from Norman Mailer but was so disinclined to believe its veracity that I took the lift up to the penthouse office of Gardner Cowles in the old *Look* building on Fifth Avenue.

Mr Cowles, now a venerable figure in the history of American journalism, looked at me with clear twinkling eyes.

'Yes, it is true, but Norman does not have all the titillating details.'

Spellbound I listened as he told me how Aristotle Onassis, George Schlee and himself planned to save the finances of Monaco.

I tell the story in full simply because it seems incredible that three such formidable brains could think up anything so audacious without even consulting the central figure, Prince Rainier.

'I had been a close friend of George Schlee for quite a number of years. Every summer Schlee used to leave his wife, the dress designer Valentina, behind in New York and go off with Greta Garbo for a month or two on Onassis' yacht in the Mediterranean.

'This particular year, in 1955, when Schlee came back he and Valentina came up to stay with me at my house in Western Connecticut. He told me that Onassis had just bought a tremendous portion of Monaco and that he wanted Schlee to help him promote it. Monte Carlo was no longer the chic place to visit on the Riviera as others had supplanted it. To maximise the return on his investment Onassis wanted to do anything he could to bring Monte Carlo back as the smartest place to go to.

'I asked George to tell me a little bit about Monte Carlo and Prince Rainier, whom I had never met. How attractive was he and so on?

' "Well, he is a plump young man but he is attractive enough," he answered.

' "Why don't you marry him off to an American celebrity and that would give Monte Carlo worldwide publicity and get the Americans going back again," I told him.

' "What kind of a woman have you in mind?" he asked.

' "Well, what about a movie star?"

' "That's not a bad idea, but which one?"

'I said, "Why not start at the top—Marilyn Monroe." Marilyn was at the peak of her popularity at the time. Schlee got very excited about it but cautiously said how could anyone persuade Marilyn to marry the Prince.

'I was publishing *Look* magazine at the time and we had done many stories on Marilyn and I knew her pretty well. She trusted me.

' "That's great," Schlee said, by now highly enthusiastic. "I know Ari would do anything to promote this. Will you put it up to Marilyn?"

'It just happened that she was staying that month with Milton Green the photographer, who had a house three or four miles from mine. He was a close friend and adviser of Marilyn so I phoned him that Saturday night and said I couldn't invite them to dinner, as we already had too many guests, but would they come along afterwards for drinks.

'They did and George and I managed to get Marilyn to walk with us round the pool so that we could talk alone. We put the idea to her. She listened very carefully and said, "Is he rich? Is he handsome?" Those were the only questions she asked. I don't think she even knew where Monaco was. But she agreed that we were to go ahead and arrange a meeting.

'As an after-thought I said to her, "Do you think that the Prince will want to marry you?"

'Her eyes were full of light. "Give me two days alone with him and of course he'll want to marry me."

'I promised to be in touch with her the following week.

'Imagine my surprise when on the following Monday morning on the front page of the *New York Times* was the story that this high ranking priest (Father Tucker) was being sent by the Vatican to reach an agreement with the Kelly family in Philadelphia.

'I called up Schlee, who wouldn't believe it and went out and got his copy of the *Times*. He just couldn't believe it. The reason that the story has stuck in my mind all these years is that the Kellys had the big advantage. They are among the high-ranking Catholics in the United States and Marilyn Monroe, as far as I know, had no religious affiliation and anyway it would probably never have come off. But it was worth a try.'

Gardner Cowles paused for breath and a chuckle. 'It was quite an idea.'

It was.

When one watches the painstaking dedication that Princess Grace puts into her work as a royal patroness, the calm and efficient way she handles people, the discipline that she imposes on herself, the effort she makes to be punctual, the genuine love she has for Monaco, 'Her Serene Highness Princess Marilyn' would not have stood a chance.

Poor tragic, vulnerable, child-woman Marilyn. How irresponsible of these cold-blooded money tycoons to meddle in emotional affairs of the heart. And how fortunate for Monaco that they did not succeed.

Nineteen

Prince Rainier and Father Tucker had arrived in New York on 15 December. Also included in the entourage was Dr Maurice Donat, the Prince's personal physician. It had been stated in the Press that the Prince was in America for his annual medical check-up and to visit the Johns Hopkins Hospital for a small sinus operation.

As soon as the Prince arrived in New York he got in touch with the Austins, friends of the Kellys who had visited him in the summer. It was a masterpiece of strategy and all part of the crafty plot of Father Tucker's to link up with Grace Kelly again.

It was felt that this would be the more diplomatic way of going about things as the Prince wanted a certain protocol to be observed. Instead of having the Prince, Father Tucker and Dr Donat to dinner as planned, the Austins telephoned Mrs Kelly and asked if they might bring their guest to dinner that night. Christmas Day night is a special one reserved for family gatherings in America, so this in itself was a little unusual.

Peggy Conlan remembers the night vividly.

'It was Aunt Eddie and Uncle Russ who asked mother if they could bring over their guests to dinner on Christmas Day night. The Prince being a prince had to have an invitation from someone, and he was always accompanied by Father Tucker and his doctor.

'When they arrived my father greeted them at the door. The Prince looked very handsome and rather shy. Father Tucker looked like a simply divinely cute parish priest with a twinkle in his eye. My father knew an Irish priest if ever he knew one and said: "Father Tucker sit down and I'll give you a cigar and let's go on from here."

'It was a very gay and lovely dinner and Prince Rainier and my sister sat and talked a lot. I think at first that Grace was a little shy and so was the Prince, but as the dinner progressed everyone seemed to warm up.

'Father Tucker left soon after dinner as he was going to spend the night with the parish priest, whom he knew. After all he was a Philadelphian himself. My father offered to drive him there.

'Mother suggested that we young ones all go over to my place. So this we did. While the rest of us played the card game *Thirty One* in one room, Grace and the Prince went into the other room to talk.'

By the time Mr Kelly arrived back from the train, Father Tucker had already had a talk with him.

'Know what the good father told me,' he said to his wife on returning. 'He said that the Prince wants to marry Grace and the Prince asked him to sound me out on the idea. What do you say to that?'

Mrs Kelly is a realist. A woman with her head set firmly on those handsome shoulders. 'What will Grace say to that?' she answered.

Over at the Conlan house a homely touch, when the party finally broke up, was that Prince Rainier's dark suit was covered with hairs from Peggy's dog and she had to get out the Scotch tape and clean him up before leaving.

Back at the Kelly household it was already late, and when Mrs Kelly asked Prince Rainier and Doctor Donat if they would like to stay the night they both accepted.

The next day Grace and her sister took the Prince and doctor to Bucks County to see a hospital the doctor was interested in. Though the Prince and Grace were never alone, when they returned the second night to the Kelly home it was very much understood by the family that there was something in the air.

'It was the sweetest love story possible,' Peggy continued. 'You know when you think of it it was all rather strange as they both came from such different shores. But it must have been love at first, or least second sight.'

During his two-day stay with the Kellys, Prince Rainier was to find his bed apple-pied one night and his pyjamas sewn up at the legs and arms. It was his first intimation that he was becoming involved with a family who enjoyed practical jokes just as much as he did!

As there could be no question of Prince Rainier, the last of Europe's absolute monarchs—even if his Principality is only 370 acres—being rejected in his suit, Father Tucker became the intermediary.

As the Father was to write in *The Philadelphia Inquirer* at the time: 'What pleased me most about my first contacts was the parents' hesitation about the romance of their daughter—even a sort of reluctance and concern about the whole thing. Mr and Mrs Kelly have shown the prudence and caution that can be inspired only by true parental love and attachment to the principles of their faith.

'Mr Kelly's first question was that of any sensible man: "What do the lad's parents think of all this?"'

Princess Charlotte, Prince Rainier's mother, who lived in an apartment in the Legation de Monaco in Paris, in fact had stated her wishes previously to Father Tucker when she said, 'All I want is that my son marries a Catholic and someone that he loves. And I hope she'll like her mother-in-law.'

Mrs Kelly, in particular, who had never been a mother to push her daughters into marriage, was not so much interested in Grace's immediate reaction as in the kind of life she would be required to lead in the future. Would it bring her the happiness that she deserved?

It could almost have been a scene from an updated *Little Women*. Peggy remembers whisking into the bathroom with Grace and each saying simultaneously and gravely: 'He is very charming.'

Grace Kelly went back to New York and over the next few days saw the Prince constantly, but it was at a private party on New Year's Eve that he asked her to marry him. As there were several formalities to be observed it was agreed that the date of the official announcement should be 5 January and that it would be made simultaneously in Philadelphia and Monaco.

On 4 January, when the Prince and Grace appeared with their friends Carylon and Malcolm Reybold in the Cub Room of the Stork Club, heads turned when the party entered the room. Already there were ripples stirring among the gossip writers.

Jack O'Brien, a Broadway reporter of the New York *Journal American*, was also there, and boldly decided to send a note over to Grace Kelly.

He wrote: 'Dear Grace, I understand you will announce your engagement on Thursday or Friday', adding two little boxes 'yes' or 'no' and asking 'Answer one please.'

The four conferred over the note and then, picking up their fur jackets, the girls made their way towards the table. Grace was peering through her pink-framed glasses to recognise the sender. When she saw it was Jack O'Brien, she paused and said, 'Hullo Jack.'

He stood and boldly said, 'Are congratulations in order?'

'I'm sorry I can't possibly answer your note tonight, Jack,' she parried.

'Can you answer it on Friday?' he dug deeper.

Astonishingly frank she replied, 'Yes, Friday.'

And that is how the first journalist got his scoop on the engagement facts.

John B. Kelly had always had a great understanding and affiliation for the Press. He not only understood the power they have in presenting the Kellys' image but respected them as people employed to do a good job.

'Grace, this is going to be a big thing,' he told his daughter, and then set about organising it all down to the last detail.

He arranged that Grace and the Prince would drive down from New York. They were to stop off briefly at the Kelly home at 3901 Henry Avenue before going on to the Philadelphia Country Club, when the news was to be officially announced at 1 p.m. at a luncheon party for twenty-nine guests.

Plans had been made that it should be simultaneously announced in Monaco by the Minister of State. Everyone was so excited about the event that no one remembered that Monacan time is five hours ahead so the news was in fact announced in Monte Carlo and back on the agency wires to New York before it was out in Philadelphia.

Father Tucker was in shining form as he chatted to the various guests which not only included the close friends of the Kelly family but several City dignitaries, including Governor and Mrs George M. Leader, and Mayor and Mrs Richardson Dilworth.

Prince Rainier and his fiancée arrived at 1.40 and entered the Country Club by a side door where the guests awaited them. There was champagne poured as Mr Kelly tapped his glass and standing tall and proud said: 'We are happy to announce the engagement of our daughter Grace to His Serene Highness Prince Rainier of Monaco. We drink a toast to them.'

It was a simple, straightforward announcement as befitted the man himself. Grace looked happy and pretty in a simple gold brocaded shirtwaist dress with a blush pink chiffon scarf tucked in her neck. Her only jewellery was a pin in the right of her lapel and her engagement ring—a large twelve-carat solitaire diamond which the Prince had had specially brought over for him from Monte Carlo.

One photographer, Dominic Ligato of *The Bulletin*, and one TV cameraman were admitted to make pool photographs of the occasion. I am told that Prince Rainier looked very shy as he watched the way Grace faced the cameras—her usual cool, calm professional self.

After Ligato had taken four shots she told him:

'Oh, won't you please take another? I think you got me cross-eyed on that last one.'

Back at the Kelly home the place was swarming with nearly 100 reporters and photographers. As there was only one telephone line which was reserved for family calls, the Press descended on neighbours, badgering them for telephones. Henry Avenue had never known such excitement before.

For a whole hour the cameras moved in to take their pictures. They climbed over the chairs, stood on antique tables, pushed and jostled, and even overspilled into Mrs Kelly's bedroom. Grace's sister Lizanne (Mrs Donald C. LeVine), obviously very pregnant, had to stand on one side in case she was pushed. Jack Kelly brought out his own camera and began taking a personal record of his sister's engagement.

At first Prince Rainier was acquiescent and patient as he listened to some of the inane questions being fired at him and his fiancée. When one woman journalist burbled what plans did they have for a family, Grace coloured pink and Ma Kelly stepped in smartly, answering: 'I should say they will have lots of children.'

After a period Prince Rainier showed signs of restlessness and was overheard to say crisply to Father Tucker: 'After all, I don't belong to M.G.M.'

After the last photographs and interviews had been completed, John B. Kelly opened his basement bar and invited the Press to celebrate with him. But there was little time for drinking as they swarmed out of the house back to their offices with first-hand accounts. For the *Philadelphia Bulletin* it was a field day to remember . . . they led all the way.

The following afternoon Grace held a small party in New York for two dozen of her friends. The Prince arrived wearing white tie and tails and his royal decorations as they were both to go on to the 'Night in Monte Carlo' Charity Benefit later that evening. The fairy-tale was now becoming a reality.

A touching moment at the party was when the Prince publicly thanked Mr and Mrs Austin for bringing Grace to him. 'You have done more for me by this than anyone else has done for me in my life,' he said.

At the gala at the Waldorf Astoria that evening Grace and her Prince were the centre of attraction. It was as if satiated, jaded New York society wanted to gaze, or even physically touch, the fairy-story couple in the hopes that some of their happiness would rub off.

Grace wore a Dior silk gown that showed off her slender shoulders and had pinned a corsage of orchids on her bosom. This time her white gloves were of royal proportions and she had chosen to wear low-heeled shoes so as not to appear taller than Prince Rainier, who stands 5 feet 7 inches in his bare feet, the reason he referred to himself always as *Shorty*.

They were suitably photographed with Grace folding her hands demurely in her lap and eyes beguilingly turned down. Standing behind her Prince Rainier looked handsome, prosperous and pleased.

According to *Time* magazine, who wrote lyrically of the event, 'They sat uncomfortably in the royal box and nibbled crystallised violets while the Press howled at the door. Later at the Harwyn Club Grace nibbled Rainier's ear and danced with him until 4 a.m.'

Both Prince Rainier and Princess Grace have made it very clear over the years that the timing of their meeting was just right.

Grace Kelly had a knack of always getting her timing right. As she was to later say with disarming honesty to friends on board the *Constitution* as she sailed for Monaco and marriage: 'If I had met the Prince six months previously I doubt that it would have taken place.'

Quotations taken out of context can be dangerous words. But two by Grace Kelly before she became engaged to Prince Rainier are relevant in that they indicate her shyness and uncertainty about life.

'Marriage is like life. You never reach a point where you can say "Now I have grown up" because you go on growing all the time. Love is a growing thing too, because it takes on so many different aspects. I'm always falling in love with other places or other people.

'There are many people, many men I could love. I think it depends on the man you want to devote yourself to spend your life with. This is the decision of marriage.'

Prince Rainier said at the time: 'It wasn't a sudden thought . . . I think that we were both ready for marriage.'

Mrs Kelly had decided to shorten the Prince's name to Rai, which she still calls him to this day. John B. Kelly was enjoying his new status.

In an interview with *Time* magazine during the week of the engagement John B. Kelly was in an expansive mood as he spoke of his future royal son-in-law.

'I told him that I certainly hoped he wouldn't run around the way some princes do, and I told him if he did, he'd lose a mighty fine girl.

'The Prince solemnly promised that he would be an exemplary husband.'

In a syndicated newspaper column at the time Mrs Kelly described the event in rapturous words.

'Through it all Grace has remained calm. At the press conference she was her usual pleasant, retiring self. There was a difference in her behaviour, however, that I believe I was the only one who noticed. . . . Whenever she looked at her Prince or her ring her feelings took possession of her face.

'She really looked like a girl who had found her prince!

' "Mother, I never knew I could be so happy," she said to me, time and again.'

The 'difference in her behaviour' may, of course, have been one of three things. A fond mother's exuberance over her daughter's royal engagement; an inventive ghost writer from the paper or perhaps, and this is what I believe, an astute mother commenting on a sensitive and fascinating facet. The making of a princess had already begun.

When *Time* asked brother 'Kell' what his reaction was he replied:

'I don't think we can make a sculler out of him. He's not tall enough. But I hear he is a terrific skin diver.'

Carroll Righter, the well-known American astrologer, who was writing at the time for the New York *Mirror*, pronounced that the romance could actually have been made in heaven.

'Comparison of the two charts finds eight out of ten points in common. Both Venus, the planet of romance, love, and concord, and the redoubtable Mars, the planet of energy, vitality, and consuming interest play a very prominent part.

'Miss Kelly has planetary positions which are stated in textbooks as being "a sign all by itself", indicating she is such a personality in her own right that she will be imbued with a unique activity, career and viewpoint that set her a little apart from others. . . . Despite wealth, talent and what seems to be a quick and easy rise to fame, there is no question that many things have been done the hard way by her.

'The horoscope of the Prince of Monaco indicates he has a decided, restless urge to go places, see people and do things. This does not interfere at all, however, with his capacity to love deeply and sincerely.

'Any woman would be happy to have him around the house because he is a born problem solver. There will be no lack of love for Grace from him because he likes to show little attentions a woman craves.

'There will be considerable problems, however, to prevent the relationship from bogging down into too great contentment. . . .'

Covering himself for all eventualities Righter continues:

'There is one danger, and that is of unconventionality or confusion from different backgrounds. However, an understanding attitude on the part of both persons can provide an added respect and a deepening of the existing ties.'

Twenty

Grace Kelly was to become the most married girl of the year. With her two weddings—civic and religious—to Prince Rainier all set for 18 April, 1956, she first had to go through a wedding in the film *High Society*, which she had already contracted to make before the Prince's arrival and proposal.

The film was a remake of that classic *Philadelphia Story* starring Katharine Hepburn, James Stewart and Cary Grant, and though I find the original a much more stylish production, the Grace Kelly, Bing Crosby, Frank Sinatra, Celeste Holm version was opulent and had a starry quality due no doubt to the new ecstatic happiness of Grace Kelly.

On the first day when the cast met on the set there was a certain apprehension. It occurs on every first day . . . the same kind of feeling of children starting school. With cosseted, egotistical actors the atmosphere is often charged with tension.

Grace had made one film with Bing Crosby and Celeste Holm had worked with Frank Sinatra before, but the combination of all four was as yet an unknown factor. The director was Chuck Walters, an ebullient extrovert. Grace was gracious on that first day, if a little shy, simply because while all the others were used to doing musicals this was to be her first.

Even with a string of successes now behind her, Grace was still uncertain when working with experienced stars. Writer Maurice Sollito explains this withdrawal: 'An actor who worked closely with her said, "She goes to incredible lengths to avoid any situation in which there is even a remote possibility that she might be rejected. She doesn't trust people. She is afraid of looking stupid and that's why she doesn't talk very much." '

Celeste Holm, who remembers that first day, confirms this. Talking to me in New York, she said: 'She kept very much to herself. At the time she was dieting like mad. She would have grapefruit, honey and tea for lunch and nothing else. She was so slender that I thought it was a little odd but she was so strong-minded, almost stubborn about it.'

On the first day of shooting Grace had one request to make of the director. She asked if she could wear her own engagement ring in the film. Next day she arrived with her diamond ring.

'It was the most wonderful diamond I have seen. Most diamonds I think look just cold and icy but the thing about this one were the colours in it,' Celeste Holm said.

When Bing Crosby says in the film, 'Some stone, George. Did you mine it yourself?' the audience were able to get a close-up view in glamorous Eastman Technicolor plus VistaVision.

In most cases when two blondes are to share honours in a film the bigger name demands that the other actress dye her hair to avoid confusion. When Betty Grable first co-starred with Alice Faye she bleached her hair to platinum so as not to interfere with Alice's corn-colour hair. Sheree North wore a black wig to contrast with Marilyn Monroe's blondness. Agnes Moorhead, a lifetime red-haired, had to switch to blonde to contrast with Jane Russell. But when Celeste Holm and Grace Kelly met there were no complications—they remained their own colour.

'No one gave it a thought that we were both blonde. Grace wastes no time on such banal matters. She was lovely to work with simply because there was not one trace of temperament even though these were harassing days for her.'

Every day during the lunchtime breaks Grace had to give an interview of some sort. The Press were relentless and M.G.M. equally keen to squeeze the last drop of publicity out of the situation.

'Grace seemed to move without any consciousness of self,' Celeste Holm continued. 'She has remarkable self-composure. The publicity demands on her were overwhelming. With it all she retained absolute equanimity which she maintained at all times. I have worked with many actresses who would have collapsed under the strain.'

Miss Holm's eyes dropped in on one such interview when Grace was being interrogated by a dragon from Associated Press 'with a voice of shattered glass.'

' "Tell me, Miss Kelly, how long do you think it will last?" the reporter asked.

' "I beg your pardon," Grace answered.

'The woman repeated her question.

' "A Catholic marries for life," came the answer.

' "Do you plan on having any children?"

' "I certainly hope so."

' "How many children are you going to have?"

' "Well . . . that is out of my hands," she replied without any hint of impatience.

'I would have punched the lady hard,' Celeste Holm remarked. 'But Grace was so courteous and gracious.

'Once after such a scene I asked Grace, "How is all of this affecting you?"

'She replied, "I'm tired. I'll catch up on my rest later—I guess!" She has a keen sense of humour and a human receptiveness.'

In between the endless interviews Grace had to have numerous fittings for her trousseau and wedding dress, answer letters and invitations and take many personal calls from well-wishing friends. She never had a free minute to herself.

Grace was determined to sing her own songs and not have them dubbed as many other stars do.

'She had a very clear contralto voice—lovely and totally appropriate. She made no effort to sound like a professional singer. On the day she was to sing that lovely, lovely song *True Love* with Bing we all hung about to hear them.'

During the making of the film Prince Rainier and his father the Duke of Polignac visited Hollywood and were invited on the set of *High Society*. A luncheon was given for them in the panelled executive dining-room which at Metro was considered rather a joke simply because it was so small and could only seat eight.

There was Grace Kelly and Prince Rainier, Chuck Walters and Dore Schary, the Duke of Polignac and Celeste Holm. The lunch rippled along happily even though Grace seemed nervous. Chuck Walters, who had a tendency to be enchantingly obscene, could not have been more correct. Then suddenly it happened. Dore Schary asked Prince

Rainier how large Monaco was. The figure of five square miles was mentioned.

'Five square miles,' Schary countered. 'That's not as big as our back lot.'

Suddenly a cold wind went through the room. Celeste Holm was so perturbed that she stuck a knife into her steak, it skidded and the sauce spluttered all over the front of her dress.

'I knew that second that Grace Kelly would never make another picture,' she recalled.

Grace and Celeste were both invited to the Red Book Party, an annual movie colony event, and planned to go together.

'Who are you going with?' Celeste asked.

'My Prince,' Grace replied archly.

As it turned out the dinner was to be late and with an early morning call the girls decided not to go.

When Prince Rainier returned to New York, Grace Kelly promised him that she would neither drink nor dance with anyone until they met again. And she kept her promise except at a party in her honour when Danny Kaye and Frank Sinatra telephoned the Prince and asked his permission.

Mr and Mrs Kelly also paid a visit to the Coast to see Grace. Mrs Ben Lyon and her former husband were old friends of the Kellys and gave a party for them.

'We made the arrangements for it at the Beverly Hills Hotel right after Grace's engagement was announced.

'We had calls from everyone wanting to come, but by that time our guest list was completed. It was a beautiful party and we had orchid corsages for both Grace and Margaret. Grace looked incredibly beautiful that night in a long white brocaded satin chongsam. Her hair was drawn back into a chignon but she outshone everyone by her simplicity and beauty.'

Members of the cast of *High Society* had a hard job trying to find the crooked roulette wheel which they gave to Grace as a wedding present.

Helen Rose of M.G.M., who was given the coveted job of designing Grace Kelly's real wedding dress, gave her a shower-party for 18 when among the gifts she was given was a shower cap with ermine tails. Guests were asked to bring underwear—'I have never in my life seen such beautiful things. They were all in white, blue and beige,' Celeste Holm recalled.

A surprise guest was Annette Kellerman, the famous swimmer, who brought a rosepoint handkerchief given her by Gatti. Nibbling dainty sandwiches with coffee and fruit, they were all speculating as to when Grace would return to making movies after her wedding.

Only the bride-to-be remained silent.

Grace was to be given three more bridal showers. Virginia Darcy her hairdresser, who was travelling to Monaco to make the French pleat hairstyle on the wedding day, organised yet another one in Los Angeles. The only shower given in New York was arranged by a bridesmaid Sally Richardson and in Philadelphia Mrs Jay Hamilton asked the guests to bring something suitable for a yacht. The Prince then owned the *Deo Juvante II*, which he had given to Grace as a present.

Celeste Holm still has the note that she received from Grace Kelly about her Central Park passion. It is typical of her that even at her busiest she found time and thought to write it. Celeste Holm is an official of the Friends of Central Park, a society which campaigned to get the park made into an historic landmark. The park was created in 1855 and designed in such a way that no buildings were visible when you were inside it . . . a piece of countryside within a city. This rural atmosphere is what its Friends are trying to preserve against the encroaching city skyline.

The note reads: 'Dear Celeste, thank you very much for doing all you are doing. Keep up the good work and be sure they keep the *bridal* path open.'

Grace Kelly's last night in Hollywood as a working actress was to prove the sterner stuff that she is made of and why with her polished façade she is the born princess.

After completing *High Society* she remained there to present an Oscar to the best actor at the Academy Award ceremony.

Towards the end of the ceremony she was called to the stage to present the Best Actor Award to Ernest Borgnine. Was it nervousness or calculated inverted snobbism when the M.C. Jerry Lewis introduced her as 'Gracie' for the first time in Hollywood history? Miss Kelly blushed a deep rose shade.

Later the stars were hustled to the basement for a photographic session. For someone who hates crowds it was an ordeal for Grace, as she was pulled, pushed and shoved from room to room. At one point an Academy official begged her to retreat to the interviewing room, but she firmly replied: 'They don't want to interview me. I haven't won anything.'

Then came a voice from the crowd, the only spark of humour in this whole witless and tasteless evening.

'Yes, you have. You've won a prince.'

One of those scenes followed that takes a thoroughbred like Grace Kelly to handle. When she was finally dragged into a newsroom full of reporters who were busy filing their Oscar stories there was a ghastly silence. She was as stunned to see them as they to see her.

'Please get me out of here,' she announced desperately to the M.G.M. publicity man, Morgan Hudgins. Once out in the corridor the frenzy began again and the only one to keep her head was our heroine. White-faced, white gowned she stood calmly like a neo-classical piece of sculpture.

'I will be delighted to pose with Mr Borgnine for a picture,' she said patiently, 'but I do have to get up at 5 a.m. to fly to New York.'

The evening was over. Hollywood with all its brash phoneyness, its schmaltzy warmth, its hard-working, insincere gospellers; the Hollywood that had turned Grace Kelly into a household name throughout the world was now behind her. It would be interesting to know the thoughts that she had as the limousine slipped away and, looking every inch a princess, she waved farewell to the crowds . . . and Hollywood.

Twenty-one

There had been much discussion among East Falls people both privately and in the newspapers when the engagement was announced. In a single vote the 20,000 residents all wanted the wedding to take place there. To be specific, in St Bridget's Roman Catholic church —just a wave's lash from the Schuylkill River—the Kelly family's parish church.

'The church is plenty old enough . . . it is 102 years . . . and Grace should be married in St Bridget's like her folks before her. If Grace and her prince want to be married for a second time then it can be Monaco, but we want to be first,' protested Mrs Angelo Bellofatto of 3678 Stanton Street.

But as an absolute monarch and head of state as well as being an astute business man, Prince Rainier had explained that the wedding of the year belonged to Monte Carlo and his Monegasque subjects.

Monte Carlo business men were reported as overjoyed when they heard that the wedding would take place there. The timing in the late spring could not have been better in order to attract inpourings of tourists in the off-season.

Leaving her apartment and the New York she loved was a poignant experience for Grace. Intelligent and sensitive as she is, she was the first to realise that it was much more than that. She was not only leaving behind her family and country but a way of life that she understood. Before her was the unknown.

In those last days Charlie Kelly, her cousin, came from Philadelphia where he was a professor of Latin and Greek, to help her.

There were still two years to go on the lease of the apartment and Grace decided to keep it on so that she could return and her family could use it. It may even have been a subconscious reluctance to sever all ties with her past.

Packing was not without humour as Grace remembered the two trunks that she had sent ahead and wondered what the staff's reaction would be at the palace in Monaco when they unpacked them. Instead of a bridal trousseau fit for a princess they were stuffed with old jeans, shirts, sneakers and sweaters. Everything dear and old and sentimental had been packed into them.

The furniture had been moved out of the dining-room to make space for the trunks of clothes and wedding presents stacked around waiting for the professional packers. Grace herself is an erratically methodical person and did most of her own personal packing herself. She even made a list of what to wear for every night on the ship and the week at the palace before her wedding. She was leaving nothing to chance.

In that last week she made an unexpected and sentimental journey to Central Park, where she went riding for the last time.

From a riding academy, which has a school of livery horses, she hired *Daisy*, a horse well known to American television audiences for its appearance in *Howdy Doody* and *Robert Montgomery Presents*. A charming animal, it made a pretty picture with Grace riding side-saddle, an accomplishment she had learnt for her part in *The Swan*.

As every hour of those last days were dogged by newspapermen her arrival in Central Park at 2 p.m. with dapper instructor Fred Birkner soon became known and the photographers began a feverish Grace-hunt round the park. To avoid the Press Mr Birkner had arranged to meet her at a police exit at 90th Street and Fifth Avenue, but the Press soon caught up.

At the family holiday ranch house at Roc Agel in the hills above Monaco, where several horses are kept, Princess Grace still rides when-ever she has time and prefers side-saddle to astride. She has a natural seat and even the Empress Elizabeth of Austria could not fault her straight back.

Princess Grace's side-saddle anachronism is very much in keeping with her character and makes her into the enigmatic and individual person that she is and always will be.

During the last week she also attended the wedding of Rita Gam, who was to be a bridesmaid at her own in Monaco. Rita, who had previously been married to film producer Sidney Lumet, was now marrying Tom Guinzburg, the scion of Viking Press publishing house. It was a charming ceremony held in the elegant drawing-room of the Guinzburg's family house in Sutton Square.

Rita and Grace, who had spent so many hours when they shared a flat in Hollywood discussing their various beaux, were now both making highly desirable marriages. There were tears amid the orange blossom. Grace was in fact the last among her group of girl friends to marry.

All Grace's trousseau shopping had to be sandwiched into one huge buying spree during one hectic week in New York between finishing *High Society* and leaving to spend Easter in Philadelphia with the family.

As time was so short she called in a friend, Eleanor Lambert, one of America's best known fashion authorities. The final choice was always Grace's but Eleanor Lambert helped in making it possible to see so many things in so short a time.

'It was a liberal education as well as a thrill to watch the world's most famous bride-to-be select her trousseau,' Miss Lambert said at the time.

'Future brides who may not boast Miss Kelly's gift for looking divine in everything, her background of wealth or her personal earning power could still take lessons from her in thrift, discrimination and firm budget control,' she added.

Grace Kelly chose middle-of-the-road clothes in the colours of white, blue and her favourite honey beige, that would outlive current fashion fads. She just plumb did not go for fussy, hard-to-care-for clothes either. As she says even today: 'I am very easy with clothes.'

Ben Zuckerman turned out to be her favourite designer and it was his clothes that mainly created the Grace Kelly look which permeated American fashion that year, and after twenty years has returned full cycle to fashion once again. The silhouette is a long moulded torso with a gently flared skirt, a fashion she loves to wear in blonde silk jerseys and crêpes. The most patient of shoppers, the only thing she was fussy about was that her clothes fitted snugly at the waistline and that the hems were immaculate.

The list of designers was formidable and I give it here simply because it reflects how much she affected American fashion that year.

For sports clothes Claire McCardell, Brigance, B. H. Wragge and Marquise. Her day clothes were designed by Adele Simpson, Mollie Parnis, Larry Aldrich, Christian Dior, Traina Norell, Branells and Suzy Perette. Cocktail dresses came from Pauline Trigere, Harvey Berin and James Galanos. The evening dresses, all so beautifully simple, were the work of Fira Benenson, Trigere, Galanos and Branells.

She confessed that she had gone wild over hats and bought far too many. All her shoes, in deference to the Prince's height, had low curved Louis heels.

The precious wedding dress of ivory silk, Brussels lace 125 years old and embroidered with seed pearls, had arrived from Hollywood where it had been designed by Helen Rose and was now packed for the voyage in a long steel wardrobe box from Metro. During the sea trip Mr Kelly was so alarmed that something might happen to it that he personally insisted on going down into the hold to inspect the trunk and cases of wedding presents. He found that the wedding box had tipped up on end and made sure it was firmly set down horizontally.

With all the grandeur of a pharaoh marrying off his favourite daughter, Mr Kelly had organised the Kelly entourage of seventy-eight which was to sail on the S.S. *Constitution* from New York to Monaco. Family, friends, bridesmaids were all invited to travel together on a voyage that was to take eight days.

It is doubtful whether prosaic John B. Kelly thought in allegorical terms, but there was a touch of classical drama in the idea of the New World bringing its favourite daughter as a gift to the Old World.

As she left her apartment building that grey April 4 morning, a small girl jumped forward and handed Grace a gay nose-gay. She believed it to be an omen of good luck.

The rain tumbled down, sheeting New York rain, as she sped in a black limousine along the West Side Highway to Pier 84 at 44th Street where the S.S. *Constitution* was berthed. The rest of the party were already aboard. She had in fact travelled on the ship before as part of an advertising campaign at its launching.

Metro Goldwyn Mayer, who still to this day keep a watchful eye on Princess Grace whenever she visits America, had sent along Morgan Hudgins to accompany their brightest star. Newsmen swarmed all over the place, pressing round her as Grace was manœuvred to her stateroom, where she made her first broadcast to the people of Monaco. It had been arranged through Radio Monte Carlo who had linked up with the Voice of America. Here is what she said:

'I am deeply moved as I prepare to leave the United States where I was born and spent my early years. But also I have the great joy today of bringing to the Monegasques the sincere affection of their American friends. All those who know the Principality want to go back there; many would like to remain. I was there one year ago and I am going back again . . . to stay.

'I would like to tell my future compatriots that the Prince, my fiancé, has taught me to love them. I feel that I already know them well, thanks to what the Prince has told me, and my dearest wish today is to find a small place in their hearts . . . to share their joys and sorrows as well as their hopes and aspirations.'

A Press conference was immediately held in the observation lounge, where Grace answered yet another hundred questions with quiet and dignified patience.

Darting among the guests were her small nieces Meg and Marylee who were to be flower girls. When they saw all the fuss being made they grabbed Grace round her skirt and demanded: 'Aunt Grace. If you are going to be a princess why aren't we?'

As the ship steamed down the Hudson River Grace stood on the captain's bridge between her mother and father waving farewell on the wharf to her sister Lizanne, who could not go as she was expecting a baby any day, and her sister-in-law Mary who was to fly over later as she, too, was expecting a child.

When Grace at last arrived in her stateroom S-5 there sitting on the bed was Oliver and beside him a gangling, temperamental puppy that turned out to be a Weimaraner. It was the surprise gift of Philadelphia friends Mr and Mrs Albert Greenfield Jr, and ultimately grew to the size of a great Dane. In the excitement he had already proved not to be ship-trained.

Oliver also had received a surprise gift from the Hitchcocks, who had sent him a chain leash deliriously decorated with white carnations and satin bows with the accompanying card which read: 'You'll love Monte Carlo. Happy barking.' It was signed 'Philip', which was the name of the Hitchcock dog.

Grace's stateroom, which had been specially decorated in beige raw silk for the trip, was brimming over with flowers and gifts and well-wishing telegrams.

Every night there were parties for the Kelly clan beginning with the captain's welcome aboard reception on the first night.

France Soir, Paris Match and *Life* as well as many American newspapers, all had teams of newsmen aboard to cover every hour of the day. During the voyage Grace made time to pose specially for every photographer aboard so that he could claim to his newspaper that this indeed was an exclusive picture. It was the kind of thoughtful gesture that had made her the darling of newsmen in her Hollywood days.

Last thing at night, when everyone was still merrymaking, Grace used to slip on an old coat, collect the dogs and take a walk on the top deck all by herself. She had much to think about on those starlit nights.

During the day there was plenty to do as Grace answered all her letters or in an old tweed skirt, shirt and sweater, with dark glasses and a scarf round her head, played shuffleboard with her nieces or lay chatting on deckchairs with her parents. During the voyage she always wore a pearl-studded charm bracelet with a large golden coin dangling from it. This was the medallion that the Prince had given her and on one side was his face in profile and on the other the royal crest of Monaco. Prince Rainier also cabled Princess Grace every day of the voyage.

One of the most memorable nights on the trip over was the impromptu sing-song when Judy Kanter and Grace gave impersonations of Judy Garland and Rosemary Clooney. Few people outside her own close circle of friends realise that Princess Grace is a brilliant mimic. Her impersonations of Garbo and Zsa Zsa Gabor have such sharp-edged detail that they must be among the best in show business. The evening ended with Grace singing some of the Cole Porter songs from *High Society*. As the New York *Daily Mirror* was to head their dispatch: 'Grace and 60 on a Showboat to Monaco'.

During one night when everyone was dancing, the *Constitution's* sister ship the S.S. *Independence* passed close by and blinked 'Good luck, Gracie!'

When the message was announced on the public address system Grace remarked to Gant Gaither: 'You know, I never really cared anything about an engagement ring or the conventional wedding gown with all the trimmings. It never meant anything to me. Now, look. All this! Isn't it ironic?'

Everyone has their own private memories of this trip. When Mrs Ben Lyon remarked to Mr Kelly: 'It must be very difficult for Grace to give up her career when she is just at the top,' he replied: 'When you get to the top where else is there to go?'

The party had fallen into two groups called 'The Seniors' and 'The Juniors'. Grace and her sister naturally spent much of their time with

'The Juniors'. One night they decided to play for probably the last time 'The Game' and everyone joined in with Grace heading one team and the family dentist, Dr George Coleman, at the helm of the other. She had to act out 'Beware of the Danger Line' which was a well-known toothpaste advertisement and became so involved in acting out 'danger' that the heels of both shoes broke off and she spent the rest of the night in her stocking feet.

The evening finished with a real Kelly family sing-song ending with the old favourite *The End of a Perfect Day*.

Instead of all giving irrelevant wedding presents the *Constitution* friends had a splendid idea. They had all banded together and, under the advice of veteran film producer Mervyn LeRoy, had bought 14,000 dollars worth of equipment necessary for a cinema to be installed in the palace at Monaco so that Grace would not fall behind in seeing all the latest American movies.

A part of the garage where the old carriages had been kept was converted into the cinema which exists today and is used whenever they have a film evening. Small individual supper tables are set and guests eat while watching a movie.

Grace did not go down to dinner on the last night but spent it quietly in her own cabin as she had to make an early rise in the morning. Peggy joined her after dinner and calmly set about manicuring Grace's nails. It was a gesture of any sister and illustrates the naturalness and closeness that exists in the Kelly family.

Normally the *Constitution* does not make a stopover at Cannes, but special arrangements had been made for this occasion. All the other passengers were delighted to have the chance of seeing the Princess's departure when she joined the Prince in the Bay of Hercules when his yacht *Deo Juvante II* met the liner.

Just as the mayor of Monaco boarded the *Constitution* the sun broke through the clouds, spot-lighting the sun deck where the official presentations were to take place. With the blue sky above and shimmering blue sea all around the yacht even Sam Goldwyn could not have planned a more impressive arrival scene.

Circling the ship was a helicopter dropping white and red carnations, a brilliant and fragrant welcome from Aristotle Onassis, who at that period was the majority stockholder in the company that controlled the gambling casinos and best hotels. His personal wedding present was a diamond bracelet and his company had given a diamond and ruby tiara. The carnations were an after-thought.

At 10 a.m. a gangway was lowered from the side of the *Constitution* and Miss Kelly and her parents walked down to board the yacht. Grace was conspicuous in her navy blue *faille* coat topped with a huge white hat of organdie and Swiss lace. The picturesque but ill-chosen hat was the first lesson that Grace Kelly was to learn about the protocol of royal fashion. As the Prince delicately pointed out to her, it would be difficult for the people of Monaco lining the streets to see her face, but by now the ceremonies were well under way and there was no chance to go and make a change as all her luggage was being unloaded.

The whistle of the *Constitution* blasted a series of farewells as the passengers cheered and yachts in the harbour all opened their voices to make a crescendo of happy noise.

Prince Rainier, dapper in navy blue, who had spent frantic weeks personally supervising all the arrangements for the wedding, now looked relaxed and smiled contentedly as he took his fiancée's arm and led her to an open car to drive through the streets of Monte Carlo up the winding road to his castle on the rock. The people cheered as they watched this real-life fairy-story unfold before them.

Within three hours, having first been greeted by her future father-in-law, Prince Pierre, and sister-in-law, Princess Antoinette, who were to stay with the Kelly family in the palace during the pre-wedding festivities, there was a large family luncheon party.

Two servants in full livery with the Grimaldi royal crest stood behind each chair.

'The servants had so much gold braid that you couldn't tell them from the generals,' Mr Kelly remarked to a friend.

Prince Rainier had elected to stay at his villa farther along the coast until moving back into the palace on their return from their honeymoon.

For the week before her wedding Grace Kelly lived with her family in the palace that was to become her home. A strange experience!

Twenty-two

All that week before Grace Kelly's wedding took place to Prince Rainier Monte Carlo was *en fete*. With the *Constitution* clan firmly entrenched at the Hermitage Hotel, there were parties and galas every night.

The Kelly family itself was something of a refreshing surprise to the old set of Monte Carlo who looked on somewhat askance as Peggy sauntered through the hotel lounge in her neat Bermuda shorts followed by a gaggle of unselfconscious children.

There were parties every night. At the International Sporting Club the programme included a ballet with Tamara Toumanova and Eddie Constantine, the American singer who made his name in Paris, came specially for the occasion. The climax of the evening was a fireworks display with the initials R and G interlaced for the first time.

Mr and Mrs Kelly were hosts to 100 guests at one of the most glamorous events of the week—a dinner and ball at the Monte Carlo Casino. It was a splendid dinner with a menu beginning with game bird soup with quenelles, golden paillettes, parboiled Loire salmon, English saddle of lamb, iced gooseberries, early fruit pie, salad Caprice, surprise omelette. The wine served was Pommery Grenot Brut 1949.

The Prince and Grace were the first to step out on the dance floor as Aimé Barelli's orchestra struck up *A Woman in Love*. They danced alone to everyone's delight Grace already looking the part of a princess in champagne peau de soie with baby puff sleeves and tight bodice.

Apart from the change of place, time and man, it could almost have been a scene from *The Swan* which she had played in just a few months before.

It was the first time their friends had seen Grace and Prince Rainier so relaxed.

'It was quite obvious that here were two people deliriously in love and they danced oblivious of everything around them,' one of the bridesmaids told me. 'It really was a fairy story come alive.'

When the second number began, *Love is a Many Splendoured Thing*, Mrs Kelly, looking every inch the one time 'cover girl', proudly took the floor on the arm of Prince Pierre. It was a night the Kelly family will never forget . . . and a long, long way from Philadelphia.

As a touch of home-town, Stan Rubin and his Tiger Town Five from Princeton had been specially flown over, but the jazz sounded so discordant in this Cinderella-at-the-ball atmosphere that Mrs Kelly quickly reverted to the Barelli music.

Grace, who is a beautiful dancer, seemed to glide around the ballroom with all eyes on her.

When the ball ended, Grace said goodnight to Prince Rainier on the steps of the Casino. They did not kiss but clasped hands and looked into each other's eyes.

Grace drove back to the palace with her parents and the Prince to his villa at Cap Ferrat.

And so the storybook romance continued with each day bringing new delights for the bride-to-be. Jewellery from Prince Pierre in the form of a large pearl that he had inherited from his mother. With superb planning the Prince saw that each day Grace received yet another piece of jewellery, including two handsome pieces from his mother, Princess Charlotte.

Whenever possible Grace used to slip along to the Hercules Gallery in the palace to see the wedding presents which continued to arrive hourly. There was a gold serving-tray from Queen Elizabeth, a fragile antique desk from the Cary Grants, a small Steuben glass rabbit, treasures of gold and silver, paintings, a great many rosaries, and a length of cloth of gold from the Ambassador from Pakistan to the United Nations, the Nawab Mir Nawaz Jung.

All Grace's friends knew that she liked picture frames, which still fascinate her even today. The assortment was enormous . . . silver from the Cornelius Vanderbilt Whitneys, white satin from playwright Lexford Richards.

There were also the 'hokey ones', as Grace described them. The hundreds of garters, a *Cook Book for Two:* numerous pot holders and a shamrock-green double bed for Irish luck.

She insisted on entering each one in the white satin bride's book that she had brought from America. By the time she was through she had used a dozen books.

One of the official presents was to be the centre of an unpleasant incident which the Prince has described as 'a sordid affair'.

The National Council of Monaco decided to give the Princess a wedding present and selected one of their members to buy it. Despite a handsome sum of £30,000 he chose an unattractive old-fashioned necklace that was most unsuitable for the Princess.

When the Council decided to return the necklace and ask for their money back the jeweller refused to return the deposit which ultimately led to a law suit. It was altogether an upsetting incident which Princess Grace took in her usual calm style. If she discussed it at all it was in strictest privacy. It was her first taste of royal diplomacy.

The Princess's gift to the bridesmaids was an original thought and made by Cartier. It was a gold medallion engraved with the initials R and G surmounted by the crown of Monaco. At the time the bridesmaids wore them on their chunky gold bracelets but today most of them have them on a golden chain as is the present fashion. They gave her a silver dressing table set from Cartier with a silver tray on which all their signatures were engraved.

Looking back on that week, Princess Grace says that so much happened that it is difficult to remember everything. It was one glorious, exhausting whirl. Over the immediate weeks before the wedding she lost ten pounds in weight and even her wedding dress, made in the Metro Goldwyn Mayer design studios, had to have last-minute adjustments.

One night she does not forget is when Prince Rainier took her by car up on to the *Grande Corniche*—a ribbon of road that stretches through the sky away above the Riviera. They drove up in his sports car to watch the dawn break. At Super Èze they left the car and climbed up through the sleeping village to a small chapel at its apex.

They returned to Monte Carlo in the hot morning sun at 8 a.m. Before them was a day when every hour was scheduled. There was the buffet luncheon for the palace staff which Prince Rainier had arranged and in the afternoon the acceptance of a Rolls Royce, the gift of the people of Monaco.

In the afternoon the children of Monaco gathered in La Place du Palais with a large plastic mail bag filled with letters addressed to 'La Belle Princesse de Monaco', 'Notre Princess Grace Patricia' and so on.

A special stage had been constructed in the Place de Palace where the Festival Ballet from London danced, followed by acts from the London Palladium, the superb choir of Monte Carlo and many other performers.

The day finished with Prince Rainier and Grace standing hand in hand at the windows of the white and gold salon watching the fantastic fireworks display. Part of the precision planning had been the turning off of all the lights in Monte Carlo and in the boats in the harbour. Not a light remained as suddenly the whole sky over the bay burst into brilliance, like ribbons of sapphires, emeralds and diamonds, as the fireworks exploded in the sky.

Prince Rainier's civil marriage to Grace Kelly began at 11 a.m. on 18 April in the gold and crimson throne room of the royal palace. Everyone in Monaco stopped work to watch the ceremony on their television sets.

Prince Rainier entered first followed by his father, Prince Pierre, his mother, Princess Charlotte and his sister, Princess Antoinette.

Grace looking like a beautiful French porcelain doll in a short dress of tea-rose mousseline de soie over lace with a Juliette cap trimmed with matching silk roses, was serene and calm. Small pink gloves had replaced her usual white ones. Though inwardly she was shaking, no one would have suspected it as she walked behind Count Ferdinand d'Allières, chief of protocol. He was to collapse a few minutes before the service began and was taken to the palace infirmary.

Seated in groups around Prince Rainier and Grace were the members of their families, the bridesmaids and their husbands and a few close friends.

It was a simple, dignified service as the bride and groom remained seated. Judge Portanier read the civil marriage rites of the Napoleonic Code.

As he looked down at this beautiful American girl, he said:

'Mademoiselle Grace Patricia Kelly, do you take as your husband His Serene Highness, My Lord, Prince Rainier III, here present?'

In a low but firm voice she answered, 'Oui.'

Turning to the Prince, who was shifting nervously in his chair, he asked:

'May I respectfully ask Your Serene Highness if he agrees to take as his wife and legitimate spouse Mademoiselle Grace Patricia Kelly, here present?'

The Prince raised his head and said in a firm clear voice, 'Oui.'

It was all over in sixteen minutes.

Grace Kelly had now become Princess Grace de Monaco, the most titled woman in Europe . . . 142 all told . . . albeit thanks to ancient titles referring mainly to villages that no longer existed.

It was a solemn occasion and despite the intimacy there was a certain amount of tension. The Prince was the first to sign the register and after that Grace. Prince Pierre, then Princess Charlotte were followed by Mr and Mrs Kelly. Next Princess Antoinette went to the table followed by Grace's sister Peggy Davis, as she was then, who was a witness for Grace, and finally brother 'Kell', John Kelly Junior.

The tension was at last broken when Grace turned and said smilingly: 'At least I am half married.'

Immediately after the service Their Serene Highnesses Prince Rainier and Princess Grace stood and greeted four thousand of their Monegasque subjects in the Court of Honour of the Palace.

It was the first time in her life that people had curtsied to her in her new role as their very own Princess.

After the last guest had gone, in a very tender private ceremony the Prince invested his wife with the Order of Saint Charles, the highest honour the country can give.

While dressing Princess Grace's hair that night for the Opera Gala two women who had been so close together the last years met in the privacy of a bedroom. Virginia Darcy, who had been Grace Kelly's hairdresser for many of her films and had come over specially to take care of her during the wedding week, was placing a diamond coronet on Princess Grace's hair. Suddenly she burst into tears and remarked:

'I have always called you Princess but this time it isn't a paste prop. It's for real.'

Just after 9 p.m. Princess Grace of Monaco took her place beside Prince Rainier in the Royal Box, which now had the initials R and G on the frosted glass sides.

She seemed to glide into the box standing there in a beaded bell-shaped dress by Lanvin wearing her new order, a family coronet of diamonds and the diamond necklace given her by the people of Monaco.

Slowly she turned her head from right to left, inclining it with a tiny motion just as she does today. It was not a smile, just the corners of her mouth turned up. No one could possibly have guessed that without her glasses the auditorium was a blurry haze. She stood still, indestructibly beautiful and unbelievably regal.

The celluloid had dissolved into reality.

Twenty-three

Today on the first floor of the Philadelphia Museum of Art on a wax model resembling Philadelphia's famous daughter, is the wedding dress of Princess Grace of Monaco.

As they shuffle past, the tourists stand and stare and one hears the odd remark: 'Look, Martha, doesn't she have a small waist . . . I'm not so sure I'd have had those bows . . . I liked her best in *The Country Girl*.'

Twenty years ago on 19 April this wedding dress was worn by Grace Kelly when she went through her second wedding ceremony and became in the eyes of the Holy Roman Empire the bride of Prince Rainier.

It was the most enchanting royal wedding of the century. No bride could have looked more fragile, more beautiful.

'My God, to see Grace was like seeing a statue of alabaster marble. I have never seen anything so exquisite in my life,' Earl Blackwell, New York's social lion, described to me.

If she was tired . . . and she must have been desperately tired . . . the Kelly discipline prevented her from showing it. It was the picture that all the cameramen had waited for as she glided down the staircase of the écru-pink royal palace at Monaco on the arm of her father John B. Kelly and walked the cobblestoned courtyard to the Cathedral of St Nicholas.

Father and daughter made their way slowly through a guard of honour of sailors and marines from visiting American, British, French and Italian warships. Grace's eyes under her veil were demure and shy. John B. Kelly was tall and proud.

The Cathedral of St Nicholas, the beautiful old church which dominates the old town of Monte Carlo, was filled with 600 international celebrities and minor royalty. It was reported that King Farouk almost skipped the wedding of his friend Prince Rainier as he could not get four extra tickets for his bodyguards. Instead he sat and sulked alone. When the Egyptian Minister arrived and saw Farouk he promptly left the Cathedral.

Aristotle Onassis's silver head was noticeable. He had been taking playful bets among friends that he would be 'bumped off' in the Cathedral. But there he sat delighted to be among the élite.

Another famous figure was Somerset Maugham, who once coined the quip 'Monaco is a sunny place for shady characters.'

The two most elegant women in the Cathedral were the Begum Aga Khan sitting next to the aged Aga Khan and Ava Gardner, who had come out of hibernation to be present at her friend's wedding.

The religious ceremony which followed the civil service the day before was to be three hours in length. Prince Rainier had already arrived at the Cathedral.

It is said that he himself designed his uniform which was based on that worn by the palace guard. The trousers were blue with a gold stripe worn at the sides and the tunic navy blue with gold epaulettes and shoulder cord. His left breast was covered with twelve impressive medals that glinted in the morning sun.

The Bishop of Monaco, Monseigneur Gille Barthe, performed the wedding ceremony which was followed by high nuptial mass. The bride's parish priest from Philadelphia, Father John Carten, delivered a homely message of good wishes to the royal couple.

The service was marred only by the technical apparatus necessary for the use of television and motion picture coverage.

There were the ordinary minor mishaps of any wedding which I recall only to emphasise that despite all the grandeur these were two people taking part in an age-old ceremony. This was a real wedding and not a rehearsed spectacle.

A page boy dropped one of the rings used in the double ceremony; at one period Prince Rainier seemed to get tangled up with his sword; the Princess's ten-foot-long train got caught on a chair, and the bridegroom seemed concerned as he had trouble getting the ring on the bride's finger.

But never once did Princess Grace show the slightest signs of nervousness or hesitation. Of all the parts she had ever played, her own wedding was her finest performance.

The Prince and Princess over the years have had only one regret about their glorious wedding. It is a regret that every royal bride in the world would understand. They wished that they had not been so involved and could only see the immediate things around them. As the Prince was to tell Peter Hawkins:

'There was such a lack of intimacy, it was the disappointing culmination of all that had gone before. For a man, perhaps, this is less important, but for the Princess it meant a great deal. It is difficult for a girl, for her wedding, if she can't be alone with herself for a moment. And the Princess did not have a minute to herself from the moment she set foot in the Principality.

'Another thing that astonished me when we actually stood together in the Cathedral was the fact that during this wedding in front of the altar there were cameras and microphones everywhere. Such lack of solitude and dignity. Reflecting on this afterwards, we both agreed that we should really have got married somewhere in a little chapel in the mountains. That is the sort of impossible desire one has after these things.'

In their family film library, collected and mostly made by the Princess, is a souvenir of their wedding.

After the ceremony Prince Rainier and Princess Grace left by open car to drive round the old town of Monaco waving to their subjects who packed the narrow streets.

They stopped at a small peach-coloured shrine under the railroad bridge of Monte Carlo where Princess Grace knelt in the dust and prayed that St Dévote, the patron saint of Monaco, would bless her marriage.

She then kissed the relics proferred to her by the robed priests and placed her bridal bouquet of lily of the valley at the feet of the virgin saint who had brought Christianity to Monaco.

Once the royal car had left, the wedding guests were allowed out of the Cathedral and began the walk across the cobbled forecourt. Many of the men, and the women, teetering in their spike-heeled shoes, were frantically looking for the *Dames* and *Hommes*. They had left their hotel just after 8 a.m. and it was now past midday.

Suddenly someone found a gardeners' *cabinet de toilette* and the word spread from mouth to mouth. In a matter of minutes a long queue of elegantly dressed women and men in their white ties, tails and top hats had formed outside the little door.

'It was incredibly funny,' said Mrs Ben Lyon, who told me the story.

As soon as someone from the palace saw what was going on staff were sent to direct the guests to special cloakrooms, but it was a sight so human that it could have been snipped from an Henri Cartier-Bresson album.

A royal enclosure had been made at the foot of the staircase where the wedding party sat at small tables. The rest of the guests mingled in the sun-filled courtyard, eating a buffet lunch.

With his hand over his bride's, Prince Rainier cut the five-tiered wedding cake with his sword.

Just before she left the palace, Princess Grace took her private farewell of her bridesmaids—her sister Peggy Davis, Judy Kanter, Maree Pamp, Rita Gam, Sally Richardson, Carolyn Reybold and Bettina Gray—girls who stretched back in friendship to her early modelling days. Virginia Darcy, always the wag, had lined them up and said: 'Now let's all curtsey to the new Princess, girls.'

Sister Peggy's goodbye to Princess Grace was in the Kelly tradition. In a fun moment so desperately needed to prevent the tears that were near she quipped:

'See you later, alligator.'

To which Prince Rainier who had just come into the room replied: 'In a while, crocodile.'

There was laughter and a forlorn moment had been saved.

While the wedding party had been in progress, outside in the streets tourists were queueing to obtain the first release of the new postage stamps which bore the head of Princess Grace. The photograph had been specially taken in New York and the denominations ranged from 1 franc to 500 francs. And so Grace Kelly from Philadelphia, now Princess Grace of Monaco, had become the first film star to have her face on a postage stamp.

By 5 p.m. the *Deo Juvante II* set sail as two rockets dropped the American and Monegasque flags in the sky. The bridal couple and Oliver stood for a moment by the ship's rails until the coastline faded. By this time the sea was terribly rough and the yacht beginning to rock.

Down in the stateroom the crew had prepared a supper of snacks, caviar, foie gras and champagne, and left the Prince and Princess alone.

Instead of eating, they collapsed into chairs completely exhausted by the day's events and slept for a couple of hours.

On the advice of the captain the yacht pulled into a small cove only a few hundred yards from the Prince's villa and there dropped anchor till morning.

That night Oliver took up his usual position at the foot of his mistress's bed as he did every night until his death some years later.

The *Deo Juvante* was an old English boat built by Camper Nicholson in 1928. She was a comfortable boat, even if she did roll, with an agreeable atmosphere and a cruising speed of eleven knots.

As long as they were at sea the Prince and his bride had all the privacy they craved for. The Prince had always loved the freedom that sailing gives, which he has compared to the sensation that you get in the mountains.

'You are really at peace with nature and existence,' he has said many times when discussing the subject.

The honeymoon took them first to Spain, where Princess Grace caught such a severe cold that she had to see a doctor. From there they went on to Corsica, Napoleon's birthplace and of immense interest to Prince Rainier whose Napoleonic collection, begun by Prince Louis II, is regarded as one of the finest in the world. It is now installed in a new museum which Prince Rainier designed and arranged himself.

Some of the honeymooners' happiest days were spent picnicking on the white sandy beaches of Corsica, totally alone. Knowing Princess Grace's dislike of hot sun, the Prince used to construct small Robinson Crusoe shelters for her and Oliver—bits of wood he collected and canvas he brought along. Pottering on the beach together, sunbathing, talking, sleeping, collecting shells. Two contented people far from the responsibilities that lay ahead of them.

On the return from their honeymoon, and after a quick trip to Paris to check with her doctor, Princess Grace calmly told the Prince that it was now definite that she was having a baby. The Prince joyfully announced the news to his subjects.

All Monaco was dizzy with delight and celebrated the news for days. Princess Grace had given them hope for the one thing they wanted most of all—an heir to the Principality.

Twenty-four

'When I married Prince Rainier I married the man and not what he was or who he was. I fell in love with him no matter how it might all turn out.'

These words were spoken by Princess Grace after she had been married ten years. They remain as unimpaired today as when she first uttered them.

What kind of a man is Prince Rainier who was now to become such a dominant factor in her life? Trustingly, gratefully and hopefully she had placed her life and happiness in his hands.

No two people could have outwardly been more different. She with her reserve strength, reserve intelligence, reserve emotion and he with his inherited Latin temperament, Mediterranean upbringing and the authority that being an absolute monarch creates.

No husband and wife could have had a more different family background. The Kellys with their boisterous family life filled with fun and caring. Prince Rainier with his disturbed and lonely childhood.

In an interview with English journalist Douglas Keay eighteen months ago, Prince Rainier said:

'I think the experience of my parents' separation when I was only six has subconsciously made me very much want my own marriage to succeed. So the Princess and I have always tried to minimise any sort of incident or little disagreement between us in the interest of keeping the family together—so that the children should not suffer.'

Born on 31 May 1923, the son of Princess Charlotte of Monaco and the Count Pierre de Polignac, Rainier's parents separated when he was six years of age. This tubby little boy, who seldom smiled, was then shuttled between his grandfather, Prince Louis II, and a nanny. With no real parental anchor of his own, he was apparently not a particularly attractive child. No one recognised that the tantrums and sulks were a cry of desperation for affection.

At eight years old, speaking little English, on his father's wish he was suddenly sent off to a preparatory school at St Leonards-on-Sea—a fearsome experience for any small French boy, let alone a cosseted prince.

He has never forgotten what loneliness meant, and far from curing his shyness it only increased it.

Speaking of his childhood to Peter Hawkins in his authorised biography *Prince Rainier of Monaco* (William Kimber), Prince Rainier said:

'When you are twelve years old you feel that the Channel is terribly wide. The plane services weren't so regular in those days, either.

'I suppose I enjoyed it—but, like most little boys who go to prep school, I was caned. This shocked me in the fact that it was a physical punishment, but no more. The attitude of all English youngsters at that age is that being caned is more of an occasion to have a good laugh, and fun, so there was nothing dramatic about it.'

He then passed on to Stowe, that stern, laudable seat of learning high up in the beautiful, cold Cotswolds. For a child from the sun it must have been a chastening experience. He was totally friendless—the only foreigner among five hundred and sixty English boys.

Soon after his arrival, in sheer desperation he did the only sensible thing a small boy could do. He ran away. He was picked up by the police in Buckingham and taken back to school, where an understanding house-master, a retired army major, gave him a cosy tea of hot muffins and jam.

One of the first shocks that the Prince experienced at Stowe was the English system of fagging from which no one is exempt. He was astonished at this feudal custom when a younger boy is expected to get up early in the morning and fag for a senior boy before getting himself ready for the day.

From Stowe he went to the École du Rosay in Switzerland, which in itself must have been a traumatic experience. Not only was he back to speaking French all day but all his mathematical studies had to be switched into the metric.

Yet he enjoyed Rosay and preferred its more liberal approach to education to the in-bred ambiance of an English public school. This was shortlived, as when the Germans began their bombardment of Lyons he was removed to Monaco for safety. It was only after some time that he went to Paris to continue for his French baccalauréat. A year at the École des Sciences Politiques in Paris completed his scholastic career.

After a period back in Monaco, during which time he found it very tough to have to live with Germans all around him, Prince Rainier volunteered for the French Army, where he went under the name of Lieutenant Grimaldi. To his chums he answered to the name of 'Shorty'. During a campaign in Alsace he won the Croix de Guerre, but at the time of the Armistice was transferred to the Economic section of the French Military Mission in Berlin.

During Father Tucker's 'reign' in Monaco, as spiritual adviser and confidant of the Prince, they had a standing joke which never failed. Father Tucker had served as a chaplain with the 103rd Field Artillery in the First World War which had seen action at Verdun.

Whenever he began with his oft-repeated remark, 'Now when I was at Verdun . . .' Prince Rainier used to jump to attention and begin singing the *Star Spangled Banner*.

In April of 1949 Prince Rainier was recalled to Monaco, where his grandfather was suffering a long illness. A few months before he died he delegated his powers to Prince Rainier.

Aged twenty-six, Prince Rainier was now sovereign over two thousand Monegasques and twenty thousand other inhabitants of the Principality.

His first job was to find a completely new staff of his own, including the Cabinet, in an effort to bring new thinking and modernisation to the Principality. And this he did with firmness and clarity.

Prince Rainier quickly developed from an awkward princeling into a man of immense personal strength who later in his reign had the courage to stand firm against two of the world's most powerful men . . . General de Gaulle and Aristotle Onassis.

When de Gaulle criticised his 'grandeur', Prince Rainier remarked: 'My grandeur only comes up to his ankles.'

Pinpointing Monaco on the map, it is tempting to make a wisecrack about this tiny Principality. From the windows in his study Prince Rainier can take in at one glance all 500 acres of his Principality. Today, skyscrapers jostle together like stacked cards, new factories have been built that by law have dispensed with ugly chimneys and have roof gardens instead, and flowers tumble down the steep cliff of the roads etched from the hillside. It is dazzlingly beautiful in the brilliant sunshine.

Two promontories enclose the new harbour. On one is the Casino and those dowager hotels L'Hermitage and Hotel de Paris, and on the other the Prince's palace, which changes colour through the day from pale apricot to Pompeian pink in the sunset, and is set in a tiny medieval town.

For many, Monaco is still a kind of Ruritania, a set from *The Student Prince* or *Perchance to Dream*. To others, escaping from the cold climes of Scandinavia, Germany and England, it is a tax haven paradise.

To its ruler, Monte Carlo is Big Business. Through his influence its gambling image has diminished. Today Monaco's Budget depends hardly at all on gambling. More than eighty per cent of revenue comes from such unromantic items as V.A.T., State Monopolies (including postage stamps) and industrial development.

During the last seven years, fifty-three acres have been won from the sea—an area set aside for Monaco to expand its light industries which in turn will attract foreign capital.

There are still the old ladies in the park. Still the chalk-faced beauties of indeterminate age who emerge in the evening from their one-roomed 'homes' to try their luck on the wheel yet again. Still the picture-postcard gardens, planted with red and white cyclamen, a floral carpet in the Place du Casino.

But there are also many more hotels bustling with scientists who have gathered for international conventions on the disposal of radio-active waste, pollution in urban life, destruction of chemical refuse and similar topics.

Given sufficient hotel accommodation, Monte Carlo could well become one of the leading conference countries in the world—a role, as much for its moral values as commercial, which the Prince would find agreeable.

Prince Rainier also sees Monaco as a kind of headquarters for a few base companies—English, American and Canadian—from which they could direct their European operations.

One of Prince Rainier's earliest schemes in the modernisation of Monaco was to run the railway through the Principality *underground* thus giving acres more land not only *in situ* but by using the old rock for reclamation. Here he ran up against the old-fashioned conservatism of the National Council, who challenged him: 'Why waste that money in making a tunnel when the railroad has been running as it is for forty-five years?'

He won his point and today the railway is one of the triumphs of Monte Carlo.

Prince Rainier is an absolute monarch . . . the only one in Europe. He rules his kingdom seriously, conscientiously and lovingly by 'le Droit Divin'.

He is deeply sensitive about any comparison of Monaco with what the French call a *pays d'opérette*—musical comedy country. 'I cannot understand for instance why Monaco has more jokes about it than Liechtenstein or Luxembourg,' he once remarked.

'It is a small country. It is a serious country. The more I go out the more I think small countries are useful. They have no eagerness to possess what their neighbours have. They should be given more latitude. They have a place in the world as peaceful mediators.'

Not everything new that has mushroomed up in Monte Carlo over the last ten exciting years has pleased its ruler. Not all modern architecture delights him, but when his business advisers persuade him that it is good for Monaco then he acquiesces.

The most convincing testimony to Prince Rainier's statecraft is that he remains an absolute monarch yet by temperament he is the least autocratic or pretentious of rulers.

Peasants in the hills behind Monaco who bring their vegetables, fruits and cheese down to the Monte Carlo market are all familiar with the Prince, in jeans and sweater, who sometimes walks round their stalls in the early morning buying from here and there. He knows them by name and remembers the details of their family life.

Though the changing of the guards outside the palace does have a toy-box quality about it, the object of the exercise, in addition to security, is that it attracts thousands and thousands of middle-class tourists every year—which is a much healthier situation for Monaco than the Casino.

In his private life Prince Rainier is a charming man. He is 5 feet 7 inches tall, but looks shorter due to a weight problem with which he continually struggles. A year-round suntan gives his face a youthful appearance and the hair, black at the time of his wedding, is now a distinguished grey. Women find him appealing once they have broken through his reserve.

Much has been written about the Prince's 'wild oats' days before his marriage. It would be untrue to say that he was ever a playboy, as his chances of even becoming one, should he have wished, were slender compared with the Duke of Windsor when he was Prince of Wales or the late Aly Khan.

The Principality is a tight little fortress of gossip and he would scarcely have escaped it. The one romance of his life worth recording was a four-year friendship with the French actress Gisèle Pascal, sometimes termed by the gossips as 'the uncrowned queen of Monaco'.

Although the Prince once explained in an interview: 'It was never intended to be serious and was good training for later on in life but never more than that,' it is unlike him to have kept up a friendship so long if it had not been meaningful to him.

Mlle Pascal, who was heart-broken at the time of their break-up, has been quoted as saying: 'People resented the fact that I was not of royal blood. They gossiped when they saw the Prince spending so much of his time at my home. I waited, hoping that everything would work out, but it didn't. It is only in fairy-tales that the prince and princess live happily ever after.'

The more acceptable explanation is that as Mlle Pascal was a divorced woman a permanent relationship was impossible.

The Prince would be the first to agree that he is not an intellectual but his interests are varied and amusing.

Above all he is a man of simple taste. He has an infectious sense of humour, a schoolboy's love of practical jokes and gadgets and is easy to talk to. A man happiest with his family or alone with one of his many hobbies.

When he was once asked what he would have liked to be had he not been a ruling prince, he answered:

'I would have liked something to do with the sea or farming; an activity close to nature. Or a circus clown . . .'

Basically a sporting man, he plays golf, tennis, skis and water skis. He also has an enormous collection of jazz records, takes photographs and moulds sculpture from metals.

As a young man he was keenly interested in underwater diving and photography and became an expert at them. He used to hunt, but his love of animals has made the sport of killing increasingly unbearable to him. Among his friends he counts Jacques Yves Cousteau, who helped him in the preparation of the new Oceanographic Museum at Monte Carlo of which he is a director and whose exploits round the world the Prince supports.

The Prince had a lightning career as a competition motorist in the Monte Carlo Rally before his marriage. Entering with a D.B. Bonnett his co-driver was a mechanic from the palace garage. Both exhausted, Prince Rainier gave him the wheel while he had a cat-nap, but they ended up against a telegraph pole. Neither of them was hurt, but the car was a write-off.

His passionate interest in football has been inherited by his daughter, Princess Caroline. Whenever the Monaco team play, father and daughter are to be seen cheering their team on.

This then is the public man that Princess Grace married. In private he is more complex, as she was to find out. He is the true Gemini—a twin-sided being. He is also a Mediterranean who can explode with anger but in a minute it is forgotten and the recipient of the wrath is bathed in unconditional *bonhomie*.

Two of his secret hobbies, at which he really excels, are writing poetry and drawing. His sketches of the children are excellent likenesses and he has made several studies of Princess Grace.

In the royal garages are perhaps twenty cars, ten of them pre-1923, which are kept in pristine order. In the early evening the Prince likes to go round the garage and chat with the mechanics. He gave Princess Grace, for her personal use, a specially refurbished London taxi which is ideal for Monaco's narrow streets.

Prince Rainier's Napoleonic collection is extremely fine. One of the treasures that Princess Grace most enjoys is the little wooden cradle of Napoleon's son, L'Aiglon. From time to time the Prince adds to his collection, whenever he sees something that he admires.

Like all Mediterranean men, the Prince can also be unreasonably jealous. He likes Princess Grace only to wear jewellery he has given her or that has come from the family, and on her marriage she gave several attractive pieces from former boyfriends away to her girl friends.

American friends pander to his unashamed delight in gadgets. One that misfired was the chicken dissector that he brought back from America. The French chef's comments are unprintable.

The Princess was also yet to find out the Prince's preoccupation with the animals in his private zoo. This was something that no American bride could possibly have foreseen.

There were many facets to Prince Rainier which Princess Grace had not even begun to know about as the *Deo Juvante II* sailed back into Monte Carlo harbour.

Twenty-five

Princess Grace, the real woman, is much more intriguing than her fairy-tale image. As she herself once said: 'I am not complicated but full of contradictions. I am easily influenced by climate, by moods and by the people round me.'

Taken in that order, her first obstacle on returning from her honeymoon in June was to face a Mediterranean summer. According to the tourist brochure: 'In Monaco there are more than 300 days of the year that have sun with an average of 10 hours a day in summer and 5 hours a day in winter, except February with 4·5 hours of sun per day.'

Princess Grace is a heliophobe . . . a moon creature. She dislikes intense bright light, avoids the sun if possible, wears dark glasses to shade the glare from her near-sighted eyes, detests heat.

She is happiest on dull, even wintry, days and does not feel the cold. She loves the gentle misty days of autumn in the New York State countryside. The soft moist atmosphere of early winter in London. The crisp embracing air of Switzerland in the winter. Sun saps her strength like a flower without water.

When the nostril-drying, eye-stinging Mistral season begins in Monaco she stays indoors to avoid the hot irritating wind. She is said to become depressed and quiet. During the hottest month, August, the family always move to their *mas* or farm at Roc Agel, where the night air is cool and the days more bearable than down by the coast.

All during that first summer in Monte Carlo, when she was pregnant, she found the heat exhausting . . . almost unbearable. She went out as little as possible and clung to the shade of the palace garden.

In California she had disliked the summers, too, but there was always the knowledge that it was only for a few more weeks, a few more months, and then the film would be finished and she would be back in New York again where the heat was sticky but less glaring.

Princess Grace's favourite sports are swimming and walking. The palace pool, around which the family practically live now in the summers, had not yet been built and the large palace gardens lack privacy as they are open to the public every afternoon.

'I never went out anywhere,' she remembered. She did not shop, go to restaurants or walk freely in the streets. Her only public appearance was at the Red Cross gala and a short trip to Paris to buy maternity clothes.

Apart from the heat, Princess Grace said that the biggest adjustment she had to make that first year was the Latin temperament. It was so entirely different from the American way of life she had been used to. For five years she had been treated like a queen in her own right as one of America's most adored women. Now she was the wife of an indulged royal prince in a country where she did not even speak the language.

She had not only to adapt to the temperament of her husband and the staff of the palace but to conform to the Mediterranean attitude to marriage. It was a completely different situation from being a wife in America or England.

There was also the court protocol to absorb in this most royal of principalities.

'There were 15 footmen to wait at table during a recent palace dinner for only 10 people,' the *Sunday Express* reported on 17 June 1956.

'Before entering the drawing-room to be received, lady guests were told by an equerry, "Will you please remember to curtsey to both the Prince *and* the Princess." . . . Friends say that Grace appears rather awed by the imposing formality insisted upon by her husband's courtiers.'

Actually, Princess Grace was not in the least embarrassed when people curtsied to her. 'They are honouring my husband's position and not me,' she explained pragmatically to American friends.

'I must say I have great respect and admiration for the Princess, because I think she came back from her honeymoon to what must have looked rather a grim situation and faced up to it marvellously,' the Prince said some years later.

Before the marriage Monaco had been going through a period of economic instability. Tourism had fallen to a decline by 1955, the famous casino was in bad disrepair and urgently needed refurbishing. There were even rumours of an attempt being planned to replace Prince Rainier by his sister Princess Antoinette, who at least had the children necessary to give the country an heir.

Among a *côterie* of die-hard Monegasque aristocracy Princess Grace had still a great deal of prejudice to overcome. They had enjoyed the pomp and importance of the royal wedding, but now the gossiping began.

'We had read all these reports about a bricklayer's daughter,' one countess explained to me. 'It is very hard for us to understand the American way of life and of course she *did* come from Hollywood. But once she arrived and we finally began to see her it was quite different. She was cultured and charming and of course quite different from what we had expected.'

This remark came from a well-travelled, highly educated, cultured woman. But she had lived within the ivory towers of Monaco for many years which she proudly described to me as 'the last outpost of elegance'.

'*C'est une Américaine*' was a phrase that was to be repeated in the vieux rose salons. Its translation into English does not carry the derogatory undertones as in the original French.

It is doubtful whether Princess Grace would have been told of these secret rumblings although there is every reason to believe that Prince Rainier was aware of them. But her sensitive—almost over-sensitive—feelings made her painfully aware of the situation.

Within the Principality Prince Rainier has his own intelligence antennae which enables him to be in touch with the thoughts of the true Monegasques who are the 'grass roots' of this small country.

Many of these local people have lived in Monaco's five square miles all their lives and there are senior citizens there today who have never ventured farther afield than Nice or Roquebrune Cap Martin. They are a heady mixture of Italian and French blood and many have names as Italian sounding as Grimaldi. To them the people of Grasse or Cannes are as suspicious as the Sassenachs are to the Scots.

Beneath the surface lies an uneasy contempt for all strangers. Tourists are different. They come and go like the Mistral. They are also business and are therefore necessary for the economy. But foreigners who have chosen to make their home in Monaco say that they are no more acceptable to the Monegasques after ten years than the day they arrived. For this reason they tend to stick together in lumps—the Scandinavians, the Germans, the Americans and so on—with their own clubs and interests.

Prince Rainier was the first to appreciate Princess Grace's fey qualities. 'A woman's intuition is much more acute than a man's and in those early days I found that the Princess was asking questions about people I'd worked with and taken for granted for years: people whose motives I had never thought to question,' Prince Rainier said in an interview some years later.

It did not help the situation either when it was erroneously reported that the Prince had banned all Grace Kelly films from the Principality. What were these films? 'There must be some good reason that he has done this. Pourquoi . . . pourquoi . . . pourquoi?'

The facts are that the Prince did not ban the showing of the films but what he was afraid of was cinemas cashing in on Grace Kelly festivals and turning her image into vulgar commercialism.

Had she been another kind of person Princess Grace may have stretched out to meet the people sooner. She could have overcome any lingering suspicion by her charismatic personality.

'It was very strange. That big wedding and then we never saw her. She should have shown herself more,' the proprietress of a small hotel told me. 'As far as we were concerned there was no difference from before the Prince was married.'

As it was, Princess Grace behaved according to her 'act' . . . the only way she knew she could cope sincerely. She went slowly, shyly, cautiously.

Although she had a smattering of French and could speak it slowly, all through that summer she took regular French lessons and continued until she became fluent. She found reading French plays and poetry more amusing than textbooks and was so thorough in her studies that she even bought a book on French slang. Today her French is grammatically perfect. She has not so much an American accent as an intonation which her French friends find fascinating.

Between themselves and in the family the Prince and Princess always speak English although the children speak French among themselves. The Prince has now a more pronounced American accent than the

Princess and all the children use American colloquial slang as if it was their native tongue.

Even within the family Princess Grace had to face delicate problems of protocol. Before Prince Rainier married, his sister, Princess Antoinette, had acted as the first lady of the land. Although on her marriage to Alec Noghes, the Davis Cup tennis player, she had relinquished all rights to the throne, she had gathered around her her own private court —many of whom would have resented the intrusion of any other woman, especially an American.

Apart from acting as Prince Rainier's hostess on official occasions, Princess Antoinette was also vice-president of the Red Cross, of which Prince Rainier was president.

Right from the start Princess Grace found allies in Prince Rainier's father, Prince Pierre, and in Madame Banac, a grand old lady of Monaco and mother of Mr Vane Ivanovic, the consul general for Monaco in London. They both loved and admired her and were conscious of the difficulties she had to overcome.

Prince Rainier's mother, Princess Charlotte, lived outside Paris in a beautiful house at Marchais and had removed herself many years before from the Monaco scene. A lively and original woman, she has devoted herself to the rehabilitation of prisoners.

Her naïve kindness caused her to employ as her chauffeur one such ex-criminal who was euphemistically known to the French underworld as 'René the Swagger Cane'. His reign came to a sticky end when Princess Charlotte applied to a French court to have him evicted from a villa on her estate which made a piquant story in the French Press.

Although a thriving American colony existed in Monaco, and it would have been natural for the Princess to gravitate towards it, this she did with considerable caution. In the hot-house society in which she lived she was sensitively conscious of the fact that now she was a Monegasque Princess and no longer an ordinary American citizen.

Although she has retained her American citizenship, as well as having a Monegasque passport, according to Prince Rainier the Princess is now more Monegasque than American.

In those first months in Monaco the Princess was very homesick, made possibly more acute because of her pregnancy and self-imposed seclusion. Her hay fever often gave excuse for red eyes which the staff were quick to notice.

'I don't think people understood how hard it was for her to be cut off from her family and friends in America. She was very homesick for a long time and even now finds it difficult to make friends,' said the Prince.

'If she was homesick she never complained. Never once,' her sister Peggy explained to me. 'Her letters were always filled with fun and the pleasures of making her own home. Grace is not one to complain . . . it is not in her character. Besides, she could always see something funny in even the dreariest situations.'

The palace with its 200 rooms was in a forlorn state. For years it had lacked the hand of a woman. Its vast rooms were lifeless, soul-less and even the roof needed urgent attention. The Prince had lived and done all his private entertaining in his 10-roomed villa at St Jean Cap Ferrat, about 20 miles from Monaco. He only entertained in the palace when it was on an official level.

Most of the palace's official rooms had been furnished in the un-yielding, traditional French style. These include the main reception and dining-rooms, the grand salon in white and gold, the blue room, red room, throne room and Duke of York room, the hall of mirrors and two rooms containing the Prince's collection—second best in the world—of Napoleonic relics.

For several months the Princess did nothing. She just sat and looked and mentally made notes. She did not move a chair. The arrival of her own furniture from her flat in New York was her first positive attempt to make the family living-quarters in the palace more homely, more livable. These included practically new damask drapes, deep grey carpets, comfortable easy chairs in light attractive colours and a charming little sofa covered with deep blue brocade through which is woven 'I love you . . . I love you.'

The box that the wedding dress was packed in and sent to Phila-delphia made the return trip. This time is was filled by Mrs Kelly and the family with gossamer-soft American lavatory paper, ready-mix cake mixes of all sorts, including pancakes and scrapple, a breakfast delicacy as dear to the hearts of Pennsylvanians as haggis is to the Scots. It looks like a cross between salami and luncheon meat and is served fried with eggs instead of bacon. It had always been a favourite of Princess Grace's and even Prince Rainier succumbed to its obscure charm.

Princess Grace had a special cupboard where she kept the cake mixes and used to delight in making chocolate cakes, angel cakes, waffles and other American specialities especially for the Prince and Father Tucker.

It was all one big joke and no one, least of all the staff who saw these miracles appear in no time at all, knew that it was all due to those magic cake mixes. Even the Prince was in awe of his wife's culinary skill. But it was her secret and she kept it.

Slowly and with great delicacy the family quarters began to come to life. She filled the palace with flowers, but not always with unqualified success.

To brighten up one of the state rooms as a surprise for the Prince she had boxes arranged down one side and planted with white chrysanthemums. When Prince Rainier saw this he was horrified and exclaimed: 'Not chrysanthemums. These are the flowers of the tomb.'

The chrysanthemums were immediately all removed as in France they are always associated with death and burials.

Neither the Prince nor Princess were very satisfied with their efforts to turn the palace into a livable home. It had the impersonal air of a museum.

Princess Grace was also to find out that her life now was anything but private. All through that summer tourists stood in the cobbled palace courtyard, which looks like a scene from a Donizetti opera, hoping to catch a glimpse of her.

'Everyone's marriage is a series of concessions,' the Prince said at the time. 'Whatever force of love there is between two newly married people, however strong the bonds, it would be very difficult for any young bride trying to adapt herself in circumstances like these. Plus the problem of dealing with the horrible old bachelor and getting him rid of his bad habits.'

And so the year slipped round till Christmas, her first in Monaco. A memorable year. A difficult year. A developing year in the life of Princess Grace of Monaco.

Though her baby was due very soon the Princess insisted on helping arrange a series of parties for the Monegasque children at the palace, a custom she and the Prince have continued ever since.

Rooms that had been bare and friendless for many Christmasses suddenly came to life as she personally arranged the elaborate Christmas decorations she had made and candles everywhere as is the custom in America.

In all, 500 children were invited and left the palace clutching small presents. In those early days the children were given a large tea at the palace before the Punch and Judy or conjuring shows which followed afterwards. It was the Princess who noticed that they wanted to take home something for their mothers. At the Christmas parties now each child also gets a small bag of cakes and biscuits, as well as his or her present, to take home. 'They absolutely love it as they go off clutching their paper bag,' the Princess said.

When the New Year dawned everything was ready for the arrival of the baby. George Stacey, a New York decorator, who was already working in France for a client, was hastily called in to hurry up the endless delay in the creation of the new nursery, next door to the private apartments of the Prince and Princess.

The Princess had chosen yellow—one of her favourite colours—and white to decorate the nursery, and Stacey installed an ingenious shelving unit for the baby's wardrobe.

At first it was planned that, like most American mothers, the Princess would have her baby in a hospital, but with the arrival of the world's Press and for security reasons the Prince asked her if she would have her baby at home. 'Ma Kelly' flew over a week ahead of schedule to be with her daughter, as due to the fact that Princess Grace had been too active over the holidays, the baby might arrive early.

It had been reported that Princess Grace had been extremely angry when her mother wrote a series of intimate articles about her daughter for a Philadelphian paper before the marriage—the proceeds for Women's Medical naturally!

The Kellys are a family, a very united family, and clearly all this had now been forgotten in the excitement ahead.

The library was transformed into a delivery room and the Princess's gynaecologist, Dr Emile Hervet, stood by.

Monaco went about its business with hushed voice and there were more than usual glances up at the palace on the hill which flew the national flag. All Monaco was waiting the birth of this baby . . . this very exceptional heir to the throne.

Twenty-six

Nine months and four days after her wedding, in the library of the palace, at 9.27 a.m. on 23 January 1957, Princess Grace gave birth to a baby daughter—Caroline Louise Marguerite. The birth had been normal, if somewhat a little long, and the Princess had her baby naturally, as she wished, without twilight sleep or any other form of anaesthetic.

The Prince and Princess had chosen Professor Emile Hervet to follow the pregnancy right through. The doctor has the eminent status of professeur Agrégè à la Faculté de Médecine de Paris, Gynécologue Accoucher des Hospitaux et Chef du Service de Gynécologue Obstétrique du Groupe Hospitalier Pitié-Saltpétrière.

Dr Hervet arrived from Paris with a nurse and moved into the palace two weeks before the actual birth.

The baby was charming, and because of her weight—8 lb 11 oz—was a complete little human being with a fuzz of peach-coloured hair and large blue eyes.

As Prince Rainier was to remark at the time:

'Apart from Caroline, I had seen other people's new-born children whilst making official visits to the maternity home and they had always appeared to me as being rather ugly little red creatures. Probably I was biased, but my own babies never seemed that way at all. They weren't red and they weren't ugly—in fact they have all been rather big babies, large children already when they were born and not all wrinkled and old-looking.'

Hungry for any snippet of news, the reporters latched on to the talkative Father Tucker, who gave his own unofficial daily bulletin. His pride and joy were irresistible.

'Prince Rainier told me with tears in his eyes: "It's a beautiful baby girl," ' he announced solemnly.

Princess Grace was extremely well after the birth and sat up in bed drinking a glass of champagne. Unlike most royal mothers, anxious to preserve their figures, she had insisted that she would feed the baby herself. To this day she is a strong advocate of breast feeding, which she considers 'wholly normal and right'.

In those first days were formed the thoughts which she was to express five years later when she delivered a paper on the subject of breast feeding at a convention organised by the La Lèche League in Chicago.

In words, very dear to her heart, she gave this imaginative message to the mothers of the world.

'It would seem to me that the closeness to the child resulting from breast feeding is somehow an extension and affirmation of that very love that has resulted in its being there. A man and a woman have united to create this little being that one is holding to oneself, and nurturing. And this nurturing is to be treasured for its relationship that is to end all too soon, the very first of many partings.

'If one but realised it, with the onset of the first pangs of birth pains, one begins to say farewell to one's baby. For no sooner has it entered the world, when others begin to demand their share. With the child at one's breast, one keeps the warmth of possession a little longer.'

At the same time she not only urged mothers to breast feed their babies but to allow other children in the family to watch and teach them 'the wholesomeness of sex and the naturalness of it'. And this she subsequently did with her own family.

On Friday, 25 January, Prince Rainier officially certified the birth of an heiress apparent before Judge Marcel Portanier and three witnesses.

One would like to think that it was genuine delight in Monaco on the arrival of a baby to these attractive royal parents, but the cynics were quick to note that at least for another generation the people of the Principality would have no taxation or military draft under French rule which would have been their fate had the royal line not produced an heir.

All Monaco went wild with joy. Flags flew, cannons boomed and the boats and yachts in the harbour hooted a non-stop lullaby. Everyone was happy and the wine flowed.

During the week after the baby's birth seven thousand messages of congratulations arrived at the palace, including one from Queen Elizabeth.

Gifts began to pour in, from homely knitted baby clothes to the pearl ring and diamond clasp that Prince Rainier gave the Princess to mark this splendid occasion.

For Princess Grace one of her first tasks was to get her figure back as she had put on a great deal of weight during the pregnancy. This again she applied herself to with her usual thoroughness and did exercises daily, with long walks with Oliver whenever she could.

Her women friends were amused when she told them that she did exercises in church. 'I do isometrics in church so while I'm doing my soul some good, I'm doing my body some good too.'

A Swiss-German nanny had been engaged to look after Princess Caroline although Princess Grace herself spent a great deal of time in the nursery and has always been actively involved in bringing up her children.

Right from the start there was a strict rule that was always kept in the palace. No one except Prince Rainier, Princess Grace and the immediate staff concerned was allowed to visit the nursery. In this way the Princess thought that she could keep her children's babyhood as normal as possible.

As is customary in court circles in France, the baby was referred to as 'Madame Caroline' by the official palace staff, but to the Princess's personal staff simply called 'Caroline'. It was not until she was several years of age that she was aware of the fact that she was any different from other children. She believed that everyone lived in a palace and had special parents called Their Serene Highnesses.

Before their marriage the Prince and Princess had naturally discussed having children and had both been anxious to commence a family as soon as possible and to have their children within a limited time. This they felt was better for the family itself and would allow the Princess to resume a normal life and take up her own interests again.

It was to become an all-absorbing occupation. Within fourteen months Princess Grace was to give birth to her second child . . . a prince for Monaco.

Prince Rainier described it as one of the most wonderful experiences of his life and it also changed the historic outlook in the Principality.

Although there was a Constitution Law which said that the first-born of the Prince should succeed, this only applied until a male child was born which would take precedence.

Again the confinement took place in the library, which had been converted into a delivery room with Dr Hervet in attendance. Prince Rainier was given the news of his son's birth by a midwife who stuck her head round the corner of the room adjoining the library shouting ecstatically: 'It's a boy.'

Both parents had been wishing for a boy, but as Prince Rainier was to say: 'Had it been a girl I would not have been upset.'

The baby boy was christened in the Cathedral of St Nicholas and given the names Albert Alexandre Louis Pierre. He also weighed 8lb 11oz, and was promptly nicknamed 'Albie', which has stuck to him ever since.

Among the galaxy of celebrities invited to the christening were two from England, Sir Bernard and Lady Docker, whose behaviour gave cause for more inches of space in the British Press than the event itself.

To understand the following incident one must also know about the English and the Dockers. England is a land where eccentrics are encouraged to flourish. It is part of their national character.

During the 1950s Sir Bernard and Lady Docker brightened our breakfast table reading every morning with their social antics. Though one did not always condone the behaviour of the pretty loquacious Norah, seen in her own English context she was more acceptable than in Monte Carlo, where they frequently visited in their yacht *The Shemara*.

Norah Docker, a former milliner, had been one of the prettiest and most graceful hostesses in the Café Royal in London. With her blonde bubbling looks, stylish figure and extraordinary acute assessment of men, she had married three millionaires who all adored her. Two of them died and left her a fortune, while the third, Sir Bernard Docker, as the successful head of Birmingham Small Arms, was at the time one of Britain's most successful industrialists.

They were rich, happily married and unconcerned with the storms that invariably broke around them.

I think my own story is illuminating and illustrates their amused status in the British Press. We thrived on them. It was the year after Lady Docker had startled the Motor Show at Earls Court by appearing in a gold starred dress to match the bodywork of a new Daimler which her husband's firm was exhibiting.

The following year as woman's editor of the *London Evening News* I was again sent to cover the motor show from a woman's angle. I reported what I thought to be correct, that Lady Docker was once more there in a slate-blue dress to match the new slate-blue Daimler. It made the front page.

The next morning I received a telephone call from a voice saying that it was Lady Docker's press agent speaking.

'You've got it all wrong. You've made a boob and Lady Docker is very angry with you. It was the Daimler that was painted to match her favourite dress and not the other way round.'

The editor was only too pleased to print an apology . . . on the front page.

This then was Norah Docker ... lovable, irascible, amusing, outrageous.

You never knew what she would do next. She played in the English Marbles championship at Tinsley Green, she stood on her head in public, she was pictured dancing a sailor's hornpipe with the crew of *The Shemara.* She was never dull. Her only crime was that under certain circumstances, when the pink champagne flowed, she tended to be remarkably outspoken.

When Sir Bernard and Lady Docker were invited to the christening of Prince Albert they asked that their own nineteen-year-old son Lance be included in the invitation as it was his birthday the same day.

'It seemed a natural enough request to make,' says Lady Docker today.

Their request was denied them for the simple reason that everything had already been planned and the number of guests allocated. The Dockers were hurt and perhaps confused.

Their first mistake was to refuse to attend the christening and instead to hold an impromptu Press reception in Cannes at the Hotel Majestic. The next day they returned to Monte Carlo, where a regrettable fracas happened in the restaurant of the Hotel de Paris.

The restaurant staff reported at the time that Lady Docker not only said some insulting things about Their Serene Highnesses but snatching the flag of Monaco from the table in full view of everybody, broke it in two and flung it on the floor.

Later from his flat in Claridge House in London Sir Bernard told the British Press his version of the story.

'As we rose to leave Norah's hand knocked a tiny Monaco flag out of the bowl of flowers in the centre of the table. In her disgust with the way they treated us, she picked it up and threw it on the floor.

' "Well, we shan't be needing any of those," she said.

'I can't think anyone saw us except one or two waiters. Norah was pretty cross. I don't blame her.'

The story exploded all over the world. It was the kind of irreverent piece of gossip that every tired news editor jumps at. It was blown up into proportions far beyond its merit.

When rumours of the Dockers' proposed expulsion from the Riviera reached her, the indestructible Norah retaliated in the *Daily Express* in true fighting form.

'As far as I am concerned Prince Rainier can go and jump in the sea. I am signing my own decree that I will never set foot in that Hyde Park Principality again. I never went to the reception. I would be glad if they sent their presents back. I will not take my yacht within shooting distance of the palace. Well, one thing is certain. They will miss us more than we will miss them.'

What should have been a forgettable incident rankled on both sides and to this day the quarrel has never been made up. Although according to Prince Rainier he has been approached several times by the Dockers' lawyer—the christening incident was only a part of an accumulation of distressing incidents—his reply has always been: 'Will Lady Docker retract what she said, and the attitude she had at the time, and will she freely engage herself not to do this sort of thing any more?' And this Norah Docker will never do.

A new addition to the royal household in Monaco that year was an English nanny, who was to stay with the family for seven years. Her engagement was purely by chance but is indicative of the unconventional attitude of Prince Rainier and Princess Grace towards their staff.

She was no traditional English nanny bristling with diplomas and nursery clichés but a plump, jolly, apple-cheeked, cherry-lipped girl from Rugby in the Midlands of England.

Maureen King had been employed by the celebrated French playwright Jean Anouilh to look after his two children in Paris after a similar position in Belgium. Her mother read in a magazine that Princess Grace was expecting a second child. Unbeknown to Maureen, her sister wrote a letter to Princess Grace asking if there was a vacancy for a nanny, which began, 'Dear Madam, it occurred to me . . .' and signed it 'Maureen King'.

Two months later when Maureen was home on leave a letter with the royal cipher was handed in by the postman and it was only then that the family owned up about the original letter. The letter invited her to fly to Monaco for an interview with Princess Grace.

In telling the story to me, Mrs Maureen Wood, now a slender mother of two, recalled:

'I said to my mother, "I can't go. I did not even write the letter." '

' "Go. You can always say that you slept a night in a palace," my mother said.

'And I went completely with this attitude. I was quite sure that I simply couldn't land the job. For one thing I had had no formal training at all. It was a chance in a million that I was given the job.'

Some years later when the royal family were on holiday in Switzerland Princess Grace asked Nanny King to invite Jean Anouilh, who had a home near by, to drinks before dinner. She had played in *Ring Round the Moon* when she had been a young actress in New York. 'It was fascinating to see how they were both obviously delighted to meet each other,' Maureen Wood remembered.

Maureen King was to join another young member of the palace staff, an American girl called Phyllis Blum, now married to Somerset Maugham's nephew Julian Earle. These two lively girls were to become firm friends and brighten up Princess Grace's life in many enjoyable and rollicksome ways over the next few years. They were filled with fun.

After a few months, 'Big Fat Nanna', as Princess Caroline aptly called her nurse, was in sole charge of the two children.

Speaking of those early years of her marriage, Princess Grace was to say:

'During the first years of my marriage I lost my identity because I didn't have ways of recharging my batteries that I had depended on before. I tended to let my husband and his life and work absorb my personality. This was wrong. I had to find ways of finding myself in this life.'

Twenty-seven

By 1958, with her two babies growing up, palace life running reasonably efficiently and smoothly, and her French much more fluent, Princess Grace was ready to take up some other activities outside her family life.

'I don't think it was because she was bored with family life, but merely that she could see so much to be done and with her American efficiency was longing to get started,' a Monaco friend told me. 'While most of us take up charity work when our children are grown up, she had to do it right at the beginning.'

On 23 May 1958, Prince Rainier named as his successor as president of the Red Cross his wife, Princess Grace.

The Monegasque Red Cross was founded in 1948 by Prince Louis II, who entrusted its presidency to his grandson, Prince Rainier. Today under Princess Grace's guidance it is now one of the most active societies with the International Red Cross. Princess Grace is what the French say in their picturesque language a 'participant président'. She is not just the nominal head but is involved with some aspect of Red Cross work almost every day of her life. Whether she is in residence at the palace in Monaco, at their apartment in Paris or abroad, she is in constant communication with the secretary and all decisions of policy are referred to her. Although there are heads of the various services the Princess reviews nearly every case taken care of herself, often personally seeing the people concerned.

Because Monaco is such a small country to operate under the

umbrella of the Red Cross, all kinds of amenities came alive despite the fact that it was not always easy and there were some misunderstandings.

Grace's main problem in the beginning was that she tried to bring a kind of American efficiency and knowhow to this essentially Mediterranean atmosphere. She would arrive at meetings complete with her notes and business-like glasses, totally briefed and ready to get on with the business at hand.

'Good morning,' she would say and then expect the meeting to be dispensed with as quickly as possible. It seemed the most polite way to save people's time.

The Monegasque members of the committee were completely confused. They felt she was abrupt, cool and impatient. Gradually she learnt that in Monte Carlo one begins the conversation with 'And how is your mother . . . and is your sister back from England yet . . . is your husband's asthma better?' Only after these pleasantries are exchanged can you then begin to get down to the business on hand. You have to coerce the people into the mood and this can take two or three times as long as in America.

As she herself explained: 'One misses that fine American custom of saying, "Of course it can be done. Why not?" '

Every year the Red Cross Gala which raises many thousands of francs for the society is one of the most important events of the summer social season.

This is a labour of love for the Princess, who not only chooses the elaborate decorations and colour scheme but is also responsible for persuading some of the world's top names in entertainment, who are also her personal friends, to come and perform. Their expenses are met, but few people could entice such a galaxy of talent to give up their time. Many of them donate their cachet to the Red Cross.

In an interview with American journalist Nancy Schraffenberger, who once asked Princess Grace if she would have chosen to take on civic involvements had she not been married to a man whose station in life required it, she replied:

'Perhaps. We were brought up to participate and enter into things—they don't happen automatically. My father didn't care what interests we had but we had to be interested in something. He couldn't stand anyone who didn't have enthusiasm.'

Princess Grace, as well as Prince Rainier, also took an active part in the reconstruction and development of Monaco's new hospital which opened in 1958 and which now carries the name 'Hospital Centre Princess Grace'. Through her reading and visits to the States, whenever she saw or heard something that might be useful, she would gather up all the information. At her instigation an Assistance Centre, again composed of volunteers, now operates in the hospital.

Three years after she was married Princess Grace went to see the Monaco Old People's Home and was desperately depressed by what she saw. 'Can't we put some flowers here ... can't we do something there?' she said to the matron.

The matron replied, 'There is no use doing anything because the old people won't even come downstairs. We have movies for them but they won't even come and see them.'

The Princess then called in her Red Cross helpers and suggested that they make a rota for people to go and visit the old people and talk to them and take them for outings—'to get them out of themselves'. She also organised that the Girl Guides went so that the old people would have some contact with young people. It worked like a charm.

The atmosphere of the home completely changed and the old ladies not only came downstairs to enjoy the movies but to the special birthday parties that were arranged for each person.

Prince Rainier and Princess Grace next arranged for them to have a new building and personally supervised the choosing of the building materials, decorations and furnishings. It is now an extremely attractive home with a completely different atmosphere.

Every Christmas there is a special tea for the old folk of Monaco and the Princess distributes not only a food parcel but something new to wear.

As one old lady summed up: 'She brought us heart.'

It is natural that children are Princess Grace's major concern. She is not only devoted to her own children but is concerned with other people's children, other nations' children, particularly suffering, needy, handicapped children or those whose mental health is in danger.

In 1963 she became honorary president as well as one of the most active founding members of the Association Mondiale des Amis de L'Enfance (World Association of Friends of Children).

During the ceremonies to mark the founding of the Italian branch the Princess spoke these words:

'The A.M.A.D.E. was born of this anguish, born with no strength except its founders' will to succeed. Its cradle lies within the smallest nation in the world. But, from frontier to frontier, we fully intend to spread over the earth a network of childhood's true friends.'

On her doorstep there were many problems that she personally took a hand in solving, When she heard that there was no day nursery for working mothers, the Red Cross acquired a dignified house in Boulevarde de Suisse in Monte Carlo and turned it into a nursery which is called 'Garderie Notre Dame de Fatima', named after the Blessed Mother.

Princess Grace personally chose the colour schemes and much of the equipment right down to the cheerful yellow-and-white kitchen with the latest gadgets for preparing meals for the children.

In the playrooms and sleeping-quarters the walls are decorated with animal cut-outs which she bought in America. In the entrance hall, under a ceramic plaque of Our Lady of Fatima, is a huge teddy bear which once belonged to one of her own children. She raided their nursery and sent most of the toys which are still in use there today.

The Princess not only discusses the children's menus with a dietician, when they are planned for the various seasons, but it was her idea that a daily menu should be put up on the wall at child-level in the entrance hall.

As the mothers deposit the children on the doorstep on their way to work there is a rush over to the wall to see what is for lunch today.

Every Christmas the Princess sends them her Christmas cards so that the staff can decorate the nursery to make it look gay.

There is also a music academy in Monaco where any child can have music education without having to pay a franc.

Another project dear to her heart is the multi-racial family of the late singer Josephine Baker. Princess Grace's admiration and friendship for Josephine Baker were immense. When she read in 1969 that the black singer, through blissful ignorance of the reality of money, had gone bankrupt and lost the château in the Dordogne Valley where she had made a home for her family, she got in touch with her.

With the aid of an initial loan from the Prince and Princess and afterwards with the help of the Monegasque Red Cross, Josephine Baker was able to install her family in a comfortable villa at Roquebrune-Cap-Martin. She was given a chance to appear at the Red Cross Gala in 1969 and because of this and other engagements she was able, and made it a point of honour, to repay the Prince and Princess and the Red Cross for all their help.

Josephine Baker was so cold in the ghetto of St Louis when she was a child that she decided to become a dancer to keep warm. Here in her Riviera villa where the blue sky meets the blue of the Mediterranean she was able to find peace and pleasure with her 'rainbow children'.

One of her greatest triumphs had been at the Folies Bergère, where she would slink on to a mirrored platform clad in a bunch of bananas. Nothing else. 'I wasn't really naked,' she liked to say in later years. 'I simply didn't have any clothes on.'

When I called one brilliant sunny day in June 1974, I found some of the children there—still bewildered and confused as to what the future held in store for them after Miss Baker's death.

Marianne, who is French and nineteen years of age, invited me in to a cool crème de menthe drink as we talked about their future. Akio (Korean) is twenty-three and works in an office, Luis, a twenty-two-year-old Brazilian, lives in Brazil, Jarri, a Finn, and Jeannot, a Japanese, both twenty-two, are students, Moise, an Israeli, is nineteen and works, Marianne and Brahima Berbers are nineteen and students, Koffi, an African, is eighteen and learning to be a pastrycook, Mara, an Indian, is seventeen and a student, Noel is French, sixteen years of age, and a student and Stellina, an Arab, is at school in England and is only eleven years of age.

Miss Baker's husband lives in Brazil most of the time, but her sister, Mrs Wallace, is in Monte Carlo. 'Tante Tante', as the children call her, will keep a family eye on them, but all the papers and official problems in their lives will be taken care of by the Red Cross.

Princess Grace is adamant that the family will remain together as long as possible or they wish.

There was a healthy respect for each other between these two women—Princess Grace and Josephine Baker—both professionals in their own spheres: the art of giving people pleasure through entertainment and the art of giving love to children.

When Sammy Davis Junior outrageously snubbed Princess Grace and her 1,200 glittering guests at the grand opening of Monte Carlo's Sporting Club Casino, Josephine Baker ... the Black Venus ... then aged sixty-seven years, joined black comedian Bill Crosby, Desi Arnaz Junior, and pianist Burt Bacharach to give an impromptu performance at less than an hour's notice.

She not only slayed the sophisticated audience with her devastating talent and charm but it was also to prove to be a turning point in the rejuvenation of her career. From then on she was offered cabaret contracts all over the world.

On the night before Josephine Baker died in Paris, Princess Grace went to say goodbye to her. Though Miss Baker was unconscious through a stroke and it was known that she would never recover, Princess Grace asked if she might visit her in hospital. She arrived at the back entrance of the hospital so as not to attract attention and the eye of the newsmen lurking round the front door.

In the cool twilight of a Paris spring evening she sat alone with her friend.

In 1965 the Princess Grace Foundation was created which was primarily used to encourage local artists and craftsmen of all ages. This was originally inspired by the Elder Craftsmen Shop in Philadelphia though the Monaco version is not strictly for older people.

She bought a shop in the old part of Monaco near the palace and gave it to the foundation. A branch has now opened in the city of Monte Carlo. Along with the knitted hats and scarves and pretties made from Provençal prints, there is pottery, ceramics and paintings. But one of the most successful sales to tourists is a scarf designed by Princess Grace.

It is charming in thick white silk with a rouleau edge in pink. There are pastel coloured flowers, drawn in the style of Picasso, or one of her children, and round the edge a stylish border that on looking closely discloses itself to be made up of the words Monte Carlo, repeated and repeated into an entrancing pattern.

The Foundation has now extended its perimeter to help people in need who don't qualify under other charities. For instance, the Red Cross cannot give money direct to people, but with the Foundation Princess Grace was able to send a boy to the New York University.

Every now and then Princess Grace adds money in the most unusual way to her Foundation. When she read extracts from the Bible on *Stars on Sunday*, Britain's popular Sunday night programme—in which the Archbishop of Canterbury, Yehudi Menuhin and hosts of other world celebrities have performed—she was offered a handsome fee. This money went directly into the Foundation funds.

When an American magazine asked her to write an article about the merits of breast feeding the Princess did it simply because it is a subject dear to her heart. But on publication, when the same magazine offered to pay her a fee, she accepted it and again it went into the Princess Grace Foundation.

Princess Grace has a great respect and understanding for all mothers. Not only for what they have achieved but in the difficult task they face in bringing up their children. Every Monegasque woman who gives birth to a baby is sent a letter of congratulations from the Princess and a religious medal.

Twenty-eight

It is generally known that Princess Grace loves flowers. She loves living with them, giving them to friends, arranging them, and drying them and making them into enchanting collages. Her life is surrounded with flowers.

In 1968 she decided that Monaco should have a garden club to develop its members' artistic sense by a knowledge of flowers and plants and decorative arrangement of flowers. At one of the early meetings Princess Grace gave a lecture herself with slides about the trees of America and the development of the great forests there.

'It was so knowledgeable,' said an American who was there.

From this club she then wanted to extend to an international flower-arranging competition. One of the judges in that first show was Julia Clements (widow of Sir Alexander Seton, the 10th Baron of Abercorn) author of fourteen best-selling books on flower arrangements and an international judge and lecturer. With two roses named after her—Julia Clements and Lady Seton—she was once described as the 'arch priestess of flowers who had led more than 5,000,000 women into the grip of flower arrangement'.

The first show was a brave little venture but, perfectionist that she is, after the show when the officials and judges were walking round the palace garden Princess Grace sent her lady-in-waiting across to Julia Clements and asked her not to leave when the others did but to go to the Princess's bureau.

'I noticed a delicate looking dry flower arrangement on the desk, then shortly afterwards the Princess walked in with a note pad and pencil in her hand saying, "Now do tell me how to improve this show." '

They discussed staging, schedule making, judges and various definitions. She took down many notes, asking pertinent questions, which resulted in Miss Clements returning to Monaco to give lessons to the founder members of the new Garden Club.

'I find that Princess Grace does not like too many principles or technicalities, even when teaching. I will make arrangements one way emphasising principles, but when working she will do it her way, which not only displays her originality but the results are often much better,' said Miss Clements.

'After one lesson, when she had made a very original arrangement, with striking strelitzias and fruit, she was so pleased with the result that she said: "Oh do help me take it back to the palace. I want my husband to see what I've done." '

The Princess became the president of the garden club and the flower show, and is always thinking of different methods of presentation or ideas to make the show more appealing.

One of her bright ideas was to have a 'Men Only' class. But her problem was how to get the husbands to enter. She invited several husbands and wives—including writers, film stars and artists—to the palace for drinks. They all wondered why they had been asked but after a few drinks she told them of the flower show and said, 'I want all the ladies to stay with me and the men to go into another room.'

The men thought the women were going to have flower-talk while they continued their drinking. They were wrong. A long table was laid out with flowers, dishes, pinholders and scissors. The Princess told them that as she wanted each one of them to enter her show, now was the time to practise. And this was how the most amusing class held in the competition every year was created. It has become the 'Men Only' class with titles which vary every year.

Some years it is sport, others a proverb and last year the theme was astrology.

On a May morning last year with the other husbands there was a blue-jeaned competitor carrying in his equipment and jocularly greeting the other men. Then seriously he set about creating a Scorpio motif with his little bags of sand, tin tray of pebbles, tiny red-tipped cacti like fat little candles and a plastic crab—or was it a scorpion?

After he had finished he meticulously cleaned up like the other men round him.

At the prize giving at the Hotel de Paris on the next Sunday, where Princess Grace was giving out the prizes, a happy and bashful Prince Rainier acknowledged the clapping when it was disclosed that he had been highly commended by the judges.

No one knows quite how Princess Grace persuades Prince Rainier and their other men friends to enter year after year. But she does. And so sincere is Prince Rainier's interest that he gives up two whole days to her gardening club events. The Prince varies his name for entering each year, usually choosing one of his other titles, but in any case the judging is done quite anonymously.

The two-day event now attracts visitors from all over the world, including Japan. Last year for the first time the South Africans, who had arrived with boxes of marvellous flowers from their own gardens, scooped most of the prizes. I was sitting with them during the luncheon at the beach club when Julia Clements came over to our table and said, 'Princess Grace would like to meet the ladies from South Africa.'

Cameras were whisked out, lipstick applied and smiles adjusted as they went over to the Princess's table where she was sitting with Prince Rainier, Princess Stephanie and Prince Albert. The Princess could have been any pretty girl in a red cotton skirt, white lawn shirt, navy cardigan, her hair pulled back into a pony tail with a strand of heavy red wool and huge trendy sunglasses. She carried a floppy navy blue and white beach hat. Nothing could have been simpler.

But for these housewives, who had come half a world away, first scooping many of the prizes at the Ghent Flower Arranging Show in Belgium and had then been persuaded to come on to Monaco, it was the highlight of their trip.

'It was worth all the expense and all the travelling. Everything. Just to go home and say I have talked to her. And she was so lovely ...'

The Princess is filled with fun on these occasions when she sees that everyone is enjoying themselves. During a children's flower parade when the royal family was throwing flower heads at the children as the floats passed by, she suddenly became tired of this and turned to the next box and threw flowers at the people in that.

Princess Grace has become so advanced in the art of flower arranging that she has been made an international judge and took part as a judge in the great Ghent Floralies last year. The other judges were impressed with her knowledge when discussing composition, colour and interpretation. Had she entered herself she probably would have walked off with many of the first prizes.

In 1970 Princess Grace was invited by the Flower Arranging Society of Solihull in the Midlands of England to be their guest of honour.

She exhausted and enchanted her hostesses. After a tiring afternoon of looking at all the exhibits she remembered that there was something else to see.

It was past 9 p.m. when the Princess asked: 'And what about the church?' The parish church, St Alphege, had been specially decorated for the occasion.

Someone quickly rang through to a church official to open up the church, which had been locked up, and the Princess spent an hour there before leaving for the drive back to London.

Although she does not always have time to do the flowers in the palace, guests always know when it is her touch. At one luncheon party she had all the children helping her make fantastic concoctions of flowers and fruit and vegetables for each of the small tables round the pool.

In the new living-room in the palace extension there was a large twisted and gnarled root out of which a cascade of cymbidium orchids tumbled. They looked just right. Princess Grace had pulled up the root from a barren part of the mountain at Roc Agel when she had been out for a walk. Some of her happiest private hours are spent in the large flower room she has made on the ground floor of the palace which is stacked with bases, containers, wire, pinholders and everything needed for flower arrangement.

Dried flower pictures, which began as a Kelly family hobby, has now been developed into a high art by the Princess. This year in Paris she will hold her first public exhibition of about fifty of her creations.

The finished product, mounted in a deep recessed frame, is a work of art. The most spectacular are the fantasy flowers which she creates herself with stamens from one flower and petals from another. They are wildly exotic and extremely beautiful. Her wild flower pictures are delicate and exquisite. No telephone book in the palace is ever thrown away. Princess Grace keeps them all and fills them with flowers she finds out walking in the mountains behind Monaco or those grown in the palace gardens. She presses them for a month before using them.

'I walk behind the gardeners and pick up the clippings,' she said.

When a Monegasque woman said to me, 'She has brought life to Monaco,' she meant it. From a beautiful faded city, forecourt to the crematorium, Monte Carlo is now bursting with tourists, exhibitions and everything to do with the arts. All this comes mainly through the Princess's enthusiasm.

Grouped in 1970 as the International Arts Festival, concerts, ballets and theatre performances, cabaret and literary events succeed each other from June to September. This, too, was originally created in 1966 at the Princess's initiative upon the occasion of the Monte Carlo Centennial.

The best ballet companies in the world have danced within a specially conceived set in the Place du Palais ... the Paris Opera Ballet, the National Hungarian, the Soviet Ballet of the Novosibirsk Opera, the Harkness from New York, the Slask Polish Ballet, the London Royal Festival Ballet, the New York City Ballet and the Mexican Folk Ballet.

The Comédie Française regularly performs there and the concerts given by the Monte Carlo Opera National Orchestra in the main courtyard of the palace have assembled some of the world's most prestigious names . . . Igor Markevitch, Mstislav Rostropovitch, Georges Prêtre, Paul Klecki, Zubin Mehta, Lovo von Matacic, Elisabeth Schwarzkopf, Tamas Vassary, Yehudi Menuhin, Rudolf Firkusny, Galina Vashnewskaya, Emil Gilels.

Few of them ever recognise during their rehearsals a small figure sitting intently behind her glasses in the back of the theatre, listening and watching. Her body is in the stalls but her mind is right there with the performers. She will be back there at night as the glamorous Princess Grace of Monaco but now, sitting in her skirt and cardigan or simple shirtwaist dress, she is Grace Kelly the professional artist.

While Prince Rainier concentrates on the developing of the business interests, in reclaiming land and watching real estate and small industries becoming big business, Princess Grace is the tourist attraction. They queue for hours just to catch a glimpse of her. Not the grand tour regulars at the Hotel de Paris but the £10 a day trippers who flood in from San Remo in Italy or French resorts along the coast.

On gala nights Princess Grace is always there ... just as breathtakingly beautiful as they imagined. As Prince Rainier has explained:

'Often when we have to go to a gala she has a stinking headache, but it doesn't show because she has this ability to put on a mask for the required time. I suppose it is something to do with her dramatic art training.'

Although Princess Grace enjoys wearing simple clothes in her private life, for galas she dresses up as she fully understands people want to see a princess. Once her elaborate preparations back-fired.

In 1968 for the re-opening of the Monte Carlo Casino which had just been redecorated, there was a grand ball with everyone wearing spectacular head-dresses. Among the guests was Sophia Loren, who had flown in from Rome.

Alexandre, Princess Grace's hairdresser, came from Paris to create many of the fantasies worn that night. She was to be his last client and as usual he arrived late. Finally her elaborate head-dress was finished as the Prince, a wily mandarin in pigtails, chafed at being late.

There is an autocratic rule in the Principality that no one is allowed to dance or have a drink before the arrival of the Prince. The Princess went out to leave in the car only to find that her head-dress just would not go in ... it was staggeringly beautiful but too tall. Everyone offered advice and every suggestion was tried but it was impossible. At last one of the palace service vans was brought round, a carpet hastily placed in the back and a chair for the Princess. She arrived at the Casino—extremely late—via the back door entrance.

Sadly to this day in Monte Carlo everyone only talks about how late the royal party was in arriving and how hot it was without a drink. Few people know the real reason. Perhaps now they will understand why she was late.

Every summer through one or other of the Princess's enterprises Monte Carlo is once again packed with celebrities from all over the world. It is doubtful whether tourists would have noticed Queen Victoria Eugénie of Spain, King Umberto of Italy or Princess Sophia of Greece, but they will stand for hours just to catch a glimpse of Elizabeth Taylor, Richard Burton, Sophia Loren, Gina Lollobrigida, Danny Kaye or Cary Grant.

It is not just the sun that brings these busy, sophisticated people to Monaco but the charm of taking part in some of the last of the fabulous social occasions left in this weary world.

Princess Grace is one of the best public relations officers in the game. It is a business that she understands and works at tirelessly . . . for Monaco.

Twenty-nine

'The most exciting day of my life wasn't the day I got the Oscar. No, it was the day when Caroline, for the first time, began to walk and she took seven small steps by herself, one after the other, before reaching me and throwing herself into my arms.'

These are words spoken by Princess Grace when she was once reminiscing about her days as a movie star. And anyone who knows the Princess intimately recognises the truth in them. Some of her happiest days have been those early ones in the nursery at the palace in Monaco with her children when they were small.

With the birth of her second daughter and third child on 1 February 1965, the Princess's family was complete. Once again it was an incredibly pretty baby and was christened Stephanie Marie Elisabeth.

'This is the most beautiful day of my life,' Caroline announced when she saw the baby for the first time. Caroline's only disappointment was that she could not look after the baby all by herself and she longed for the day when she could take her to school!

Albert looked for some time and then said quietly, 'Next time, could it be a boy?'

Once again the library had been turned into a delivery room. Princess Grace now preferred to have her children at home. As she told an American magazine:

'Perhaps it is less hygienic to have one's baby at home rather than in the hospital but it's much more pleasant. Even if one has a baby in the hospital the husband and other members of the family can only see it and not hold it. That practice of keeping the baby away from the father behind a sheet of glass is so impersonal. As for the baby, to come straight from the mother's womb and almost immediately be placed in a room full of screaming infants—I'm not at all sure that that is a good practice. I feel that the system here of having babies at home if you can is much better than in America.'

And as before, to the magazines who were quick to note that Princess Grace had put on weight, the truthful answer to *Look* could not have been more appealing:

'I always have a weight problem after the birth of a baby because I breast feed my babies for at least two months. I feel it gives them a good start and would continue longer, only my many obligations do not permit. In order to feed a baby properly, a nursing mother should not diet. And I am too concerned about the well-being of my children to worry about my own line. It is not that important at this time.'

The centuries-old christening ceremony took place in the Cathedrale de Monaco, the same cathedral where the marriage had taken place. Eugene Cardinal Tisserant, a prince of the Roman Catholic Church and a senior member of the Sacred College, came from Rome to officiate at the baptism.

After the ceremony from the flower-decked palace balcony Princess Grace showed her baby to the people of Monaco. Prince Rainier gave this message:

'She comes to us in all her innocence and purity, bringing us once more, as did her sister and brother, joy, happiness and pride. Yes, indeed pride! For she, like them, is a symbol and the bond of a family and patriotic union of which we can justly be proud. And these three children, who certainly belong to the present, also represent for us all the future.'

There would have been another child in 1967 had the Princess not had a miscarriage when attending *Expo 67* at Montreal. She became ill after a reception and dinner for 200 Canadian artists and government leaders who had been invited by Prince Rainier and Princess Grace to the new Château Champlain Hotel.

The dinner had followed a gruelling day when 10,000 visitors jammed the Place des Nations in hot muggy weather to celebrate Monaco's National Day ... and get a good look at Princess Grace. Despite the heat she weathered a Press conference but looked drawn and distracted during dinner. The Princess was later rushed to the

Montreal Royal Victory Hospital, but the doctors were unable to save her baby.

People in France were at first quite confounded about the way Prince Rainier and Princess Grace decided to bring up their children. To begin with it is not customary for children to address their parents in the familiar *tu* (thou) instead of *vous* (you). Even in these enlightened days among the aristocracy of France children still use the formal form of address.

'We have deliberately not brought up our children in a princely manner,' Prince Rainier has said on many occasions. Both parents right from the start made it clear that they were opposed to how children were brought up even today in many aristocratic homes in Europe. They are often shuttled off to their own quarters with a nanny and only see their parents at set periods. There until the age of five they are practically invisible. This is followed by a brief period in the nursery before once again being banished—this time to preparatory school.

The Prince has too many sorrowful memories of his own childhood when this is exactly what happened.

Right from the children's babyhood the day began with breakfast with their parents in the library. At 8.30 a.m., while the Prince and Princess were still in their dressing-gowns, a trolleyed table would be wheeled in with breakfast on it and the children would come tumbling in from their nursery which adjoined their parents' private apartment.

In the small private kitchen the Princess usually prepared the breakfast, which consisted of a grapefruit popped under the grill and boiled egg. The Princess likes tea for breakfast and the Prince coffee. She would tempt the children to eat with fingers of hot buttered toast.

In many French families where the mother of the family is rarely seen until lunchtime, these American-style family breakfasts were quite an innovation. Thursdays and Sundays were always kept free so that Prince Rainier and Princess Grace could join the children for lunch, and when they became older, on any other day when they were free of school work.

All through their school days in Monaco and even today the Princess has breakfast with her children. In Paris, instead of allowing any members of the staff to take Princess Stephanie to school she prefers to do it herself at 8.30 before settling down to her desk and the day's work. In the afternoons whenever possible she is always at the gate with the other mothers to meet Princess Stephanie after school.

The children were never spanked if they were naughty. Instead their parents and their Nana punished them by refusing privileges. It worked like this. On one occasion when Prince Albert had needed chastising, Nana King had said quite firmly, 'No television for you tonight.' Some time later she entered the library and found the little boy sitting with Prince Rainier glued to a Western.

'I thought I said to you that there was no television tonight,' she admonished.

Prince Rainier asked why and then on hearing the reason promptly turned off the set.

The Princess invariably bathed the children herself and when she discovered teeth marks on Prince Albert's body she inquired of Princess Caroline if she knew anything about it. It appeared that she had in fact been biting her brother at play. Princess Grace immediately bit her daughter on the arm and remonstrated, 'You must not bite your brother. You see it hurts.'

Even when the children were as irritating as only normal lively children can be, Princess Grave never raised her voice to them. Once when they were about four or five she went into her dressing-room and found a mess of lipstick and powder. Calling Princess Caroline and Prince Albert to the room she said:

'Now I want the truth. Who has done this naughty little job?'

One of them said, 'I didn't do it,' and then the other, 'I didn't do it.'

As thousands of mothers before her have said, Princess Grace remarked, 'Well, somebody must have done it.'

In the same breath they both answered, 'I did it.'

Far from being cross, Princess Grace was delighted that they had not told on each other and the incident was forgotten.

The children are extremely kind and considerate and have been brought up to respect other people. Right from the beginning the Princess was determined that her children would have good manners.

'People who are overly indulgent with babies are inclined to say, "Oh he is just a baby,"' she once said in an interview. 'But how a teenager behaves depends very much on how he behaved before he was a teenager.'

A typical example of this was one occasion when Prince Albert was young. The story comes from Nana King.

'Albert was getting ideas one evening. You know the butlers were standing around and he was late finishing his dinner and when he did finish, he said, "I'm ready" in a very imperious tone of voice. The

Princess quietly said, "Just a minute. Just a minute. That is no way to speak to anybody. You get down and take your own plate out."

'The humiliation of having to get down from his chair and walk past them all with his own plate was punishment enough. Little things like that. They weren't allowed to get away with anything as children by either the Prince or Princess.'

When she was young Princess Caroline was touchingly solicitous—and still is—to the people around her. Whenever she saw someone at the palace with a cut finger or injury she amusingly offered them advice or wanted to bandage them up from her own first-aid kit.

Usually on birthdays the children had a few of their friends to celebrate with them. On her fourth birthday Princess Caroline went to Princess Grace and said, 'This year, Mummy, I want to invite all the children in the palace (the palace staff). You see, I didn't invite them last year. They must have been very upset.' So they were all invited to a glorious ice-cream and balloons party.

All the children have been brought up not to have expectancy of any privileges because of their royal parentage. Prince Albert is a particularly kind boy. When he won a swimming competition and received a medal he noticed a little girl crying because she had not won one. Without any ado he went straight over to her and gave her his medal.

When Princess Stephanie won a prize in a flower arranging competition for a bouquet she had made she was so surprised, and so overcome with emotion, that she promptly burst into tears and ran to her 'nana'. Although Princess Grace was present the child knew that it simply was not done to embarrass her mother with her tears.

Both Prince Rainier and Princess Grace always speak English to the children who call them 'mummy' and 'daddy' or if by chance they are speaking French 'mama' or 'papa'.

On evenings when he was present the Prince would always have a bedtime game with the children. The old apartments were especially well laid out for this and he would romp around with them. One hilarious game they all enjoyed consisted of the children running after Nana and calling her 'fat'. They would continue to do so as she would grab them and tickle them, and the more she tickled them, the more they continued saying it. This went on until they could not breathe and she would stop when they finally admitted, 'You are not fat, you are thin.'

'Of course, the Prince would egg them on and then he would be chasing them around in a glorious game of hide and seek. Typical father, of course, get them all excited before they went to bed,' Mrs Wood recalled.

'Princess Grace was particularly good at story telling. I have never heard anyone better. I couldn't help but listen myself,' she remembered. 'She put such feeling into her stories.'

One night when he was still very little, Princess Grace decided to read a story to Prince Albert. She was just about to sit down and read when he said to her: 'Are you going to do it in French or English because your French sure needs improving.'

As the children at that time did not get any pocket money they invariably made their parents' presents. They did paintings or cut-outs, made up bouquets of flowers and learnt little poems to say to Princess Grace on her birthday. One of their favourites was the Robert Louis Stevenson book of verse. Prince Albert's gift to the Princess on one birthday was reciting *The Land of Counterpane* to her.

There was always lots of laughter with a completely free atmosphere. One day Prince Albert and Princess Caroline were watching the *Sound of Music* Trapp family on television. There is a part where the mother has to go for an audition and she does not come out of it very well. She is told to go away and practise sex-appeal.

A few days later the Princess was in the library walking up and down and coo-ing to Princess Stephanie who was a small baby at the time. Princess Caroline was watching and asked: 'Are you practising your sex-appeal, Mummy?' Princess Grace nearly dropped the baby in surprise.

One of the children's great delights was to help choose their mother's clothes when she was getting dressed. Even as a child, Princess Caroline was typically feminine and used to love to try on her mother's hats. She also enjoyed offering her advice, 'I like this dress best, Mummy. Won't you wear this one tonight.'

Both Prince Rainier and Princess Grace were determined that their children should grow up with healthy bodies and an enjoyment of sport. Today Prince Albert is a fine swimmer and has inherited his father's enjoyment of underwater swimming. Princess Caroline lives in the water during the summer at Monaco and Princess Stephanie is catching up fast.

To the rich mothers of Monte Carlo it was quite a shock when they saw Princess Grace at the Monte Carlo Beach Club teaching her children to dog paddle. In these circles it is usual for a professional to take complete charge.

Not only did the Princess teach the children to swim but also to dive without any self-consciousness along with the other children. During the children's early swimming days she frequently presided over the children's swim-meet which was a regular occurrence at the select Beach Club.

'I've loved every age of the children. We try to include them in everything we do,' the Princess once said. Wherever they went or whatever they did the Prince and Princess made sure their children were not left out.

Princess Grace maintains that her children are able to have a much more normal and natural life than people think.

'Perhaps they are isolated in certain ways but during the winter term at school they are all exposed to various social and economic levels and meet children of all languages and cultures,' she said.

During the Vietnam war, in order to make their children conscious of the suffering there, all the family wore a copper bracelet on which was engraved the name of an American prisoner-of-war.

This was done through an American organisation who also forwarded on the letters the family wrote to their adoptives.

Princess Grace had two cousins fighting in Vietnam and one Christmas Prince Rainier invited ten boys who were recovering from Vietnam wounds to Monaco as the family's guests.

She places discipline high on her list of values. Perhaps this is best explained in her own words as told to John Bainbridge of *The Philadelphia Inquirer Magazine*.

'In Monaco there still exists a respect for authority. This is so important, particularly for young people. On television, in pictures, and in books, there is so much effort expended in trying to be funny or clever, which often has the effect of actually tearing down the important qualities that young people should hang on to. It seems to be the case that young people who are in search of truth and reality are afraid to admit that something old can be something of value.

'I was just reading an article in which Margaret Chase Smith said that the word "square" has become outmoded. It used to be one of the most respected words in our vocabulary. We talked about the "square deal" and the "square shooter", and they were honoured words. She said that nowadays the person who seems to get the attention and applause is the one who plays the angles. "What we need today," she said, "are more square people, more people who are dependable in the old-fashioned way . . ."

'I'm always appalled when I see parents intimidated by their children and I must say that I see that quite often when I go to the United States. If I say something about the discipline in our household they say, "Can you do that?" Now, really parents do have to take a stand. So far we've been very fortunate with our children. So far so good.'

It was the irrepressible Father Tucker who finally summed up the early years of the marriage of Prince Rainier and Princess Grace:

'Since their marriage I've gotten this impression. Both of them take much more stock in being married, man and wife, father and mother, than in being Prince and Princess.'

Thirty

At this stage, after twenty years of marriage, it is time to explode some of the myths that have surrounded Princess Grace during her years in Monaco.

They were bound to be created simply because there are some sections of the European Press which thrive on destructive sensational stories about royal personages. It could be subconscious envy because they invariably appear in the republican Italian, German and American Press.

Last year Prince Rainier had legal negotiations with a German newspaper which wrote a story that Princess Grace was seeing a well-known doctor in Paris who specialises in cancer. Not only is the story wickedly untrue but the sequel is that it was ricocheted round the world through the medium of the popular Press.

There are certain elements in France who have made a point in saying that Princess Grace abhors gambling and wishes to see it stamped out in Monte Carlo. Nothing could be farther from the truth. She is not out to reform Monaco, as it needs no reforms. The element of gambling, once a mainstay of the Principality's revenue, is no longer so important. Of Monaco's revenue, which fluctuates round the £25,000,000 point, the Société des Bains de Mer, the quaintly named company, is obliged to contribute no more than 4·5 per cent of Monaco's annual budget, and often it is far less.

As a member of the ruling family of Monaco, Princess Grace is by law not allowed to set foot inside the Casino gambling rooms as can no other Monegasque except as an employee. The Princess gambled once in Cannes before her wedding and once in San Remo eighteen years ago.

One of the most frequent stories in the European Press in those early years of her marriage was that it was her hand behind the Americanising of the traditional casino by the introduction of one-armed bandits at the entrance, and crap tables.

As one who remembers the casino in the faded but elegant days just after the war, the intrusion of these ugly, vulgar reflections of modern-day living seems undesirable. But neither the Prince, let alone the Princess, had any say in the matter. The casino is owned and operated by a privately owned corporation: Société Anonyme des Bains de Mer et du Cercle des Strangers du Monaco. What the Prince *did* advise is that if they had to be there why not install them in a room in the basement and not in the elegant, period foyer?

It is the same society in which at one time Aristotle Onassis owned 35 per cent of the shares and was the largest single minority shareholder.

In 1958 it was decided to close the casino on Good Fridays and in Monaco one hears that it was in fact a wish of Princess Grace's. But she has never privately or publicly conceded to this. The nearest one gets to the possible truth is that when she was once asked this by an American journalist, instead of one of her usual noncommittal silences she did reply: 'I would rather not say.'

There was also the episode of the pigeon shooting for which she was blamed and had nothing at all to do with. According to that esteemed *New York Herald Tribune* journalist, Art Buchwald, whose word I would never doubt, it was Prince Rainier who wrote to Aristotle Onassis and said: 'The best wedding gift you can give me is to stop the sport of pigeon shooting in Monte Carlo.'

Mr Onassis then told Mr Buchwald, 'All right, I'm going to give the Prince his wedding present. . . . Frankly I did not know until I came down here that they shot live pigeons. I thought they used clay ones.'

International pigeon shooting matches had been held for a long time in Monaco and it is an old European custom. The birds, which were a special breed from Spain, had their tails and one wing clipped so that they flew on an erratic course. This not only makes them harder to shoot but the marksman also had to shoot into the sun. The birds used to be released from boxes on the terrace outside the casino and the shooters did not know from which box they would fly. There was a tremendously unattractive element in that many of the birds were wounded and fell into the sea or on the terrace. The pigeons retrieved were sold to restaurants and hotels, and presumably eaten.

In many ways it was no more disagreeable than some of the low-flying pheasant shooting that is done in the name of sportsmanship by affluent businessmen in the home counties close to London.

The story reported was that Princess Grace was walking on the terrace and saw the 'sad spectacle' of pigeon shooting. She is said to have gone straight to Prince Rainier in his 'office' and demanded that this bird slaughter be stopped.

The result was that many of the hotels and restaurants were unable to serve pigeons and the spring of 1960 was known in Monaco as the 'Grace Kelly Recession'.

The truth behind this story is that, like Prince Rainier, she did not enjoy the sight of the pigeon shooting. She loves all animals and birds and, if anything, is a conservationist. But it was something in which she could not, and would not, interfere. It was the patrons of the Hotel de Paris who complained as the birds began to drop on the terrace and it was the management of the casino who finally abolished the sport.

Another legend that has to be disavowed is that Princess Grace had anything to do with healing the breach that occurred between Prince Rainier and Onassis over the Greek's interference in the policy of how to run the Société des Bains de Mer, the holding company which owns not only the casino but the sporting club, seventeen hotels, restaurants, night clubs and many other tourist attractions in Monte Carlo.

It is true that the two men differed over the future of Monaco. Prince Rainier wanted a much more healthy approach of 'democratising' Monaco so that it was not so dependent on the fickleness of the big gamblers but more on middle-spending tourists. Prince Rainier visualised 2,000 beds in new hotels for middle class tourists. The 'Golden Greek', as Onassis was dubbed by the columnists, preferred to create his own little domain where he could be 'king' over the two to three hundred extremely wealthy patrons who were making the casino pay. All Onassis wanted was a base for his business interests which he was then operating in Paris, and the social cachet that being the un-crowned king of Monaco would bring him. In the international world of finance in New York or London he was still a minnow in a large pond, but in Monte Carlo he was the big fish who desired to control his own pond.

Onassis' final decision to break with Monte Carlo was, in fact, a business deal and the Princess would have had nothing at all to do with this. It was a matter between Prince Rainier, the S.B.M. and the National Council plus the help of some shrewd outside advisers whom the Prince brought in.

What Princess Grace did do was to keep the social doors open even during the difficult period when Aristotle Onassis and his beautiful wife Tina parted. She reportedly tried to bring about a face-saving reconciliation, but this proved unsuccessful.

It has also been said that Princess Grace strongly disapproved of Onassis' relationship with Maria Callas on the grounds of her devout Catholic approach to divorce. False again. Princess Grace is far too sophisticated to have been shocked by this extraordinary romance. The Prince and Princess joined a large party as guests of Onassis and his beautiful diva in 1961 for a four-day cruise on the *Christina* to Majorca. What people did in their private life, Princess Grace felt, was no concern of hers. She always admired Maria Callas as a supreme artist.

One of the highlights of the trip was attending the opening of the newly decorated Hotel Son Vida. The talent that night was immense with Elsa Maxwell bashing the piano, Prince Rainier pounding the drums, Maria Callas shaking the maracas and Princess Grace clapping to the beat. The next day they all went on to the bull fights in Plaza de Toros.

During Mr Onassis' last illness in Paris, although Princess Grace did not visit him in hospital, she was in fact kept informed of his condition. After he died she was to say: 'He was very tough because that is the way he was. But he was also a man of great sensitivity and was thoughtful and interesting. I also believe that he was a deeply religious man with a sense of family and responsibility.'

The clear, dispassionate newspaper image of Princess Grace receives a jolt every so often when, unlike any other European royalty, she rushes into print to vindicate any injustice that she feels has been made to herself or her family.

It has long been speculated that Princess Grace and Jacqueline Onassis are not on good terms. When President Kennedy was suffering from a back injury in a New York hospital, his wife took Grace Kelly to see him knowing how enchanted he was with her films. Both Prince Rainier and Princess Grace were the guests of the President and Mrs Kennedy at dinner in the White House.

From an American television personality who was at the Red Cross Ball in Seville in 1966 I have this on-the-spot coverage of an extraordinary occasion when Princess Grace met the President's wife. 'Each of them had their own camp following,' she told me. 'There was Grace as a senorita driving in a carriage and looking incredibly pretty and riding on horseback was Jackie looking absolutely stunning in a matador outfit. No two women could have looked more different.

'But the real crux came when Grace got up to open the Red Cross Ball in the evening and Jackie left the room.'

In covering the event *Newsweek* reported:

'The way it seemed to wondering newsmen, Jacqueline Kennedy all but snubbed Monaco's Princess Grace at the Red Cross Ball in Seville, Spain. At first a Madrid newspaper noted, Jackie walked past Grace without a word. Then there was a brief, "cold" greeting, after which "they not only didn't talk to each other, they didn't even look at each other". A similar account in the European edition of *The New York Herald Tribune* referred to a "cool conversation", adding that "reports blamed it on fatigue". That fetched a sharp letter from Grace Kelly Grimaldi, as she signed herself. After complaining about the Trib's coverage, she wrote: "I was delighted to meet Mrs Kennedy again, for whom I have a great admiration and respect. If there was any coolness or fatigue that evening, it was caused only by some of the many dozens of photographers who pushed, shoved and relentlessly pursued us all night." '

In addition to the reports given by these esteemed newspapers, Princess Grace was also on the defensive in an account as run by *Time*.

The Princess wrote that she was 'deeply hurt' by the *Time* report.

'What you call my frostiness and pique was directed at some of the hundreds of photographers who spoiled the evening for many of us, and certainly not at Mrs Kennedy, for whom I have admiration and respect.

'And let me add in refute to your snide and unnecessary remarks that I am delighted to be "upstaged" by Mrs Kennedy at any time.'

When President John F. Kennedy was assassinated in November 1963, neither Prince Rainier nor Princess Grace attended the funeral. This was thought to be unusual in many American circles. But it was that sharp-tongued columnist John M. Cummings of the *Philadelphia Inquirer* who drew public attention to the fact.

With Mr Cummings' permission I quote:

'If you want to know why Prince Rainier and his Philadelphia princess, the former Grace Kelly, were not among the notables at the funeral of President John F. Kennedy, you may be satisfied with the explanation of the State Department.

'It seems that Monaco, the tiny principality ruled by Rainier, has no diplomatic representative at Washington. So Rainier and his Princess, because they could not, under protocol, be considered heads of State, were not eligible for recognition in the cortège.

'For a pair that manages to horn in on a lot of functions, diplomatic and otherwise, it seems strange that, in effect, they gave the funeral the brushoff. They displayed no such reluctance when they attended a luncheon in the White House as guests of President and Mrs Kennedy. Of course, the Kennedys were gracious enough to extend an invitation at the time the Monacoans were here as guests of the city, and honour guests at a great wingding in Convention Hall.

'It would be difficult to estimate the number of people who attended the President's funeral without invitation. By the tens of thousands they lined the streets over which the President's body was borne to his last resting place in Arlington Cemetery.

'As reigning heads of a dice table, it would appear natural enough for the Rainiers to establish diplomatic relations with Las Vegas to qualify for protocol in this country.

'It has been suggested by an expert in protocol that before sulking in their mansion on the Mediterranean they should have consulted with their "prime minister" and "Ambassador at large", Aristotle Onassis.

'Perhaps the Prince and his Princess could have received some advice from Maria Callas, one of their "ladies-in-waiting", who knows her way around.

'The late, free-loading Elsa Maxwell, had she been around, would have been of inestimable value to the royal and regal pair. Elsa would know how to duck a funeral gracefully and leave a stream of speculation behind. Elsa, who spent her rent-free summers in Monaco, did have a reputation for telling upper crustaceans how to deport themselves in public and how to drink their soup from silver service.

'The Rainiers couldn't get over here to pay their respects to a man who befriended them. But Eamon De Valera, well past 80 and nearly blind, could come in from Ireland, where the Kelly clan as well as the Kennedy, had their origin.

'Rainier has the proper raiment for a State funeral conducted with military precision. When on the go here, which is frequently, he plasters his manly chest with more medals and ribbons than you'd find on the prize bull at a county fair.

'While her native land was in deep mourning for the slain President,

Princess Grace was on an outing in a Monaco park. A photograph shows her in a shooting event on that tragic weekend. She is taking aim at the imitation ducks found in a shooting gallery.

'It was on Sunday that the great of the world were arriving in Washington for the funeral of the President the following day. Anybody who wondered why the Rainiers didn't come over to join in the last sad tribute to the martyred President might have been shocked to know that in Monaco it was pleasure as usual and never mind the expressions of sorrow.'

Princess Grace was quick to retaliate with the following letter, which was published the following week in the *Inquirer*.

'Dear Mr Cummings:

'Your article of Friday, November 29th, was brought to my attention this morning. I cannot tell you how shocked and deeply hurt I was by the things you had to say, particularly as you have always treated me with fairness in the past.

'As a responsible journalist, I should think the first step in attacking someone would be to make sure that you have the correct facts. You obviously have not taken the time nor the trouble to do so in this instance.

'I have ignored many newspaper criticisms against my person, family and life as I consider that everyone has a right to his own opinion, but this unfounded and cruel attack on my loyalty to the country of my birth and my sentiments regarding the atrocious assassination of the late President cannot be passed by without a strong protest.

'To begin with I am as grieved and heartbroken as any American over this tragic loss to the country and to the world and I am very sorry not to have been at the funeral. You say that my husband and I "manage to horn in" on many occasions—that is exactly what I tried to avoid doing in Washington last week.

'My relationship with President and Mrs Kennedy has been more on a personal basis rather than an official one and I preferred to express my condolences and grief also in a personal and private way.

'For your information, the photograph published with your article was taken on Thursday, November 21st, the day before the tragedy when I accompanied my children and a few of their friends to a local fair. I was hoping to win them a prize at the shooting gallery.

'After the death of the President, my husband, the Prince, declared a week's period of mourning in the Principality and a Requiem Mass was said at the Cathedral of Monaco on the day of the funeral.

'As an American in Europe, I was very touched by the way Europeans showed a deep sense of personal loss and to see to what extent the President was respected and loved. Your criticism has wounded me greatly in its heartlessness and I want your readers to know, and I want to go on record saying that it is completely untrue and I bitterly resent being pictured in this fashion to my fellow Philadelphians, for whom I have great love and affection.

'Sincerely yours,

'Grace de Monaco'

In a postscript to the article the *Inquirer* had the final say:

'It will be noted that Princess Grace refers to her picture at the Monaco shooting gallery, which was published with the Cummings column, as having been taken on Thursday, November 21st, "the day before the tragedy".

'The caption of the UPI Telephoto used in the *Inquirer* column is dated "11-26-63" and reads: "MONACO: With steady hand and keen eye, Princess Grace of Monaco sights target at fairground shooting gallery here 11-25." The date 11-25 was the Monday following the assassination of President Kennedy and the day on which he was buried.'

The truth behind the story is in fact much more interesting. The reason that the UPI date line was Monday was that all news not concerning the death of President Kennedy was blocked for the four days from the time of the assassination until after the burial. Whatever had piled up in the newsroom of other events was released on Monday and updated for release on that day.

The hour of the assassination of President Kennedy was 1 p.m. in Texas, which meant 8 p.m. European time. The Princess had been to the carnival with her children and their friends that afternoon, that is before the assassination.

The local paper, *Nice-Matin*, printed the photograph the following morning, Saturday. The UPI date line and the *Philadelphia Inquirer* story caused a great deal of upset in Monaco and the photographers themselves offered to sign letters stating the exact time and date the photographs were taken.

When the de Gaulle altercation was at its height the myth was that Princess Grace was brought in to charm the not too unsusceptible seventy-one-year-old president, A 'cold war' had developed between France and the tiny Principality. France had told Monaco that by 11 October 1962 it had to accept fiscal alignment with France; that the people living in Monaco and the international business organisations who had made their headquarters there must pay French taxes. Prince Rainier was adamant.

In Monaco you not only do not pay personal income taxes, but if you own a business you do not pay direct corporate taxes. Negotiations were begun in Paris and the Monegasque delegation offered to meet practically all the French demands except 'fiscal alignment'. They based their refusal on the grounds that it violated the 'Declaration of the Rights of Man'.

Had it not such serious undertones and threats to the Monegasques, on hindsight it had the ingredients of one of those delicious Ealing movies like *Whisky Galore* or *The Lavender Hill Mob*.

Undoubtedly Princess Grace was an asset during the visits that were exchanged between Prince Rainier and Princess Grace going to Paris and the General returning to Monaco, but in such matters of state the Prince does not earn his title 'the Benevolent Autocrat' without cause.

What she did do, and what any other sensible woman would have done, was this: she had not read the General's memoirs herself, so she had her lady-in-waiting make a précis which she swotted up. At dinner she titillated his vanity by charming references to the great work. What man could resist that!

In answer to the various rumours that he would abdicate if the situation got much worse, the Prince said: 'The rumours are absolutely ridiculous and, it goes without saying, without any foundation. I have no reason to abdicate. I will never do it. Such an idea never came to my mind.'

Nor did it to Princess Grace. During that critical weekend in October 1962, in a green and yellow raincoat she went about the streets of Monaco doing her shopping. To anyone who asked about her feelings she replied, like Marshal MacMahon at Sebastopol in 1855, 'J'y suis et j'y reste' (Here I am and here I stay).

'Naturally we are very concerned, but I am optimistic that everything will turn out all right.'

A few years earlier Princess Grace would not have been ready to face the crowds. This day, with her royal act superbly intact, she gave the Prince the best possible support by going among his people.

One piece of blatantly unkind reporting in the British Press that really did upset Princess Grace was the remark made after Princess Anne's wedding that she should not have worn a white dress and tried to upstage the bride.

As she already had the elegant cream-coloured outfit, and it was warm enough for the vagaries of the English climate, she chose it simply because she also had a mink toque to match. She had already discussed it with both the Prince and some friends, who all advised her to wear it. 'This has nothing to do with a wedding dress and is just the very thing as it is practical and chic,' one woman friend suggested.

The truth is far stranger than the myth. The Princess had, in fact, intended to wear a blue outfit but she did not have the right hat and there was not time to get one. As she was sitting watching the guests arrive at the Abbey on colour television, just before she and the Prince left the Connaught Hotel, she turned to him and said: 'There are plenty of off-whites and pale shades in the Abbey,' and did not think a thing about it.

When she did arrive at the Abbey and saw the Queen was in the identical blue that she had intended to wear she felt relieved. Princess Grace was not only one of the most strikingly dressed women in the Abbey but was in fact complimented on her outfit by several members of the royal family. When she read the criticism in a newspaper next day she was totally unprepared. She was so upset that she has never worn the outfit since and it hangs tucked away in one of her clothes closets.

Thirty-one

'She is such fun . . .' Paul Gallico said. 'Being with her you laugh a lot,' said Fleur Cowles. 'You always knew that you would have a laugh with Grace . . .' said producer John Foreman. 'We turn our differences into jokes,' said Prince Rainier.

This, then, is the side of Princess Grace that the general public, alas, never sees.

This joyfulness in the family life of Princess Grace permeates through to the people who work around her. She and Prince Rainier both have the ability of enjoying the absurd and seeing the funny side.

Through the years that they worked in the palace both Phyllis Blum and Nana King were to contribute to many hilarious escapades. That these two engaging girls were able to get away with so much flippancy only illustrates the humanity and normality of their royal employers.

When Princess Grace went to Switzerland in 1959 to have her appendix out both Phyllis Blum and Maureen King accompanied her. The whole entourage was installed in the Beau Rivage Hotel in Lausanne, where Phyllis attended to the secretarial side and Maureen looked after Princess Caroline. Prince Albert, still a baby, had been left in Monaco.

Phyllis and Maureen were noted for their healthy appetites, so much so that Nana King earned herself the title 'Killer King'.

'The Prince always said that Phyllis and I cost him more on this trip than the whole of the Princess's clinic bill because we ate so much,' she recalled.

'One morning we decided to really give him something to talk about. He had been teasing us about our breakfasts for so long. We called for the menu card and literally ordered everything on it. We told the waiter it was for a joke and said, 'Just put everything on it. We won't eat it but put it there.'

'The Prince normally came in when we were having breakfast with Caroline. There we were with a table groaning with food and Phyllis and I sat passively either end.

' "Good God," he said. He was so amazed that he was almost speechless. He didn't really believe it so he rushed into his room and came back with a camera. Still in his dressing-gown, he was leaping around taking pictures of Phyllis and I having this fantastic breakfast. He said the Princess would never believe him unless he could show her proof.

'When the Princess who was convalescing in the hotel, saw them she laughed so much we were worried that she would burst her stitches.'

During the same visit Prince Rainier happened to mention to the girls that he was worried that the laundry were starching his shirts. Maureen King immediately suggested that she would wash them for him. The Prince was slightly apprehensive of her ironing and begged that she was careful and not burn them.

That was sufficient for a joke to be born in Maureen King's mind. She acquired a piece of old white linen that at a distance could have resembled the Prince's fine poplin shirts and made a large scorch mark on it. She then waited for the moment when she knew that the Prince would be in his room. Filled with apologies she took the scorched fabric into the Prince who on seeing it exploded with anguish. Only after a few minutes did she let him see that it was just another joke.

While his real shirts were hanging up to dry in their bathroom the girls took a series of photographs of how to wash shirts, step by step.

Long after, when they had returned to Monaco, for his birthday the Prince got a do-it-yourself washing kit, with a clothes line, soap powder, minute instructions and the photographs from Switzerland showing step by step: No 1 Wash. No 2 Rinse. No 3 Rinse again, etcetera.

It was a battle of wits with the Princess in between as the Prince and the two girls vied with each other to get up to pranks. Prince Rainier in fact won on points but the girls took the bun on invention. One of his best efforts was the Hungarian pianist episode. Here is the story as Phyllis Earle remembered it:

'In the bar playing every night at the hotel was a Hungarian pianist. One night we had gone in the bar and said to each other, "Let's be rash and have a sherry," and somehow we talked to him just for a minute or two. A few days later I had a day off and went to see a school friend in Geneva. When I returned there in a vase in my room was a single red rose with a note tied to it.

'I've kept this note to this day. It was a declaration of love from the Hungarian to me and asking me to go downstairs and meet him in the bar carrying the rose. Of course I immediately recognised the Prince's handwriting but Maureen was so excited about the whole thing I thought I would carry on and see what happened.

'I arrived downstairs with the rose and, of course, the poor Hungarian didn't know what was going on. But there standing in another doorway appearing to be preoccupied was Prince Rainier waiting to report it all back to Princess Grace.

'Prince Rainier carried the joke on for a long time, constantly asking me, "How is your friendly Hungarian?" so I decided to play along. About a year later when we were in Paris Maureen and I did a whole long thing where we made out that the Hungarian had reappeared on the scene and was taking me out. I think the Prince was never quite sure whether it was true or not.'

Despite her outwardly robust appearance, Princess Grace is in fact quite a fragile woman physically. While she was still recuperating, she asked Phyllis Blum to go for a short walk with her as she felt some fresh air would do her good.

'We came back and I could see that she was suddenly very tired. I thought the best thing to do was to get her upstairs as quickly as possible so we came in through the side door of the hotel. As we walked in she immediately noticed that the Prince was sitting there talking to a tall, very portly man. As we drew nearer we realised that it was ex-King Farouk with one of his daughters at his side. The Princess stopped to talk to King Farouk and asked me to talk to the daughter.

'After five minutes Maureen came running down and said, "The Queen of Spain is upstairs," so the Princess excused herself as she did not know exactly what Caroline, left alone with the elderly Queen, might be doing, or saying. When the Princess arrived in the room there was tiny Caroline quietly showing the aged Queen how to do the hula hoop, the Prince having bought her one in a Lausanne shop.

'But the remark that I will always remember is when the Princess turned to me in the lift and said: "Kings to the right of us, Queens to the left of us. We don't know which way to turn."'

Ex-Queen Victoria Eugénie of Spain was Prince Albert's godmother. Her visits to see the Princess in the hotel were something from another era. This stately matriarch used to arrive on time to the second that she said she would and then after exactly one hour, without at any time consulting a watch or clock, she would get up and leave. No one, let alone Princess Grace, could work out how she gauged to the second the length of an hour.

On their last evening in Lausanne the girls decided to have a 'really good spread'. When the wine waiter came over to ask what they were drinking, they jokingly said: 'Whatever His Serene Highness would like to offer us.'

With horror they watched the waiter go over to the Prince who was dining with some business friends and whisper in his ear. About ten minutes later a jumbo bottle of chianti arrived back at their table with two red tulips stuck on it and tied to the top of the bottle was a note 'And bloody well see that you drink it to the last drop.'

The girls drank what they could before going off to the cinema. When they arrived back at the hotel and returned to their room the bottle was standing outside their bedroom door with another note: 'Please finish.'

There was always plenty of fun on the Swiss holidays. Far from palace protocol, everyone was ready to join in. Away from official duties the Grimaldi family is probably the most relaxed of all the European royal families.

One year Prince Rainier rented a chalet at Gstaad for the family, including Oliver and one of the other dogs. On arrival the Princess, always considerate of other people, became anxious about the thick white carpet covering the floor and how the change of environment would affect the dogs and their house-training. The moment she mentioned this to Phyllis Blum and Nana King the temptation was irresistible.

During their day off the girls had found a 'gag shop' and bought a selection of accessories necessary for their joke ... 'plastic puddles and "big jobs"'.

As Mrs Wood now remembers back: 'We waited for an appropriate evening when we knew they would be coming home late. We went into their bedroom and dropped our props into appropriate places ... a large puddle on the sheepskin rug by the Princess's side of the bed just where she would step to climb in and the "big jobs" scattered round the place.

'We went upstairs and waited for them to come back. It was a wooden chalet so you could hear everything and suddenly we heard a shriek, "Rainier ... Rainier, come and look at this." The Prince rushed in but quickly spotted what it was. He got a brush and pan and handed it to the Princess telling her to get on with it. There she was in the dim light cleaning it up and it wasn't until it was all in the pan that she realised it was plastic. Of course, we were convulsed with laughter, as were the Prince and Princess.

'They were so marvellous to play jokes on simply because they always responded in the right way.'

On another occasion in the same chalet the incorrigible two were feeling bored one night, and with them boredom was an invitation to practical jokes. When the Prince and Princess had gone out they decided to make a couple of bodies and put them in their beds.

'We borrowed one of the Princess's nighties and stuffed it with paper to look like two enormous bosoms and we whipped a pair of the Prince's pyjamas and stuffed them also. I remember making the faces with paper and covering them with a white tea towel and putting specs on them,' Maureen Wood recalled.

'I think we gave the woman a headscarf like something she might wear over curlers and we sat them up in bed. We made the man look as though he was reading some sexy magazine propped up in front of him. It looked terribly realistic—it really did.

'They came home very late and we heard the Princess go into the room which had a very dim light. She let out a blood curdling cry for the Prince to come. He dashed in and put on the light: "Oh, those girls upstairs" we heard him saying as they doubled up laughing.

'I suppose looking back that we were both very naughty, but I think for the Princess we were almost a link with "family" and because of this she obviously enjoyed our jokes very much.'

They probably would not have got away with it so much as they did if Phyllis Blum and Nana King had not been two very pretty, intelligent and charming girls. It is highly unlikely that any French members of the palace staff with their traditional mentality would have dared to have played these jokes ... .

One of the best practical jokes that the King-Blum team ever played on the Princess concerned a dinner party to be given by one of the palace staff:

'She had invited the Prince and Princess to an Indonesian dinner,' Mrs Earle recalled, 'and would have liked to have asked me but explained that already there were too many women and too few men. There and then we decided that I should go as a man. Maureen was only too willing to help, as was Louis Chiron the former famous racing motorist.

'Louis and his wife Didi were invited to the party and they were also great practical jokers. He promised to "take me in hand".

' "First of all," he said, "we'll have to take you to Nice and get you a man's wig," as I had to have something to cover my long blonde hair. Because I didn't have much time he suggested that he drive me there in my lunch hour because when I finished working the shops were all shut. You can imagine driving to Nice from the palace, getting fitted and driving back all in two hours. When I got back, shaking, I turned to Louis and said: "Now I know why you were world champion." '

From one of the male dancers at the casino she borrowed a black suit because he was the only man they could find who was tall and thin. Chiron lent shoes, and socks, shirt and jacket came from the dancer.

'It was summer time and I was very tanned so Didi insisted on my taking off my ring and with make-up erased the white mark around my finger. They were so thorough that they made me file down my finger nails. The final touch was a pair of slightly tinted glasses and sticking on a stubbly sort of beard.

'We arrived at the dinner a bit early and I still remember our hostess coming up to me and saying, "You really make a very attractive man—I could go for you myself," ' Phyllis Earle continued.

They had all decided that Phyllis was to be introduced as a Polish pianist cousin of Didi Chiron's and as she was of Polish extraction and this was the International Chopin year it all slotted into place. This also made it conceivable why the Pole did not speak English and only spoke a few words of German, which Phyllis could manage. Princess Grace was the only other one there who knew German, but it was not really sufficient to test Phyllis.

The Prince had, in fact, his own private joke by arriving at the party with the Princess dressed as a down-and-out seaman. As their hostess opened the door she took one step back before she realised that it was the Prince.

Phyllis Earle took up the story:

'As the only "stranger" present I was presented to the Princess. I bent over her hand, being careful not to kiss it, clicked my heels together and she passed on. I stood there by myself because, of course, no one could speak to me. Over drinks I did hear the Prince say in French to Louis, "Your cousin, he's a little bit on the effeminate side." And Louis replying, "Well, yes, but you know how it is with these musical people." '

They all sat down to dinner. The first course was clear soup with noodles. Louis noticed that a few got caught in his 'cousin's' beard, but worse it had begun to peel off. Pretending he was giving the musician a pat on the cheek he pushed it back into place.

'All the time the Princess was smiling at me and trying to put me at my ease. Leaning towards me at the table she said in her best German: "Die Suppe ist gut," and then aside to her neighbour because I didn't answer, "Maybe he doesn't like soup," ' Phyllis continued.

Suddenly the conspirators knew that the joke was getting stale as the whole dinner party was being ruined especially when Princess Grace whispered to her hostess: 'This young man is spoiling everything. You should have warned us that we would not be alone. The Chirons should not have brought their cousin with them.'

From across the table Louis Chiron said: 'Don't you know who it is? Don't you know who this is sitting next to me?'

The Princess left her seat and went round to have a good look. Even then she did not recognise her secretary. Finally Phyllis Blum took off her glasses. The Princess screamed with joy and took her face in her hands and kissed it. She admitted that the make-up and everything had been 'absolutely fantastic'.

On another occasion it was the Princess who dressed up. Alexandre, the hairdresser, had sent her a brown wig from Paris so that she could wear it when travelling incognito during her trips abroad.

One evening when they had invited some friends to see a film the Princess put it on and was introduced to everyone as a friend of the Princess. Madame Banac, a delightful elderly lady and mother of Vane Ivanovic, the consul general for Monaco in London, was perturbed as she thought that it was improper of the guest to be wearing one of the Princess's dresses. Prince Rainier entered into the whole spirit of the affair and kissed Princess Grace's hand. It was some time before anyone guessed the identity of the flirty young woman with the lovely brown hair and Wedgwood blue eyes.

The Prince has a collection of practical jokes which all his friends send him from various countries. When their old friend the actress Jessie Royce Landis went to dinner once the Prince bent tenderly over her and pinned a red rose on her bosom. Miss Landis was enchanted and bent to smell it when out popped a plastic snake.

On another occasion when guests were invited to dinner there seemed to be a particularly bumbling old butler who bumped into things and mumbled to himself all the time. This, of course, was Prince Rainier.

Princess Grace can also be one of the most amusing of guests. Once she is in the mood she can tell stories in every kind of dialect as well as any professional. No one who has heard her can ever forget how she tells stories in the Jewish idiom and reduces her audience to near hysteria with laughter.

All the family have this gift of laughter when things get out of hand, but none more than Princess Grace. As Fleur Cowles remembered: 'When she was staying in Spain last Easter with us at our restored Spanish castle she was followed by the police, the Guardia Civil, the riot squad, photographers and mobs. She viewed it with a detached calm when in public and with peals of laughter when safely private in our garden.'

Among the intimate staff of the palace there is a freedom of manner. When Nana King once pointed out to Princess Grace, the minute before she was to make an official appearance on the balcony of the palace, that her petticoat was showing she slipped into the next room and reappeared in a few seconds.

'It's in the Chinese vase,' she murmured out of the corner of her mouth.

Christmas in Monaco is a tremendous occasion as it combines the best of American tradition with the best of French. There is the tinsel and fun of the New World balanced with the religious aspect of the Roman Catholic Church. The Princess gives over the entire month of December to prepare for their official and private Christmas.

There are 700 Christmas cards to be sent out, 700 parcels for the children of Monaco, parcels for the children of the palace staff and Red Cross parcels for the aged. In the palace there are two women busy on knitting machines making sweaters for the staff children.

Four big Christmas trees are brought in which the Princess and her children decorate. There is one in the middle of the twin seventeenth-century staircase in the court of honour in front of the palace, one in the formal living-room where official guests are received, the family one in the children's playroom and one in the servants' dining-room.

It also means wrapping hundreds of Christmas parcels and filling the family stockings. In the Kelly family the stockings were always hung on the chimney piece, but as Prince Rainier was brought up by an English nanny his was hung at the end of the bed. The family agreed the British way simply because it was also a way for the Prince and Princess to get another hour's sleep when the children were young.

After Midnight Mass there is always a buffet supper in the formal living-room. Close friends are invited to this with a handful of officers or ratings from any American warship that may be in port.

All this was too much one Christmas for Phyllis Blum and Maureen King. They concocted to enliven Christmas Eve in their own special way. They decided to give themselves to the Prince and Princess in a Christmas stocking! In telling the story today Phyllis Earle remembered:

'It would have looked very funny if we had not gone to the midnight service in the chapel so we sat way back. All our plans had been made several days before. The women in the *lingerie* had sewn up a huge red Christmas stocking, big enough to contain even me and I am 5 feet 10½ inches and Maureen who is 5 feet 6 inches.

'On this particular Christmas the captains of the ships in the 6th fleet of the American Navy had been invited to the Mass and supper and the sailors from one of the ship's choirs were going to sing carols after the Mass, serenading the party as they walked back to the palace for the supper.

'As Maureen and I left the church just before the end of the service, they immediately thought that this was the signal that the service was over and began singing *Silent Night*. We almost jumped on them to shush them up but fortunately inside the chapel the singing was so loud that they did not hear the false start.'

Back in the formal sitting-room the girls were slid into the stocking which was propped against the tree, nearby the roaring log fire. The top was covered with white cotton wool and the only air they got was through peepholes that had been carefully placed in the stocking.

As the royal party entered the room there was a cry of surprise from the Princess who later confessed to the culprits that she thought it could only have come from Aristotle Onassis.

Tied to the top of the stocking was a note which read something like 'We thought hard what to give you but as you have everything we decided to give ourselves.' But the Princess was too busy with her guests to look. It was not until the stocking began to bulge and wobble that anyone was suspicious and then, of course, the joke exploded. No one laughed harder than Princess Grace. It was just the kind of thing she might have done herself.

All these pranks are naturally kept within the family circle or close friends but they do disclose that this is a very intimate and happy family. Although they occasionally join it at St Moritz, New York, London, Paris or Sardinia, Prince Rainier and Princess Grace have no permanent place in the smart international jet set. They prefer to work hard and play hard within the concepts of their own world.

Thirty-two

Will Princess Grace ever act in a feature movie again? This is the question that has been asked so many times over the past twenty years.

It all began when Prince Rainier went to Hollywood after their engagement and unbeknown to his fiancée made the announcement that she would not be making any more pictures.

'Now what would make him want to say that?' Miss Kelly is reported to have said when she heard the news.

The other interested party was of course M.G.M., who still had an option on a further picture from her. When Grace Kelly had called on her agent Jay Kanter to tell him of her good news he immediately asked how it would affect her working arrangements. As he explained:

'She said, "I guess it will have a rather profound effect on my working arrangements." I got the message, but many still hoped.'

Finally M.G.M. did waive her contract on the grounds that had she been going to continue her career they would have had first option within the length of time covered by her contract.

A month later it was reported in the *Daily Sketch*: 'Her Hollywood studio has stopped Grace's £530-a-week salary because "she does not feel like returning". A studio official said; "She might come back in a couple of years. We'll wait." '

Hollywood had left the door open. 'I never say never and I never say always,' Grace Kelly had said enigmatically and thus a hope still flickered in the hearts of some movie directors . . . and one in particular, Alfred Hitchcock.

During the next few years after her marriage it was well known that her agents, M.C.A., had often sent her scripts with the hope of luring her back.

It had already been reported that His Serene Highness had 'desired' that the Princess turn down a Hollywood offer to play the Virgin Mary in *King of Kings*.

It was Alfred Hitchcock who nearly pulled off the picture deal of the decade. In 1962 after weeks of telephone calls and letters, Mr Hitchcock had put the idea to Princess Grace that he would like her to play the title role in a film to be made called *Marnie*.

It was a strange story of a beautiful, poised, bewitching girl who substitutes passion and love with safe cracking and lying. It was a part that Hollywood's Grace Kelly could have played superbly and Monaco's Princess Grace even better. It required enormous sensitivity and style.

For many weeks there had been negotiations between Mr Hitchcock and the Princess. They had not only an intelligent working rapport but there had been a cosy friendship between the two families over many years.

The plan was that the film would be made during the two-month summer vacation of Prince Rainier and Princess Grace in America which had already been planned. Hitchcock had offered to find a suitable location so that it could be a holiday combined with work and Prince Rainier would most likely be present during part of the 'shooting'.

Princess Grace's fee, according to Hitchcock, would have been around £357,000 plus a percentage of the profits.

When the final commitment had to be made Mr Hitchcock went himself to Monaco. With superb finesse Princess Grace let the producer tell Prince Rainier about his plans as she knew that he was a man of tremendous tact, wisdom and selling power.

It may also have been a much more womanly wile in that she was making it easy for Prince Rainier to say 'no' to Hitchcock rather than to refuse her. Everyone, including Prince Rainier, knew how much she longed to make this film that summer.

It was on 19 March 1962 that a minor bombshell hit Monaco. Earlier that day Princess Grace had invited four court officials to her study and told them: 'Gentlemen, I have news for you.' She then proceeded to tell them that she had accepted an offer to appear in a film to be made during the summer.

Within an hour the news was relayed all round the world. No one, least of all the Princess, could have foreseen the chaos that followed. The message read as follows:

'*A spokesman for the Prince of Monaco announced today that Princess Grace has accepted to appear during her summer vacation in a motion picture for Mister Alfred Hitchcock to be made in the United States stop The Princess has previously starred in three films for Mister Hitchcock bracket Dial M for Murder Rear Window and Catch a Thief bracket stop The film to start in late summer is based on a suspense novel by the English writer Winston Graham stop It is understood that Prince Rainier will most likely be present during part of the film making depending on his schedule and that Princess Grace will return to Monaco by the beginning of November stop*'

What was not included in the message given out by the Palace Press Office was the fact that the Princess had intended to donate all monies received to her favourite children's charity.

Looking back at the whole episode after fourteen years, what the Princess did with the proceeds was surely her business and no one else's. But at the time, had the news that she intended to use it for her special children's charities in Monaco been made patently clear, it might have had a better effect there.

As it was, when the news broke in the Principality the people were stunned. They felt abandoned, deceived and shocked. Into what should have been a joyous summer experience they read all kinds of sinister motives. Why was their Princess going back to Hollywood? Was the marriage in danger? Why had they not been consulted on such an important step? It was reduced to such basic trivia as declarations of horror that their Princess might be required in the script to kiss another man.

Princess Grace was appalled at the reaction to such an extent that she was physically ill. First and foremost she was a Princess of Monaco and it hurt her deeply when she heard of the bad effect it could have, not only on her own position in Monaco but, because of the bad publicity, on an already delicate situation which existed between France and Monte Carlo. But what worried her most of all was the suggestion that she was abandoning her role as wife and mother and preferring instead to return to a Hollywood career.

Hitchcock was consulted, then suddenly, while the air was still thick with speculation, it was all over. From the producer came a terse announcement that 'his busy schedule ' would not allow him to shoot during the Princess's summer vacation.

A simultaneous announcement: 'The Princess regrets . . .' was also given from the palace.

At the time it was speculated that it was President de Gaulle, the Pope, or even Prince Rainier who had persuaded the Princess to abandon her plans. It was none of these. It was the wishes of the three thousand-odd Monegasques who made her change her mind. She would never let them down.

When asked recently if she had ever regretted her decision she answered non-committally in a voice void of emotion: 'I don't look back. When people are maturing they all have certain things to conquer and we have to face our own inadequacies. The one thing to do is to improve and grow as a human being and this is what I have tried to do.'

Twelve years after the *Marnie* fracas, in April 1974, Princess Grace stood before an audience of 2,800 in the Lincoln Centre in New York at a gala tribute paid to seventy-four-year-old Alfred Hitchcock.

In a night loaded with emotion and nostalgia Princess Grace had flown over from Monaco to be there along with the other stars who had gained fame through his loving direction and superb craftsmanship.

She stood there, honeyed hair and white chiffon. There was not a person not affected by her presence. The women wondering how she kept her flawless beauty. The men so regretful that she had ever left Hollywood. And the police guard affectionately calling her 'Kelly'.

The Princess led the procession of stars on to the stage. In a short tribute she said:

'Alfred Hitchcock took the thriller—once thought to be second-class entertainment—and made it an art. He is the master of suspense.'

She also brought ripples of unexpected laughter when she reminded the audience that when she arrived on his set for *To Catch a Thief* wearing a sensual gold lamé dress Hitchcock had whistled, 'There's hills in them thar gold, Grace.'

In 1963 Princess Grace did in fact play herself for the first time after her marriage in a film which was made in Monaco for Columbia Broadcasting Service's television.

She was still smarting after the *Marnie* hubbub but when it was pointed out that this was for Monaco she agreed. The film, which was called *A Look at Monaco*, was in fact the forerunner of several similar films which have since been made over the last years and shown all over the world.

Writer Cynthia Lindsay was brought in to supervise the dialogue with Bill Fryer as producer and that great cameraman Lionel ('Curly') Lynden.

Such was the impact of the six weeks she spent working on the film that Cynthia Lindsay today speaks with a memory packed with minutiae. We walked and talked about it, drinking champagne 'splits' at the Château Marmont Hotel in Los Angeles where she now lives.

Prince Rainier and Princess Grace opened their palace—and hearts— to the American television team. There were evening dinner parties and screening of old American films. At one of these parties Princess Grace wore a sheath of beige chiffon encrusted with silver sequins. She looked fabulous. As the guests arrived she told Fry: 'I'd better put on my glasses to see who's here.'

One of the most vivid memories Mrs Lindsay has is Princess Grace's passion for children . . . all children . . . and animals.

'When we arrived at the children's home near the palace (Princess Grace changed the name from orphanage) the children plus their dog called Mélange all ran around her with the great sense of here comes a friend.

'One little girl in an overwhelming burst of affection kissed her and perched a doll's hat on her head. The Mother Superior of the home immediately removed it. Princess Grace gently took the hat, pretended to study it and said, "But Ma Mère, it's so pretty," and put it back on again.'

During the school play-breaks Princess Grace had noticed the endearing scene of the children all sitting on their potties gossiping, reading or just thinking. She thought that this would make a charming sequence in the film especially as all the chamber pots were a different colour. She mentioned this to the producer, who did not want to film it in case it was offensive.

'But this is an honest part of the day,' the Princess insisted. And so it was filmed and was surely the most captivating shot in the whole film.

Princess Grace was also concerned that the image of Monaco was right. Despite all the enchantment and flowers of the Principality she and the Prince wanted to portray it as a place run by serious people very seriously.

At the beginning of the filming everyone was slightly apprehensive about 'Curly' Lynden, who has since died. One of the great cameramen in the business, he was also a notable drinker. Not only did 'Curly' Lynden rise to the occasion but also became a lifetime friend of Prince

Rainier and Princess Grace. It was a question of three professionals recognising and respecting another.

Some time later 'Curly' Lynden went back to the South of France to make another film. The Prince and Princess invited the entire company to the palace for dinner. He was asked to stand with the Prince and Princess in the receiving line and introduce the rest of the company. It was just one of those thoughtful gestures that makes Princess Grace the special person that she is.

When *A Look at Monaco* was made Prince Albert and Princess Caroline were still small children and were sometimes reluctant to take part in it.

During the working hours making the film the Princess was always prompt and professional and only once did she 'fluff' a line. For some of the crew, who were all decidedly nervous, it was a little difficult to remember to always address the Princess as 'Your Serene Highness'.

When the first scene began director Douglas Heyes was so overcome when he saw the beautiful blonde in front of the cameras that he said, 'Now, Your Highness, honey . . . '

'Princess Grace has a decent respect for herself as a human being,' Cynthia Lindsay said. 'She never tells a good story about herself. Rather she makes a light kind of joke. Although she is less rigid than other highly placed women, she can turn on authority, if necessary, very quietly. It just couldn't happen that anyone could go too far with her. By one quiet, almost invisible look, she can stop any nonsense— from adults or children. Actually she really looks astonished and *you* become surprised and wonder. She has a kind of "this couldn't be happening" look and the other person responds immediately.'

There was one scene in the Prince's zoo, which is open to the public every afternoon. Prince Rainier was wandering round with a chimp on one shoulder and the children following. Prince Albert began to imitate the way the chimpanzee walked and Princess Caroline just looked and said: 'Look at Albie's little bare behind,' which is exactly what the chimp had at that time.

The director then turned to her and said: 'Now you make like a monkey.' But she was not to be made a fool of. Even then Princess Caroline had her own mind.

She just looked at the director very solemnly and said: 'No, I am not going to. I don't like your games and I am not going to play them,' and walked off the set.

Instead she insisted on taking Mrs Lindsay to the small kitchen off the dining-room where there was a lion and two cubs curled up in a cage which had been placed near the warmth of the stove. She was terribly proud as she pointed out the cubs which she said she was 'helping to bring up'.

The small girl stood and looked at the big cat for some time then sighed: 'Oh, Mrs Lindsay, wouldn't you adore to sleep with that lion.'

'I said I'd kind of like to know whether he would like to sleep with me first,' Cynthia Lindsay remembered.

Princess Caroline answered: 'Think of the cold nights and you could put your feet in and out and all cosy and warm and you could cuddle up.'

At that moment a lioness came out of the back and Princess Caroline asked: 'Is that his wife?'

'Probably,' came the answer.

Then pushing her small eager face against the bars of the cage she said: 'What a fortunate lion you are to have such a lovely wife.'

The film was shot with enormous warmth and gaiety and happiness. When the film unit arrived at the palace the first day Princess Grace took them on a small tour to show them what she and the Prince wished to be included in the film.

In the hall of mirrors the producer thought how wonderful it would be to have this beautiful woman reflected seventy-three times. Cynthia Lindsay made a note about the throne, the hall of mirrors and finally the subterranean tunnels which used to be the palace's own aqueduct.

After the tour she found she had lost it and was horrified if one of the security guards should have found it. It read: 'Shoot Princess in Hall of Mirrors and what shall we do with the throne?'

English racing driver Graham Hill has also had a happy experience in filming with Princess Grace. In his brilliant career he has won the Monte Carlo Rally five times. He related:

'I wrote to the Prince and Princess and asked them whether they would agree to take part in a film that was being made about myself called *Graham* which was to be shown on British television.

'We had a meeting after the Grand Prix in 1973 in their garden by the swimming pool where we had a short chat. I was most impressed that she was so knowledgeable about the Grand Prix ... very observant in discussing the start for instance. The interviewer talked with Prince Rainier and Princess Grace separately and then we just sat around and chatted and they filmed it.

'One of the most charming things about her is that at the reception after the race for a lot of officials and dignitaries she is always there and circulates remembering everybody's name. She always seems to be pleased to see them and is very frank and open.

'It seems that America is forming its own aristocracy that has nothing to do with line of blood. It is a very young country and in a few years time these will be the aristocrats of America. They must be very proud of Princess Grace that she has brought into one of the royal families of Europe this frank and refreshing way and opened it right up. I think it is very nice for the Prince to have somebody like her. She is so in touch ...

'The one thing that surprised me is that after the official prize giving at the Hotel de Paris which ends about 2 a.m. or something like that a lot of us English types all flock down to a little bar called the Tip Top. It has nothing except a bar but everyone goes there for a plate of spaghetti. And she knew this and commented on it, I was so surprised that she knew . . .'

The Princess is revered at the Grand Prix parties because of her concern for her guests. One year there was a big dance, at which as usual she danced better than anybody. Suddenly there was a signal to one of the Italian drivers that the party was over and instead of there being a formal withdrawal he started a conga line and the entire group from all the nations who had been invited joined in and simply conga'd through the door and disappeared out into the night.

Standing enjoying it all until the last guest had disappeared were Prince Rainier and Princess Grace.

Mrs Lindsay had taken her own ten-year-old daughter with her to the South of France and on hearing this Princess Grace invited her to the palace to play with Princess Caroline. She had brought with her as a gift some small dolls which were welcomed. Previously Princess Grace had spent a lot of time with Princess Caroline making shoe boxes into beds and using cut-outs and pasteboard and any little thing that was around. Happily the dolls just fitted.

When Cynthia Lindsay's daughter left, well brought up as she was, she curtsied as she would have done to anyone older, and thanked for a lovely time. Once they were outside the door she asked her mother:

'When are we going to meet the Princess?'

'But darling, you just have,' Mrs Lindsay answered.

'Oh, that cosy lady . . . was *she* the Princess?' the child replied.

Thirty-three

'I've had an interesting and wonderful life, and I like to think I have made it so. If I've had unhappy moments, I've probably made that so too. We do it to ourselves,' Princess Grace recently said.

In this sentence is much of her philosophy for living. She abhors self-pity and places loyalty high on her list of qualifications. Friends who have known her right through from those early Hollywood days find her totally unchanged.

'Grace has the capacity for friendship and once you gain her trust she never lets you down,' said John Foreman, who has known her for twenty-five years.

'She is a real friend and she takes that situation seriously. She never says "no" when a "yes" would be helpful or give pleasure,' said Fleur Cowles, who was first introduced to her in 1950 by Cary Grant.

There are lesser known friends, too, who have experienced the depth of her friendship. In Monte Carlo recently an elderly English woman, Lady Doverdale, died. But she did not die alone. Princess Grace sat with her for almost two days.

The point was not that Lady Doverdale had lived as a revered citizen of Monaco for many years—it was more personal. She had no one of her own to be with her so the Princess filled the gap, sitting with her and comforting her—day and night.

Most of Princess Grace's friends are scattered round the world and can only be cherished on her many travels. She has her own captivating way of 'keeping in touch'. On her many trips abroad whenever she sees something that reminds her of someone ... a handkerchief for Edith Head, a scarf for Vera Maxwell, a crazy invention for David Niven ... she buys it and sends it off.

'These things are so spontaneous, so individual,' Edith Head observed. 'For instance, she knows that I collect handkerchiefs as she used to collect shoes and gloves. Attached to a beautiful lace one she sent me from Africa once was a little note, "Here is a pretty for you." A lot of people would write, "Here is a pretty thing for you," but Grace has a very special way of expressing herself and here she uses pretty as a noun.'

Near neighbours and friends at Cap d'Antibes are the David Nivens and Paul Gallicos. David Niven's friendship goes right back to the Hollywood days but he and Prince Rainier share more than that. They both have a zany sense of humour and are constantly playing gags on each other.

When the Prince and Princess went to dinner once at the Nivens' villa Lo Scoglitto—the little rock—they were confronted by a grave and consummate butler who wore with ponderous aplomb a startling ankle-length frock coat, originally white and many sizes too large. The butler had acquired his summer uniform from the milkman and could not be persuaded to remove it even for royal guests. Princess Grace thought he was the doctor and could not understand why he was serving dinner. It was just another Niven joke.

Virginia and Paul Gallico's friendship with Prince Rainier and Princess Grace is a close and meaningful one. One senses that here are two couples in the same happiness stage and wish to share it with each other. In addition to this, the men have a common bond in their love of animals and circuses.

Friends are constantly amazed that Princess Grace finds time to make special presents for them in a life already packed with too many busy hours. For Paul Gallico's birthday once she made him a tapestry in the Leo sign, which is his birthday, and for his wife Virginia she embroidered a cushion, copying the famous medieval tapestry *La Dame à la Licorne* (the lady with the unicorn) now in the Cluny Museum in Paris. It is kept today in the dining-room at the Gallico's house in Antibes. Fleur Cowles has a piece of Princess Grace's embroidery ... one of her own delicate flower pictures transferred into petit point.

Perhaps the most beguiling proof of her friendship for Paul Gallico is a small book called *Manx Mouse* which Gallico wrote and dedicated 'For Grace'.

Manx Mouse is the charming consequence of Princess Grace taking lessons in ceramics. When she told Gallico about this at dinner one night he promptly said:

'I want to give you your first commission. I want you to make me a mouse.'

The next day the Princess went back to her class in Monaco and began making 'a teensy weensy' mouse. She gave it big ears and a skinny little tail which it held in its minute hands. She wanted it to be grey with pink ears. The teacher pointed to some colouring 'over there' and Princess Grace mixed it up and applied it to her clay before firing. When the mouse came out of the oven it turned out to be bright blue and the tail had fallen off in the firing. It was the most pathetic mouse and she decided there and then to make him another one.

Some weeks went by and Paul Gallico had a birthday which is quite often shared with Prince Rainier and Princess Grace. She arrived with the funny little broken mouse.

'It is only a small mouse,' she said as she put it on his plate. 'I am so ashamed because he lost his tail, he is the wrong colour and everything's wrong about him.'

Paul Gallico insisted that he did not want another mouse.

'No,' she said, 'I made you another mouse.'

'Well, this funny little one will be Manx Mouse and the new one Mrs Mouse,' replied the writer who gained a kind of immortality with his enchanting book *The Snow Goose*.

Today Manx Mouse and Mrs Mouse sit on his desk, together with a small silver one given by Prince Rainier, where he sits writing his books every morning.

Nor does the story finish here. The following year for her birthday Princess Grace received a book *Manx Mouse* (Victor Gollancz) written by Paul Gallico for children of all ages. The book begins:

'There was once rather an extraordinary old ceramist who lived in the village of Buntingdowndale in the heart of England. Ceramics is the art of making pottery into tiles or dishes or small glazed figures. What was unusual about him is that he only made mice.'

Princess Grace is much too sensitive and realistic not to realise that in her royal position she has power to make people happy or to disappoint them. For this reason she is, perhaps unconsciously, extremely careful in keeping any promise she makes to a child. It may take years to fulfil, but her promise is a bond.

When Virginia Gallico's daughter by a previous marriage, Ludmilla von Falz-Fein, was a child of eleven, she first became aware of the Princess through the parents' friendship. From the age of six she had always sewed, first making flower-patterned tapestry cushions and then developing into fabric collages filled with mystery and fantasy.

'One day when you have enough of those pictures for an exhibition I will come and open it,' the Princess told the child. By 1973 Ludmilla Nova, as she now called herself, was not only a promising young actress in London but had enough collages to give her first exhibition. Remembering the Princess's promise she wrote and received back two dates on which she was free to come to London and open it.

The result was two-fold in that she had kept her promise to a child but more important, Princess Grace realised that by her presence an exhibition that may have been lost in the limbo of London's countless exhibitions was given maximum Press coverage.

On the opening night there was a crush in the gallery as Princess Grace and Princess Caroline arrived and a radiant Ludmilla went out on to the pavement to greet them. She was wearing the stage costume that she wore twice daily as one of the bel canto singers in *Babes in the Wood* at the London Palladium and the picture made every newspaper next day.

The following day Princess Grace had lunch with the Gallico family and when Ludmilla arrived home from the show there was a small box on the stairway. Inside was a pretty flower-shaped piece of jewellery in gold with a turquoise centre to be worn on a fine chain. With it was a happy appreciative note 'From Grace'. Again it was a very special choice of gift as Ludmilla signs her name (even on her printed cheque book) with a small flower dotting the 'i' in Ludmilla. The gold flower was an exact copy and had been made by a jeweller in Monte Carlo.

Princess Grace's influence on Ludmilla is profound. Ludmilla sat amid bundles of materials in her studio in Belgravia which was once a garage and told me about it.

'In this modern world women like her are to be admired. She is so disciplined. I don't know how she fits in as much as she does in a day. She once told me, "Never stand when you can sit down." But she is so feminine and graceful and doesn't mind wearing gloves to go out shopping, or enjoying flowers and doing tapestries.

'In show business people look at you if you bring out your sewing and say, "You must be mad," but in fact I have watched Princess Grace do just that and when I first started in the business I thought, "Well, there's nothing wrong with it if she does it and it became part of me by just watching her.'

For Easter one year Princess Grace made Ludmilla a white ceramic Easter egg topped off with her own tiny signature flower. The egg divided in two and inside one half was her Easter greeting. Virginia Gallico also received an egg which opened to reveal a tiny fantasy bird amid a personal message.

It was the Gallicos, too, who suggested to the Prince that he enter his Dion Bouton 1903 in the London to Brighton veteran car rally in 1968. The Gallico family went to England ahead of the Grimaldi family and did a dry-run in three hours.

On the morning of the run only Scotland Yard and the Royal Automobile Club were aware of their celebrity contestants. In the first car was Prince Rainier, Princess Grace and Princess Caroline and Prince Albert. Following behind was the Gallico family.

Princess Grace who looked fabulous muffled up for the part in a thick coat and a large fur hat had organised a picnic to be eaten en route and the whole party had booked in to stay the night in Brighton.

The Prince was making such good time on the route that, despite the fact that for part of the journey Princess Grace was so cold that she transferred to the Gallicos' car, he arrived in one hour twenty minutes.

To celebrate they decided to have the picnic in the hotel suite. There was a funny moment when the hotel manager opened the door to ask what time Their Serene Highnesses would like lunch served to find everyone sitting on the floor eating their picnic amid much laughter.

The whole outing was topped off with a visit to the celebrated *Lanes* and the return trip to London on the *Brighton Belle* singing American camp songs.

One of Princess Grace's closest friends is Vera Maxwell, the distinguished dress designer in New York. Theirs is typical of the lasting quality in Princess Grace's friendships as it began in 1955. They had both been given an award by Neiman Marcus for their contribution to fashion, and had travelled to Dallas to receive their accolades.

Sitting in her unique little office above the belting traffic of New York's Third Avenue, and surrounded by bolts of material and fashion drawings, Vera Maxwell talked of this friendship which has spanned twenty-one years.

In their own special way these two women have the same kind of elegance. Vera Maxwell with her porcelain skin, grey hair pulled back into an unobtrusive little knob, face void of make-up, eyes clear, frank, alert. Her artist's smock becomes chic because of the way she wears it.

'I was old enough to be her mother and here we were thrown together in the same hotel suite. We each had our own bedroom and shared the same drawing-room. There were wonderful parties going on and I watched at the sheer genius of this girl of twenty-three, then at the height of her film career, in the way she handled people. There were flashy smiles and mini actresses around but I never once saw Grace give a false smile.

'I remember at the time thinking what a remarkable young woman. Not because she was a supreme actress but just because she was such a marvellous person. We invariably left the hurly burly of the parties and went upstairs to our rooms with a glass of milk.

'The real bond came when I discovered that she liked Shakespeare's sonnets. We discovered that we both carried copies with us, the only difference was that Grace knew many by heart. I was so impressed by this young girl reciting Shakespearean sonnets that one of my first gifts to her was a tiny very old copy of them and I always think of her in this connection. I am a great reader of eighteenth-century literature and we also had a common interest there although I think she only has time to read biographies now.'

Despite being a dress designer Vera Maxwell has a healthy respect for Princess Grace's squirrel hoarding of her clothes.

'I think it is heavenly that she keeps clothes and the last time we met I said, "Don't throw away anything you have of Zuckerman—a well-known American designer of the fifties. You must give them to the Smithsonian."'

Princess Grace's shoe closet is also a cupboard filled with memories. At Roc Agel every summer she brings out and wears the blue and white sandals that she had made in a village during her stay in Africa for the filming of *Mogambo* over twenty years ago.

For many years Vera Maxwell had a small flat in Monaco and regularly went there and whenever Princess Grace is in New York she invariably stays in the small guest unit in Vera Maxwell's apartment. Here she can have complete privacy which is more difficult when staying in New York hotels, where she is constantly recognised and stared at.

For her fortieth birthday Princess Grace decided to hold a Scorpio party and invite as many friends as she could who had been born under the same sign.

She has a blind confidence in the stars because, as a struggling young actress before her climb to movie stardom and later her role as a royal princess, it was all foretold in her horoscope.

In his book *Astrology and Prediction* (B. T. Batsford) Eric Russell defines the Scorpionic character thus:

'It is, if anything more prone to schizophrenia than Geminian. Mars rules it and Mars can indicate either great strength or great cruelty; it is watery and fixed, indicating great possibilities of great depth of character. In sum, the Scorpionic native could either be a person of immense will-power and ambition, sensitive but forceful, or a person delighting in his power over others and using that power sadistically. All astrologers agree in crediting the Scorpionic native with great sensuality, which can amount to eroticism.'

It is intriguing to find not only Princess Grace but Martin Luther, Mata Hari, Queen Elizabeth the Queen Mother, Goethe, Marie Antoinette, Maurice Chevalier, Prince Charles, Billy Graham, Madame Curie, Katharine Hepburn and Robert Kennedy were all born under the sign of Scorpio.

Guests were sent a crimson red invitation in the form of a horoscope reading.

Day for travel ... journey to Monte Carlo is indicated. You are being invited by H.S.H. Princess Grace of Monaco, High Scorpio, to come to her Scorpio party in Monaco. Miss this at your own risk.

Love . . . Venus enters your sign

Romance is favoured and may become highly inspirational by mid-November.

Social Activities . . . You may meet many interesting people who might influence your career.

    —Saturday November 15, 9 p.m.
                       Dinner and dancing
                       Hotel Hermitage, Monte Carlo.
    —Sunday   November 16, 12.30 p.m.
                       Brunch
                       Hotel de Paris swimming pool.

Health . . . If you survive these two events you are a very healthy person and can look forward to an untroubled old age.

Advice . . . Ladies Do . . . not ignore the colours of your sign . . . red, black or white only

                  Dinner jackets propitious for gentlemen
                  For brunch: Studied Casualness.

Hotel de Paris wholly converted for Scorpian occupancy. Your private nest awaits you ... Courtesy of the High Scorpio. Other signs married to Scorpians tolerated.

It is easy to spot whose hand was behind the preparation of this invitation and the many giggles that must have ensued during its conception.

The dinner was splendidly festive in the newly decorated dining-room of the Hermitage. Because I believe that most people love to know what the 'Beautiful People' eat in festive mood here is the menu.

Coulibiac de Saumon
Consommé Chaud aux Profiterolles
...

Coeur de Carolais
Bouquetière de Legumes
Fond d'Artichaut Florentine
Yorkshire Pudding
...

Plateau de Fromages
...

Crêpes Suzette
...

Corbeille de Friandises
...

Tasse Moka.

And the wines even more splendid:

Chevalier Montrachet 1964
Chateau Margaux 1945
Pommery & Greno Brut Rose 1961
Cognac, Liqueurs
Marc de Champagne.

Among the notable Scorpians present was Richard Burton who had just given the Cartier diamond to Elizabeth Taylor—this was to be its first official wearing. The story behind the delivery of the diamond to Monaco is worthy of a movie script especially when viewed in the context of their on-and-off marriage.

The actual sale of the stone had been completed in the first-class section of a Pan American aircraft in mid-Atlantic between a representative from Cartier's and Aaron Frosch the American lawyer of the Burtons. This had been done to avoid American or British taxation.

When the news that Elizabeth intended to wear her diamond to Princess Grace's birthday party reached Monaco a whole security plan had to be put into operation. First Miss Taylor had to be reassured that she would not have to pay any sales tax if she brought the jewel into Monaco. Then she and Burton requested, to the French préfecture at Nice, for a police escort to accompany the real stone and a copy which they always carried with them.

There was a slight hitch when it was discovered that no police escort is allowed for material goods but only if a life is in danger. The French police also pointed out that they could only be responsible for the jewel until it reached the Monaco border and then the Prince's police would have to take over. All this in the name of friendship—Elizabeth Taylor and Princess Grace have been friends for many years—and publicity value was arranged even down to producing two safes in which to keep the real stone and the fake.

As Elizabeth Taylor entered the restaurant all eyes were riveted on her bosom where the diamond quivered between two white cushions of flesh, smooth as satin.

During the afternoon of the party she had been playing ping-pong with Burton. The match became quite intense. Richard thought he could beat her and naturally Elizabeth decided to win. In the heat of the game he had said: 'If you win this match I'll buy you another diamond.'

So with that incentive Elizabeth naturally won and Richard kept his promise by presenting her with a second diamond. Only this one was about 1/10 carat, the smallest diamond that can be set in a ring.

During the evening when asked to show her diamond Elizabeth said: 'You want to see my latest diamond?' She then showed everyone the ring.

Princess Grace wore an emerald and ruby ring and quipped: 'I like to know which is my starboard and port side.'

Princess Grace, who is now forty-five years old, makes no effort to conceal her age.

'It's cosy and not so bad,' she says.

She rates thirty-five as the best age for a woman simply because 'she is old enough to know a lot of things, yet still young and fit'.

Thirty-four

The royal palace at Monaco with its two hundred or so rooms is a kind of village within a village. It has a distinctly medieval flavour about it not only in the charming buildings and courtyards but in the almost feudal set-up of the palace staff which number 150.

Within the palace many families of the senior members of the staff live in their own apartments. There is the Prince's aide-de-camp and gentleman in waiting, the head of the Carabinier unit, the private secretaries of the Prince and Princess, the palace chaplain, majordomo, head butler, ladies-in-waiting as well as the normal living-in staff in any household of this stature.

A *régisseur* takes care of the palace logistics—the store rooms, laundry, food buying and so on. All the household bills are paid by the secretary to the Prince and his cabinet handle budgetary matters. One of the most important additions Princess Grace made to the domestic staff early in her marriage was to appoint an English housekeeper, Miss Christine Plaistow. She had formerly been a guide but grew into the household duties and has remained there for the last fifteen years.

Like most husbands the Prince takes a cursory interest in the household accounts and when they become too high there is a cutting down. In most Continental households of any size the *châtelaine* keeps a small pad and pencil beside her place at the table in which she writes down any remarks about the food. This is then forwarded to the chef, but in the Monaco palace the Prince has continued this habit from his bachelor days. It is probably true also that along with the notes on the menu are small personal reminders in his busy life.

One of the most handsome decorations in the living-room in the flat in Avenue Foch, which the family used until they moved into their new Paris house last autumn, was in fact a direct result of one of the Prince's economies.

In the remodelling of the apartment the Princess wanted to have a proper fireplace where she could burn logs. The Prince thought that this was too extravagant. Instead she installed an aquamarine ceramic stove which had been buried and dug up in the palace garden. Much of it was missing or broken and with painstaking craftsmanship the potter at the ceramic school repaired it until today it looks perfect, despite the fact that it does not work. As the centre-piece in a blue-green room it is exceedingly handsome.

In the Prince and Princess's own personal quarters at the palace the staff is usually about ten. For everyday work they wear green striped jackets and trousers and red waistcoats with gold buttons. Formal official protocol is rigidly observed in Monaco and for State occasions the staff wear full livery with velvet knee breeches, white silk stockings and buckled shoes. All the staff get one month's holiday a year and are well cared for if they fall ill.

Both the chef and his assistant are French and most of the food is therefore French or Italian but the Princess occasionally manages to persuade the chef to bake American cakes. Her greatest triumph was the day he cheerfully made pumpkin pie from a recipe from one of her own books.

Lunch times are usually busy during the summer season with parties of anything between six to twenty for lunch every day. The menu is simple but delicious with plenty of salads and fresh fruit, and is served at round tables in the tropical garden by the swimming pool. It is a beautiful fragrant setting with orange and lemon trees and splashes of bougainvillaea and other flowering trees. Cages with tropical birds are often set amid the trees, turning it all into a kind of fantasy garden. Now that the children are growing up they often join their parents for these semi-official luncheon parties.

'One thing I enjoy in France is that people take the time to live in a pleasant way,' the Princess has said. 'They are not rushed, not as hurried as in the United States. I think the midday meal when the whole family is together is very pleasant.'

Within the Grimaldi family it is as informal and cosy a life as could be imagined within the confines of a royal household. There is a free flow between parents and children, who come and go as they wish. Instead of being given a stuffy afternoon tea served by a butler, a guest is just as likely during the summer to be offered a Coca-Cola by one of the children.

Early evenings for the Prince and Princess in Monaco are usually taken up with people to be received, exhibitions to visit or projects to be inspected. Prince Rainier usually does not get home from his 'office', which is in one of the towers, until 7.30 and dinner is at 8 p.m. The children often eat earlier simply because there is lots of homework to be done just as in any other French family.

After dinner if the Prince and Princess are alone, she goes to her desk or does one of her hobbies and the Prince looks at television or writes his personal letters. They both try to leave official work behind them but often there are mutual things to be discussed and the work schedule overlaps.

The Princess likes to go to bed at 10.30 and often reads late, but these are rare treats during the busy months. Sleep recharges her strength and all through her life it has been her refuge in times of stress. Today whenever she can she takes a couple of days off and 'gets lost'. Her only concession to age—and she is the youngest looking forty-five-year-old one has ever seen—is that she appears to conserve her energy and sits whenever possible.

Mondays are always busy days for the Princess when she is at the palace because then she does all the housekeeping chores. There is the governor of the palace to be seen, guest lists for the week to be studied as Princess Grace does most of the placing of guests at the tables. Although the chef makes his suggestion for the menus, which are usually done three days in advance, the Princess studies them carefully and often alters them if she thinks that she can bring a better balance to the meal. The flowers, which are a feature of the private part of the palace, are carefully discussed with the housekeeper, Miss Plaistow, who usually does them with the gardener simply because the Princess does not physically have the time.

Even in their private entertaining Princess Grace prefers to sit her guests at small round tables with cloths that fall to the ground. In her early days at the palace this idea, beloved of American interior decorators, caused some concern among the palace butlers, who were used to the conventional long table. But now, as with everything else that she persists with, it is an accepted fact and is even proudly acknowledged as a feature of the palace hospitality. The tablecloths are a range of soft pastel shades, with tight posies of flowers to match, but at Christmas they are holly-red. Each year Princess Grace herself makes the centre-pieces for the Christmas tables from white and silver sprayed cones, tinsel, artificial Christmas roses, spruce, holly and candles.

Throughout the year informal entertaining can also take place in the recreation room which was originally one of the old coach rooms and converts to a cinema. Here movies are regularly shown and the Prince once kept his electric train there. Nowadays, with the children growing up, friends are asked to bring their families and it ends up with a party-for-all-ages. There is a bowling alley and pin-ball machines where teenagers and fathers are to be found, and a bar and buffet at one end of the room laden with all the delicious cold food and salads that are a speciality of Provence. Women guests usually follow the Princess and wear long skirts and shirts or caftans while the men are informally elegant.

On one occasion when Sir Winston Churchill and Mr Onassis went to the palace the meal of *bœuf bourguignon* and champagne was served in this room. An amusing aside was that after the event, Sir Winston's and the Princess's secretaries compared notes and found out that each of their employers had been 'very excited and very nervous' to meet the other celebrity.

That the Prince is totally aware of the difficulties in running such a large establishment as the palace household is evident when he com-mented: 'No woman can really feel at home running a palace. For example, if she wants to make a change she is often faced with tradition. Moreover it is difficult for a woman to run a house that has 150 employees.'

The Princess's 'office' is in the twin tower to the Prince's. It is a pleasant airy room, nostalgic and personal. The walls are soft green and the furniture French Provençal. It is a gay room filled with sunshine and flowers and personal memorabilia such as the gold record presented to Grace Kelly and Bing Crosby for their record-breaking song *True Love*, the Film Critics Award, a painting of New York in a snow storm and dozens of pictures of the Kelly family and her own.

The Princess's large antique desk looks 'lived in'. There is a French saying that she applies to her desk: *l'Ordre est le plaisir de la raison et le désordre est le délice de l'imagination*—Order is the pleasure of reason and disorder is the delight of the imagination. But with her extraordinary ability for total sight recall she knows where everything is, down to such details perhaps as a small blue button hidden at the bottom of a pile of papers.

Most of her mornings are taken up with answering letters and the routine work of the palace. The Prince and Princess both take their royal roles with dedication and sincerity. As in that other absolute monarchy, Saudi Arabia, there is a rule that permits any Monegasque with a problem to bring it to his ruler in person. With the Princess the request is more likely to be contained in a letter.

One of the most poignant letters she received was one written in 1973 and came from Émile Mangiapan, a Frenchman who was in prison for life after a conviction for killing a policeman during a robbery in Nice in 1949.

After twenty-four years in prison, on the basis that his family once lived in Monaco, he wrote to Princess Grace.

'Émile's letter touched me,' the Princess said at the time. 'He told me how he loved to paint and how painting materials were sometimes difficult to get in prison. He also asked me to check on his case.'

The Princess corresponded with Mangiapan and sent him Christmas gifts and money to buy painting materials. Mangiapan said that it was the Princess who took his case to the president of the Monaco Court of Appeal—'a move that finally got me paroled. In France when you get a life sentence, it means exactly that . . . a life behind bars. I'd still be in prison if she hadn't decided to help me.'

From newspaper photographs Mangiapan had painted a portrait of the Princess which still hangs in the palace at Monaco. After leaving prison Émile went to live in a commune of painters in Lille.

'I'm a free man and I owe it all to the Princess,' he said.

Whenever the children have birthdays the palace is inundated with letters from children of the same name from all over the world. These all have to be organised and acknowledged. The daily requests for a family photograph of Prince Rainier and Princess Grace are answered with a coloured postcard of the now famous family group taken by the Italian photographer Gianni Bozzacchi.

After lunch, for the Princess there is always Red Cross or other charity work to be done. It is also during these hours that the hairdresser and personal shopping is slipped in.

Several of the Paris couture houses have dummies of the Princess so that when she is in residence in Monaco she can shop by post in between her regular seasonal visits to the collections in Paris.

She buys from the houses of Lanvin, Givenchy, Dior and used to patronise Balenciaga. She also gets many of her leisure clothes from New York, where she is guided by her close friend Vera Maxwell who dressed her in her private life all through those early years when she was a movie star. Other clothes she buys in Nice and Monaco and some of her dresses are made to her own design by the seamstress in the *lingerie* at the palace.

'I am nostalgic about clothes,' she said and this seems to be the case. 'If you think that I am a hoarder you should see my husband and his sister,' she told friends when accused of being a miser with her possessions. An amusing result of the Princess's painstaking garnering is that with the fashion swing last year to clothes of the fifties Princess Caroline came in for a bonus.

'I never give her my clothes ... I only lend them,' is how Princess Grace explained her daughter's appearance in clothes from her mother's wardrobe. One of the most successful 'loans' last year was a suit, complete with square shoulders and pleated skirt, made for the Princess twenty years before by the English tailor Huntsman. Another shared triumph was the Dior white crêpe pyjamas which did double duty with mother and daughter wearing them on alternate occasions.

The much photographed silver crocheted cloche which Princess Caroline wore to nightclubs last year was not bought at a Paris boutique. It was in fact crocheted by Princess Grace for a few francs.

Princess Grace chooses her wardrobe extremely carefully, mindful of official functions where she is liable to wear the same dress many times if it pleases her. In no way is she a slave to fashion and prefers the same classic styles that made her one of Hollywood's best dressed stars.

Gardner Cowles has a charming story of Princess Grace which though twenty years old is just as relevant today as then.

'I used to live in Desmoins, Iowa, and at this time I had moved to New York just after my wife, Fleur Cowles, and I had separated. In a feeling of nostalgia I invited eight of my Desmoins friends to see the Iowa University football team play in Los Angeles and they were to be my guests at the Beverly Wiltshire. I asked the four wives who they wanted to see most in Hollywood and they all answered, "Joan Crawford and Grace Kelly."

'I arranged a cocktail party on the Sunday afternoon after the Rose Bowl game. Joan and her late husband Al Steele, head of Pepsi Cola, arrived first. She fascinated everyone by her flamboyant dress, flamboyant fur coat and flamboyant stories about everyone. She held forth for about three-quarters of an hour and then the telephone went, which I picked up to answer.

'Joan turned to me and said, "Who was that?"

' "Oh nothing, it's just Grace is on her way up," I answered.

'Joan turned to her husband and said, "Darling, it is later than I thought and we must leave," and just as they did, Grace came through the door. Now the point of the story was that Joan Crawford was quite well along in years and was not going to get caught next to Grace Kelly who was so young, fresh and beautiful. Grace was so demurely dressed with her hair in a simple style and little white gloves. The impression that she made on this crowd from Desmoins was immense—the contrast between one of the most flamboyant females in Hollywood and one of the best dressed and most successful.'

Today, wherever she goes, Princess Grace is the focal point when she enters the room. It is not only her immaculate and pretty clothes nor indestructible beauty but a kind of inner tranquillity that she seems to radiate. She masks her great sense of fun by a dignified but easy exterior . . . the sort expected of a princess.

She has also acquired over the years more confidence since she is surely aware of being a success at her job. When she and the Prince were present at the gala celebrations at Persepolis which were given by the Shah of Iran and the Empress Diba to mark the two-thousandth anniversary of their dynasty, Princess Grace was talking to Prince Philip and said:

'Oh, Tito's an interesting man.'

'How did you meet him?' Prince Philip asked eagerly. 'I'd love to speak to him.'

'Oh, I just went up to him and said, "I'm Grace of Monaco", and he said "I'm Tito", and from then on we went on talking.'

This could not have happened earlier on in her marriage. She would have been too shy.

'Being a princess was a job I accepted to take on and spent a while trying to learn how to do it,' she explains.

Being the wife of Prince Rainier, a complicated, indulged Gemini, cannot always have been easy. Talking with Leslie Bennetts of *The Philadelphia Bulletin*, Princess Grace gave one of her rare insights into her attitude to marriage.

'Today there is so much talk about freedom and finding oneself. I'm all for the dignity of the individual but I don't think anyone has a successful marriage or career or anything without sacrifice. Discipline seems to be a word that has almost disappeared from today's vocabulary. I learned discipline in Catholic schools, by being brought up in a strict family, and in the theatre.'

When asked about deference to her husband the Princess replied, 'You can't wait for the sacrifice of another person. You have to develop your own terms of sacrifice. It's a woman who keeps the family together. She is the heart of the home and thereby must be the strongest person in the family structure .... It is the man who must be the head of the household. I would say it is the Prince who makes the ultimate decisions.'

Though not an active women's libber, Princess Grace has strong views of women's place in society today. In one of few Press interviews given in Monaco she recently said to a reporter from *Nice Matin*:

'Woman's first vocation is to be a wife and mother. In this domain no one thinks of disputing her supremacy, do they?

'More than ever women have an important role to play in modern society only it is perhaps not the role people think it is ... they can be the moral regulators of society. This is linked with the role of educators. Our civilisation is passing through a period of upsets which we all know about and that sometimes give strange consequences. In the field of sex, for instance.

'It's not for me to express a view on the role of censorship for theatres or publications. After all, everyone is free to go and see any film he wants or read his favourite "specialised" magazine. But what I do think is intolerable is the aggression committed against our children by advertising which is displayed in public places. Not because I'm excessively puritan but because I consider that this amounts to de-stroying—and in what a sordid fashion—the element of mystery without which love whether physical or sensuous loses its magnificent charm . . .

'I know that many mothers secretly agree with me because it's fashionable nowadays to proclaim the woman's opposite major role, and her real role might perhaps be to demonstrate her opinions effectively. One of the most important things in life is to act according to your conscience.'

To mothers whose children discard them and find them out-dated Princess Grace has these words to say:

'In her time, my mother was considered to be a woman of very advanced ideas. That didn't prevent me from finding her old-fashioned. I think we are all inevitably a bit old-fashioned in comparison with our children, but I must add up to date we have nothing but satisfaction from our children.'

Last year Princess Grace was not particularly interested in Women's Year although she thought it was an opportunity for countries where women live in inferior conditions. In Western society she wants to see women fight for certain injustices like unequal pay but she does not like all the talk that women should fight for female conditions as against masculine ones. 'I find it rather ridiculous.' One of her firmest convictions is that women ought to found a new organisation to smooth out the differences between working women and women in the home as this is an area where much misunderstanding occurs.

Thirty-five

Roc Agel is not only a place it is a state of mind. For the Grimaldi family it means complete happiness. In 1957 Prince Rainier bought a small farm at Roc Agel, 750 metres above the sea up in the mountains over the border in France. It was to be a retreat so that the family could get away from the artificiality of Monte Carlo and live a normal life. The Prince and Princess also have a theory that children need a change of sea and mountain air.

Roc Agel was originally built in the Provençal style of a *mas* (farmhouse) with sturdy stonework and massive beams. In 1959 the *mas* was enlarged until now it looks more like an American ranch and is in fact referred to by Monegasques as 'The Ranch'. Even the plumbing is functional and American which the Princess supervised with the French architect.

George Stacey the American interior decorator who had worked previously for Princess Grace and knew her taste, helped turn it into an extremely comfortable family home.

Set in sixty acres of land, Prince Rainier has also enjoyed turning the rocky soil into a pleasant home farm.

'It is a sort of playground for everyone,' said Prince Rainier. Here the whole family do *their* thing as *they* wish. Prince Rainier enjoys getting behind the tractor, and in addition to planting 400 fruit trees—apples, cherries, apricots, pears—likes to work in the vegetable garden. All the salads and small vegetables for the palace are grown there in organic gardening conditions.

As well as having their own chickens, Prince Rainier put in a small model dairy where there are always several cows as he thinks home-produced milk is so much more nutritious for the family than commercial milk. They even make their own butter for their own use.

Hay-making is a family occupation and helps feed the animals so that they are more or less self-supporting. The vegetables are fertilised by manure that is collected from the few horses on the farm and as Prince Rainier tells friends, 'My vegetables taste a lot better than those in the shops.'

It has not been easy cultivating this rocky area but with his tractors he has scooped out large areas in the rock and used it for pocket cultivation. This not only shelters the gardens from the stringent winds but conserves water, which is scarce up in the mountains.

Princess Grace has her own garden. She plants the bulbs and looks after the roses and climbing vines on the house. She is such a bemused gardener that she was absolutely delighted when her publicist friend Rupert Allen sent her some special tapes that you merely twist to attach plants to the wall. Costing a few cents, she prizes them like gold.

Her main joy, however, is pottering in the superb American-style aquamarine coloured kitchen. Here she sometimes cooks for the family and the very few close friends who are allowed to share Roc Agel.

The children and their friends enjoy barbecueing and making hamburgers, hot dogs and waffles with maple syrup.

On her return from America once the Princess brought back with her a quantity of American T-bone steaks as a treat for some of their friends. They were invited to the Palace where the Prince had set up his barbecue in the courtyard. It rained that night and it all had to be moved into a covered part of the palace building.

'It was not the sight of the Prince in his apron and asbestos gloves that amused us but the palace staff in their white cotton gloves as they solemnly took the steaks from the Prince as they were cooked and handed them round. They clearly thought we were all mad,' one of the people present told me.

Since then barbecueing is mainly done at Roc Agel.

The Princess loves to experiment with all kinds of Provençal dishes which include the Monaco speciality pisaladière (a dough base covered with onions, tomatoes and black olives), cannelloni and when the aubergines are ripe, ratatouille.

Prince Rainier is fastidious about food and dislikes slabs of meat such as American king-size steaks. Instead he prefers delicate flavour and preparation of food as found in Indonesian and Provençal cooking. He is also a great salad man, and likes Chinese, Indian, Mexican and Polynesian food. Princess Grace has her own collection of these recipes, especially curries.

Life at Roc Agel is joyously informal and is much more like that of a comfortably-off American family than a French counterpart. For both the Prince and Princess, normally tied to official duties, it means complete relaxation.

The Prince often plays golf at the nearby links in the afternoon. Sometimes they leave Roc Agel in the evenings to try out small restaurants farther along the coast or, during the month of August, go down into Monte Carlo if there is some international artist they particularly want to see.

Hours are elastic with meals when it suits everyone. The only help in the house comes from an Italian couple who see that the house is in order for the family's arrival. After that they more or less look after themselves.

Just as the Kelly children had their own play houses at the bottom of the garden in Germantown, when the Grimaldi children were young they each had their own house at Roc Agel. When friends came to stay Prince Rainier would often put up tents in the grounds so that the children could play at camping.

For two summers the whole family went to America, where the children went to a typical American camp while Prince Rainier and Princess Grace took a house near by in New Hampshire. From here the girls in the family learnt songs from the summer camps, but the Prince does not care much about them and makes disparaging remarks when the girls pipe up.

Prince Rainier has a strange and interesting theory that, like human beings, animals need holidays too. Each weekend he likes to take some of the animals from his private zoo up to Roc Agel so that they can get a change of scenery. It is quite a performance shifting the large 'cats' which are loaded in their cages on to a lorry that has a special drop side. Once up at Roc Agel, if they are in the least bit tame, they are allowed out of their cages, sometimes tethered or roaming free.

Lion cubs have always been a problem for Princess Grace as not only does Prince Rainier enjoy them but young Grimaldis have collected them up as other children do puppies and kittens.

'Whenever they went to a circus they were always presented with a baby chimpanzee or lion cub,' said Princess Grace. And there was also the same talk. She would say, 'I am not having anything to do with this. I'm simply not cleaning up after this one. I'm not feeding it. I'm not doing anything. If you want the cub it is your responsibility.' But always in the end the children won, and the cubs stayed.

At Roc Agel it was nothing to come into the large family sitting-room and find two lion cubs growling and playing on the rugs or scampering over the chairs. As house training did not come into the lions' or chimps' schedule there were other difficulties, too. Lion urine is not a pleasant smell.

They once had a friend there who was doing some sculpting. Every time she got her clay ready for use a baby chimpanzee would scuttle along and steal the clay, and then sit and eat it. It happened so often that in the end the sculptor had to give up.

Like her father, Princess Caroline has no fear of animals at all. As a thirteen-year-old she handled her lion cubs like another child fondles a kitten. At one period she had a cub which she called Elsa. She played with it all day, cuddled it like a doll and fed it from a bottle. There was only one thing wrong. 'Elsa' was a young male lion, began growing a mane and finally had to be put in a cage. Princess Caroline was heartbroken. It took all Prince Rainier's parental persuasion to keep her from sneaking into the cage to be with her pet.

Princess Grace has taken many home movies of their life at Roc Agel and of the animals on holiday with the cubs playing with the children. Her favourite one is of the dogs' birthday party she gave.

At the time there were seven dogs in the family and the Princess thought that they should have a communal birthday party. Incidentally, it was also a way of using up all the cake mixes that had stacked up in the kitchen cupboards.

Everyone helped as the Princess organised making paper hats for the dogs with elastic to fit under their chins. The invitation list read for four poodles, Oliver's widow Cannella and daughter Gamma, Chester and Lindy, the Prince's Labrador called Kim, a pointer named Bella which was the most neurotic dog they have ever had and a Rhodesian ridgeback called Fanny.

Princess Grace spent the morning cooking up the cake mixes . . . chocolate, angel, devil's food and so on ... and setting the lawn with paper napkins. The party was extremely funny simply because each dog behaved according to its character. Cannella was very grand in powder blue and would not have any part of it at all while the others came and stole their bits of cake and ran away.

After the food the children played games with the dogs just as at a proper children's party. All the time the party was going on Princess Grace, in stitches of laughter, was making a home movie which they run through from time to time.

Oliver had died tragically in Switzerland. The Prince and Princess had taken him there while they were on winter sports. On returning to their villa Princess Grace heard a terrible scream from near by and rushed to find that Oliver had been attacked by another dog and was dead.

Her grief was almost unbearable. Oliver had been like a human being to her, knowing every mood, understanding every word and was her constant friend during those early difficult transition days when she arrived in Monaco. She asked Father Boston, the palace almoner, who was on holiday with the family, to bury Oliver.

Seeing the Princess's grief, made all the more difficult to bear as there were other guests in the house, the Prince ordered as a surprise a black poodle called Chester, the same size as Oliver, to be sent by air from Paris as soon as possible.

The thought was meant kindly but the Princess was desperate. She was even more bitter about the whole incident and resented the new dog terribly. She said that it was one of the worst things to foist a new dog on her, especially to replace Oliver so soon.

'I don't think my husband would have done it except that he was influenced by our friends and he thought it might comfort me. He is very knowledgeable and sensitive about the relationship between human beings and animals,' the Princess commented afterwards.

As pet lovers the world over know, so many strange telepathic happenings occur in the animal world. Gamma, Oliver's daughter, who had always been the wicked one rushing about and chasing the chickens, went straight away after the accident and lay at Princess Grace's feet, and that same night when the Princess went to bed Gamma was lying in the same spot which Oliver had previously occupied. From that day on she selflessly and devotedly did her best to replace Oliver in Princess Grace's life.

When Princess Caroline was small she was given a first-aid kit for animals. Gamma bore the brunt of this with fortitude. When the mood came over her Princess Caroline did a complete first-aid job on the dog. She must have been the only healthy dog in the world who, from time to time, was bandaged from nose to tail.

Today Princess Grace has as her special pet a tiny, beguiling little apricot poodle called Timmy which the Prince gave to her. His colour is so rare that at the time of his birth it was not recognised by the American Kennel Club.

Roc Agel is a wonderful house with its own special atmosphere of freedom and happiness as the dogs, children, chimpanzees, birds, 'big cats' all live together in total acceptance. Few children in the world have such a heritage.

Prince Rainier also has his own stables.

Princess Grace does not ride as much as she used to, but when she does she prefers side-saddle and has her own hunter. It is Prince Rainier and Princess Caroline who love to take a couple of Camargue ponies out for a gallop far away over the blue-hazed hilltops, the wind in their faces and below the drop cloth of an azure blue Mediterranean fringed by the Riviera.

In the evenings there is television and each has his or her own hobbies. Princess Grace disappears to press flowers for her collages. Princess Caroline loves to play pop and often has discussions of jazz versus pop with her father. Prince Rainier is a hi-fi expert and has a vast collection of jazz records. He has everything that Al Jolson ever recorded and many Negro spirituals.

Prince Rainier also has his own workshop where he likes to do metal sculpture. Some of it is abstract art, others strange modernistic whimsical flowers. One of his pieces stands in the modern sitting area in their apartment in the palace. He is also clever at carpentry and tries to encourage his children to use their hands as, with the Princess, he firmly believes that in so doing they will be more balanced and happier people.

Princess Grace always has needlework at hand. Apart from the waistcoat she made for Prince Rainier, she has also embroidered him slippers and a carpet for Princess Stephanie's bedroom which depicts Winnie the Pooh characters and is inscribed 'To Stephanie . . . with love . . . from Mother'. Princess Caroline is at present going through a non-embroidery phase but little Stephanie often sits with her mother doing hers. Twice a week at school she takes lessons in sewing and embroidery.

It is in this relaxed and unpretentious atmosphere that Prince Rainier and Princess Grace try to instill into their children the fundamentals of living today.

Among the American virtues which Princess Grace would like to have superimposed on her children's European culture is the openness that Americans have—their forthright self-reliance. Life at Roc Agel she hopes will give them just this.

The relationship between Princess Grace and her children is a wondrous thing. She is endlessly patient with them and treats them with gentleness and grown-up understanding. People who surround her say that she is seldom impatient but can be firm if the occasion arises. A Kelly family endearment which is used constantly is 'Lamb'. As said by Princess Grace it is exceedingly pretty. She uses it as other mothers say 'darling'.

In the early days of their marriage, before the new modern wing was built in the palace, Princess Grace regarded Roc Agel as her real home. Here she felt comfortable, happy, self-sufficient in the family life she enjoys. When the heat of Monaco is at its worst in August, the whole family move there.

Now she feels that the modern addition to the palace which was completed in 1969 has become her real home.

No matter how hard she tried, Princess Grace always felt that the original apartments which she and the Prince used when they returned from their honeymoon could never be a real home. It was nothing that she had created . . . the structure and atmosphere were already there. The sleeping-quarters were also cramped. At one period Prince Albert and baby Stephanie had to sleep together in the day nursery while Princess Caroline slept in the night nursery. Princess Grace had to store her clothes in cupboards alongside the nursery.

In the new apartments the Prince and Princess have their large airy bedroom plus a dressing-room and bathroom each, and the children all have their own rooms.

In spite of its marble floors and two-storied living area the new wing has a homelike quality. The whole effect of the room is light and contemporary with lots of glass counterbalanced with a big fireplace made of smooth stones taken from the sea below. There is a large squashy American-style sofa in a clotted cream colour and occasional tables of glass and metal. Set amidst a wall of glass is a huge brass telescope which the Prince uses constantly to scan the harbour. He can recognise all the yachts of well-known international celebrities as they enter the harbour into his Principality.

Besides his private zoo, which he visits most mornings, the Prince likes to have some of the animals and birds actually living in cages in the house. In the first apartment he kept his favourite pet, a black and white lemur, in the dining-room. The Prince would go over to the animal, put his arms through the cage and give him a hug and a kiss.

All through dinner the lemur would sit on the top of his tree hanging on with his six-feet-long tail. If he was ignored too long he would reel in his tail like a fisherman reeling in his line and sit cradling it in his arms and singing a song to it. No guest could resist it.

As the dining-room in the present apartment is like a cool, pretty tent in blue-and-white cotton ticking and only seats eight, alas there is no room for the lemur. On the wall hangs a sketch of Prince Pierre, Prince Rainier's father, and three Vidal Quadras portraits of the three children all done when they were three and a half.

Another pet is Coco the parrot. His party trick is that he can not only sing the national anthem and the theme song from *The Bridge on the River Kwai* but imitates the drawing of a cork superbly. Whenever the telephone rings he begins, 'Hello ... hello ... hello.' He also calls all the various dogs by their right names. A most engaging bird.

There is not another royal household in the world where animals and birds are accepted so naturally and fit into the family pattern.

The Princess was once standing in the old library talking to her secretary when the Prince rushed in, terribly impatiently. He waited for the Princess, who did not hesitate giving instructions to the secretary. Finally he burst in: 'You don't seem to understand how important it is. Tanagra is pregnant. It is very rare for a chimpanzee to breed in captivity.'

'All rightie,' quipped the Princess, 'I'll knit her something.'

Thirty-six

To families all over the world and not only in Monaco Prince Rainier and Princess Grace give an attractive picture of family life.

'I don't much like the word example as it gives a terrifying responsibility, but if the picture of our family gives help and confidence to others I am very pleased,' Princess Grace once commented.

For a royal family, in a golden goldfish bowl, Princess Grace has managed her job as a mother with miraculous skill. To see how all four members of her family dote on her—and she on them—is a lovely experience.

Right from the beginning of their family life Prince Rainier and Princess Grace vowed that they would be caring and concerned parents. Within the structure of royal life—and its advantages and disadvantages—they have managed to give their children as balanced and normal a life as possible. The result is three charming, intelligent, uninhibited young people. The Prince and Princess's present concern is to be able to carry through over the next expansive years until their children are self-sufficient adults.

In Princess Caroline the popular Press all over the world found a constant headliner. With the looks of Ali McGraw and the vitality of Liza Minnelli it could not be otherwise, but the Prince and Princess are fiercely protective of their children who are unable to fight back at incorrect publicity. When an Italian newspaper falsified photographs to make it look as though Princess Caroline were sunbathing in the nude, Prince Rainier sued them. When an English woman's magazine ran a story under the sensational headline 'Why Mother Doesn't Know Best' by Princess Caroline of Monaco, the *Centre de Presse de Monaco* immediately notified the editor that the story was a complete fake, which indeed it was.

One of the most exacerbating untruths in recent years concerned a story that Princess Caroline was alleged to have had a secret romance with Prince Charles.

The truth was that at that stage Princess Caroline had never met Prince Charles nor was likely to in the immediate future. Apart from difference in age, which is not insurmountable, the religious difference would make a union highly unlikely. Princess Caroline is Roman Catholic and Prince Charles will one day be head of the Church of England.

Princess Grace herself takes a remarkably modern and philosophical view about her daughter's future. As she said to one American reporter:

'I would like to see Caroline marry a Catholic. It makes it easier. But I guess if she really had her heart set on marrying somebody who wasn't Catholic ... well, Caroline is a strong, positive character and she probably would end up doing it no matter what we thought about it. Like all parents we wish for her happiness.'

When another newspaper scurrilously wrote that Princess Caroline's studies at the *Institut d'Études Politiques* in Paris were falling behind because of her gay night life, Princess Grace was angry. She immediately wrote to the editor of the newspaper and gave a factual account of her daughter's educational achievements.

Princess Grace has many acute and original observations to make in the bringing up of children which is something she totally understands.

'Children need to be told constantly over and over again by their parents that they are loved. This French parents do so well while American ones tend to take it for granted that the children know. I think this is a very subtle difference,' Princess Grace has said. From the shining open looks of the Grimaldi children they are suffering no lack of being told of their parents' affection. They have given their children a childhood overspilling with the goodness of security, fun and love.

All the children have pocket money but 'it is not nearly as much as some of their friends,' Princess Grace said.

The decision made last year between Prince Rainier and Princess

Grace that a more permanent home had to be created in Paris during the period of their children's education did not come easily. For them both it means a tremendous sacrifice in living apart for much of the time.

Even before his marriage the Prince has always had an apartment in Paris and during the last few years he and the Princess acquired a much larger one on the Avenue Foch. With the children needing more space for entertaining their own friends, the Prince has now bought a permanent house in Paris into which the family moved last autumn.

For the Princess, who dislikes travelling, and especially by air, the present arrangement means almost weekend commuting to Monaco, but this she feels is necessary and worth while until her children are old enough to stand on their own feet.

'Caroline is too old for a governess and too young for a lady-in-waiting, so it seemed the only solution,' the Princess explained to inquirers.

Had it been in America or had the Prince and Princess had members of their own families, with children of a similar age, living in Paris undoubtedly Princess Caroline would possibly have stayed with them.

Prince Albert, with the clean good looks of his mother, will remain at school in Monaco until he is ready for university. The Prince, especially, is concerned that Prince Albert will not have the same experience as he had as a boy who was educated abroad. When he finally returned to Monaco as a grown man he knew few people of his own age. Prince Albert is growing up among the boys who will one day help him in the ruling of the Principality.

It is unlikely, too, that Prince Albert will be sent to an American University for any long period. His destiny lies in the new Europe.

Although Prince Albert is more like his mother in character, as well as looks, the Prince and his son have an excellent rapport.

'Albie is much too keen on swimming and keeping fit to ever be bothered with the drug problem,' a family friend told me. 'He and the Prince are like a couple of brothers when they lock themselves away in the palace gymnasium. He will make a fine ruler one day. He is intelligent, dependable and trustworthy with a great deal of compassion.'

Prince Albert is already being gently eased into his royal role and attends various functions with his parents. As Prince Rainier has said:

'Albert should have time to enjoy himself and not be parachuted into the job. I should like him to work alongside of me for at least a year or so to get the feel of the ropes.'

Last summer he spent in America at a camp teaching swimming to other children.

It is generally conceded in Monaco that Prince Rainier will step down from the ruling position in his early sixties.

Princess Stephanie is a beguiling little girl. She is bright, indulged and has the quick wit of her father.

Although both aware of the generation gap, Prince Rainier and Princess Grace have tried to minimise it as much as possible in their relationship with their own children. They go out for meals together, sit around in the evenings together and play together, just like millions of other parents.

In 1973 when Princess Caroline turned sixteen and was beginning to go to grown-up dances, with felicitous concern Princess Grace felt that it was time that all the family knew how to dance properly as opposed to disco-dancing. She did a most astonishing thing to rectify this. A telephone call was put through on her behalf to Peggy and Frank Spencer from the tulle and sequin world of the BBC's television programme *Come Dancing*. They were invited to Monaco for ten days to teach the whole family what Frank Spencer quaintly calls 'Couple Dancing'.

A class of young people, friends of the royal children and Princess Grace, met daily in the Hermitage Hotel where they were given a ten days' crash course in the waltz, quickstep, fox trot, jive, tango, Viennese waltz and Zorba dance. The Spencers took a collection of the top band records with them.

On the first day the children turned up in jeans and casual clothes. By the second day the Grace-line had got working and they all arrived immaculate in party clothes.

The climax and test came at the Red Cross ball which Princess Caroline attended for the first time. As the music commenced an extremely proud—and elegant—Prince Rainier took the floor with his daughter for the first waltz while the rest of the dancers stood and watched. They did not put a foot wrong.

Neither the Prince nor Princess is concerned with the constant speculation in newspapers that their marriage is in danger of breaking down. They have learned to live with it.

They have an unequivocal closeness which becomes even more

apparent as the marriage enters its twentieth year this April. Neither have ever tried to minimise the differences which occur in any marriage at its onset, the proof of their adjustment is their outward approach to the world.

For a marriage that began with so few interests in common it is a remarkably successful one. The Prince's hobbies include shooting, boxing, underwater swimming, soccer, ski-ing, automobiles, fishing, yachting, none of which the Princess enjoys. Nor does the Prince share her genuine enjoyment for walking.

The common denominator is the family plus an engaging sense of humour. Princess Grace is quick to point out that her husband is wittier than she is and finds it easier to talk to people than she does. This is not the impression among her friends. Her humour can be devastatingly pungent and individual.

Another bond between Prince Rainier and Princess Grace is their deep religious conviction. At a table by his bedside Prince Rainier keeps the *Cardinal Spellman Prayer Book*, which he takes everywhere, and a crucifix he found in a battlefield which had belonged to a German.

Princess Grace has expressed the view that like many Catholics she is concerned with the changes in the Church. Some she can accept and others not.

'We are all looking for answers,' she has said. 'But your answers don't apply to other people—and that may account for the generation gap. Life is constantly changing. What was valid and true five years ago is not true any more. My ideas are constantly changing . . . As a Christian I think I've improved over the years . . . I may not be the best Catholic.'

All the children have been brought up with an awareness and involvement in religion. There was never any question of allowing them to drift until they were old enough to decide for themselves.

As the Princess has said: 'It's like telling children to wait until they are twenty-one before they brush their teeth. By then their teeth might have fallen out.'

Next to the birth of her children Princess Grace says that her trip to Ireland was one of the most profound experiences of her life.

In memory of that trip in 1961, along with her platinum wedding ring the Princess also wears an old Irish ring in the design of the cladagh. She also bought a collection of 500 books including Irish literature, poetry and plays which she is assiduously reading through. Princess

Grace travelled to Dublin last September to attend the funeral of Eamon de Valera, an old friend of the family.

She has a spiritual as well as physical identification with Ireland. When she heard that her friends the Paul Gallicos had bought the Shannon Pot in Derrylahan, Glangevlin, County Leitrim, in 1968, purely for the romance of owning the source of the Shannon river, and by doing so hopefully protecting it from the evil promoters and constructors who love to ruin nature, she was overjoyed.

Before going on a visit to make the final arrangements Virginia Gallico had told the Princess that she intended to take a Hermès scarf for Mrs Maguire from whom they were buying the Shannon Pot.

'Perhaps she may not know who I am but would you take her one of my scarves,' Princess Grace asked. 'Please tell her to use it and not to put it in a drawer.'

It so happened that Mrs Maguire had two American heroines . . . Princess Grace and Mrs Jacqueline Kennedy. When the Gallicos arrived with the pretty scarf Princess Grace had designed and gave it to Mrs Maguire, she took it and held it in front of the crucifix. At least one of her heroines had not let her down. And doubtless today the scarf lies alongside one of her religious relics.

During the years Princess Grace has lost much of her initial shyness. In the early days she suffered agonies before any great event on their official trips abroad. Besides being nervous—and it always went to her stomach and she could not eat—she found the endless protocol boring. Now she takes it with bemused resignation.

Both Prince Rainier and Princess Grace are sensitive to any reference to Monaco being a Mediterranean Ruritania. They take the Principality dead seriously, including its standards of princely protocol and behaviour. In the colourful soldiers guarding the palace which are drawn from the Principality's army of eighty-nine, they recognise a powerful piece of tourist propaganda. Ditto the galas and the big names Princess Grace lures there every summer for the various fêtes.

To the Monegasques the royal family is held in tolerant affection. They have brought stability and permanence. 'We have no drug problem, no serious crime, no taxes, a fine health system and our children are well educated ... what more do we want? If we were to be a republic or part of France all this might disappear. We are well satisfied,' an elderly Monegasque told me. 'The royal family, pouf, they are harmless.'

To the thousands of foreigners, warming their ageing bones in the golden sunshine, there is also a strict code of behaviour. If they have any criticism of either the Prince or Princess they keep it to themselves. 'We are guests here,' they say conspiratorially. 'We don't discuss any problems with anyone.'

They are all aware that the Prince is the supreme authority in all Monegasque matters with the power to suspend the Constitution and disband the elected legislature (which he did in 1959)—and also to expel any undesirable foreigners!

In *Nice Matin*, the newspaper which circulates along the whole of the Riviera Coast, one is conscious that little crime is reported in the section from Monaco. Perhaps it does not exist or perhaps it is suppressed in the hope of giving Monaco a crime-proof image for its many rich residents.

There is also another facet to this interesting little Principality. The scientific work being done there is stretching out into the world. On my television recently I watched Jacques Yves Cousteau in a programme concerning the mystery of an unknown poison affecting the fish on Lake Titicaca in South America – an economic factor as serious to the Indians there as drought is to the Ethiopians. Samples of fish were taken back to the laboratory of the Oceanic Museum in Monaco and there a diagnosis resulted. In this way both the Prince and Princess feel that the small nations have a positive contribution to give to the world and they want Monaco to be out in the lead.

To Princess Grace, with no inbred royal hang-up, the role of princess is just another job. 'I work hard in social work, public relations and raising the Grimaldi heirs. But that's what I get paid for,' she says.

For a woman whose entire life was wrapped up in her work as an actress Grace Kelly has made the transition to full-time princess with ease and credibility.

'Most women want to be married and have a family and I found that I was no different from anybody else,' she says with disarming honesty.

At forty-five years of age, Princess Grace is still at her prime as a woman. She has phenomenal beauty, health, diversified talents and professionalism. With one career as a world film star behind her and midway in her role as a reigning royal princess, she is well on the way to completing her third one—that of a conscientious mother to a lively, growing family.

In addition to this, I feel that there is still an untapped source of energy and creativity that may well provide further surprises. The 'act' is far from complete.

When asked once if she was happy, she replied:

'I have peace of mind and occasional moments of happiness. Happiness isn't a perpetual state. Life isn't that way.'

Thirty-seven

Those untapped sources of energy began to take shape when Princess Grace began to create pictures from pressed flowers, an art form that she had first seen in America. Old telephone books were quickly stuffed with flowers she gathered from friends and her own gardens and she scoured antique shops for old-fashioned flat irons. Although she later was given several presses she always preferred to use her own makeshift ones.

Her daily walk became a flower picking expedition and she always carried a pair of folding scissors in her handbag. When Madame Drount, who owned a fashionable gallery in Paris, saw one of her pictures in a friend's house, she immediately asked the Princess if she could hold an exhibition of them. It was typical of her innate modesty, the Princess signed each painting in the right-hand corner with the small initials G. P. K—Grace Patricia Kelly.

The Princess invited me to Paris for the champagne opening of the exhibition and no one was more surprised than she was when she saw the red 'sold' spots appearing on the pictures. Before the gallery closed that night there were only a few pictures left. They ranged in price from £200 to £1,000 and are now considered collectors' pieces. When the Prince swept us off to a green-bowered restaurant for a family supper party, Princess Grace was as sparkling as any eighteen-year-old at her first dinner party.

What makes these pictures so special, I feel, is not the fact that she used simple field flowers like poppies, cornflowers and daisies, but that she had created her own flowers by superimposing, for instance, a tiny daisy onto the petals of a pansy. This imaginative flair ran right through her character giving everything she did a special pixilated touch.

It was on Thursday, 26 February 1976 that John Carroll telephoned me to say that he was looking for a star American name to read poetry at the Edinburgh Festival. As it was the year of the American Bicentennial, his programme was to be given a special American flavour. As it happened, I had recently seen Princess Grace reading a passage from the Bible on the popular Sunday night *Stars on Sunday* television programme. Wearing a frilled chiffon blouse that framed her classical beauty her voice was as mellow as peach juice.

'Why don't you ask Princess Grace,' I asked John Carroll, who has devised programmes for everyone from Ashcroft to Olivier.

There was a long silence at the other end of the telephone as he gasped 'But she'd never do it, surely.'

A meeting was arranged in Paris between the Princess and John. 'I was very fortunate because she liked me on sight—I certainly couldn't fail to like *her* on sight. The important thing was that we clicked. Perhaps we have the same sense of humour—my grandfather was Irish and so was hers.

The programme—*An American Heritage*—ran for four performances and was a great success. With his consummate skill, John Carroll had chosen poetry that suited her personality and would not strain a voice that had not been used to performing for many years. Wearing a flame-red, chiffon dress she was flanked by one English actor, Richard Pasco, and one American, Richard Kiley.

Knowing of her great love of Shakespeare (she always travelled with a small book of his sonnets in her luggage), John suggested that she might like to take part in a programme at Stratford-upon-Avon where he had for many years arranged programmes as part of the summer season. The result was 'A Remembrance for Shakespeare' which was presented on a summer evening in July 1977 at Holy Trinity Church, where Shakespeare is buried. For this one performance her co-readers were Richard Pasco, and John Westbrook, with Sir Peter Pears singing unaccompanied songs from Shakespeare's plays.

John remembers: 'I was waiting outside when Princess Grace arrived at the church. She had brought with her a lovely golden rose. "I've brought this rose to put on dear William's grave," she told me.' Together they went into the church where she placed her rose on the famous tombstone near the High altar.

The news of the Princess's debut as a poetry reader had crossed the Atlantic and she soon received an invitation from Dr Samuel Hazo of the American International Poetry Forum to give a poetry reading under their auspices. He suggested that she brought over the programme she had read at Edinburgh, but when she told this to John Carroll he said firmly: 'No, dear Grace. This would be like taking coals to Newcastle. We will make a special programme for America.'

He then told her of an idea he had to devise a poetry reading using various themes to do with nature. They called the programme 'Birds, Beasts and Flowers', and it had its premiere at the Carnegie Hall in Pittsburgh followed by a tour to Minneapolis, Philadelphia, Washington and the universities of Princeton and Harvard.

Princess Grace bloomed on the tour just as John Carroll had hoped. Reciting poetry was a means of using her gifts of theatre days in a way which was right for her present position as Princess of Monaco. It was the compromise that she had been looking for all those years.

During her stay in Pittsburgh there was a most moving ceremony in which she received her first honorary degree from an American university. She was awarded a Doctorate of Humane Letters by the Duquense University of Pittsburgh. She was the belle of the campus that day with every student at her feet.

The following June she appeared at the Aldeburgh Festival, and she was back in England again in November for a shorter version of 'Birds, Beasts and Flowers' in the presence of Her Majesty the Queen Mother at St James's Palace. The performance was given in aid of the charity Family Service Units, of which the Queen Mother is patron. It was the last time Princess Grace was to see Lord Mountbatten, whom she had known since her early film days. He was tragically killed the following year.

A shortened selection of this programme has now appeared as a record as well as being made into a handsome book in a limited edition. The proceeds go to help the work of the World Wildlife Fund. I was staying in Paris with the Princess when she signed the books. I was doing my knitting, she was signing her books and we were both watching a Tarzan film on television!

Monday, 9 March 1981 was to be a very special occasion. Princess Grace had agreed to take part in a gala recital programme in aid of the Royal Opera House Appeal. Again John Carroll was in charge and it was presented at Goldsmith's Hall in the City of London. The Prince of Wales, as patron of the Royal Opera, had promised to attend, and as he had just announced his engagement to Lady Diana Spencer, she came with him on what was to be her first official function. It was the night of the famous strapless black dress. Noticing the young girl's shyness, Princess Grace made a special effort to put her at ease, and this typical Grace gesture remained in Princess Diana's memory. After the performance, Princess Grace and John Carroll were invited back to Buckingham Palace for a supper party given by Prince Charles. The event itself raised just over £7,000.

On 29 July 1981, the Royal wedding day, Princess Grace was again in London with her son Prince Albert staying as a guest of Her Majesty Queen Elizabeth II at Buckingham Palace. It was the beginning of a real friendship between the two royal families and between Princess Grace and the young English princess in particular.

In recent months John Carroll, who has contributed to the Windsor Festival since it first began in 1969, asked the Princess if she would like to take part in a special programme he was planning as part of the 1982 festival to be held in the historic St George's Chapel. When the news of Princess Grace's death was announced, it was decided that the programme would go on, just as she would have wanted.

Although Princess Grace's life blossomed in Hollywood and bloomed in Monaco, her roots were in Philadelphia and Ireland and her faith was the Roman Catholic Church. It was to her Church that she turned whenever she was perplexed or needed comfort. I was staying with her in Paris when Princess Stephanie sat her final school examination. 'Where have you been this morning?' she asked me at luncheon. 'To light a candle for Stephanie,' I replied. 'And I went to my church to do exactly the same,' she laughed.

Prince Rainier is the head of the Principality but Princess Grace was the pivot of their family life. Her concern for her husband and children was immense and they all turned to her for their wants. Whenever she read untruthful reports in the newspapers about her children she was like a lioness protecting her cubs. 'What they say about me doesn't matter but the children are defenceless,' she told me time and time again.

It is now common knowledge that neither Prince Rainier nor Princess Grace were pleased when Caroline chose Philippe Junot, a renowned playboy seventeen years her senior, as her husband. When the engagement was announced, I was at Roc Agel writing a book about flowers that the Princess and I were creating together. Though Princess Grace was obviously distressed about the engagement, and had little faith that the marriage would survive, she publicly supported her daughter's right to choose.

'Naturally you hope that your children will listen to you. You want to give them your experience but they have to learn for themselves. I only hope that Caroline, who is so eager for life, will not get too hurt,' she told me. We were walking in the herb-scented hills behind the farmhouse and she suddenly stopped and looked straight into my face. 'Caroline is not only a very bright girl but she has so much tenderness and compassion in her nature. I am very proud of her.'

'Being a mother is a very creative job,' was one of her favourite sayings and she was both amused and delighted that all three of her children were so different. She has always had a very special understanding of Prince Albert, the child who most resembles her in looks and character.

Outwardly Prince Albert appears to be a serious studious young man—'the philosopher of the family' is how his mother described him—and undoubtedly his recent period of seven months in the French Navy has toughened him up. In the family he is the joker and is perhaps the best mimic of all the Grimaldis. There is always plenty of laughter and wholesome American 'ribbing' when Albert is around.

Princess Grace completely understood Albert's public shyness as she herself had suffered so much from this when she was growing up. She and the Prince were in the process of giving the young Prince the courage and confidence to face a future which has been more or less mapped out for him. Prince Rainier may abdicate and allow his son to take over the ruling of the principality on his next birthday when he becomes twenty-five years of age.

The child who will miss her mother most of all is the quick-silver, seventeen-year-old Princess Stephanie. A lovable, oftimes wilful girl, she idolised her mother as I have never seen any other daughter. As a little girl she used literally to hold onto her mother's skirt and emotionally is still doing so. She is slower to mature than her older sister was but as Princess Grace explained to me, 'Stephanie is still in the process of growing and maturing and finding her way. I have no doubt that she will do extremely well in the end. She has a good mind and works hard.'

Princess Grace was always in favour of her children 'doing their own thing' and was behind Princess Stephanie's decision to join the staff of Dior and work under designer Marc Bohan, whose clothes the Princess loved to wear.

I am constantly asked whether I agree with the recent newspaper reports that the marriage between Princess Grace and Prince Rainier was going through 'a difficult period'. During the entire twenty-six years they were together the Princess has often referred to the fact that it was not always easy to adapt from being an independent American woman to the wife of an autocratic European.

The truth is that what appeared to be a banal Hollywood script of the pretty film star marrying her prince was false. The reality was much more interesting. From a tremulous beginning, when she not only had to adapt to being married but accept a new language and different culture, the relationship strengthened. Princess Grace's stabilising influence on Prince Rainier's volatile Mediterranean temperament was without question. When the ties with France were strained it was Princess Grace who charmed de Gaulle, and her adroit handling of the bombastic Aristotle Onassis is legendary in the Principality. As any Monegasque today will tell you, life in the Principality will never be the same again.

The real basis of Prince Rainier and Princess Grace's love for each other was founded on mutual respect and their total involvement in family life. In recent years Prince Rainier, a man of simple tastes, has tended more and more to stay in the four lovely homes that the Princess created for him. Even in the ancient old pink palace at Monte Carlo their private rooms had a special Grace cosiness about them, and were always filled with flowers. During the last months she had almost completed refurnishing the château, an hour from Paris, which the Prince had inherited from his mother.

Princess Grace's decision to live in Paris while Stephanie was finishing school was not an easy one as both she and the Prince knew it would alter the pattern of their close family life. But they were determined not to repeat the mistake made with Caroline of sending her to a school in England. Caroline had been very homesick and unhappy when she was away. The Prince, too, had memories of his schooldays at Stowe in the Cotswolds. They also knew that by her very nature Princess Stephanie could not be separated for long from her mother, and the whole family respected this.

The Princess told me just a few weeks before her death that since Stephanie had now finished school she would probably be spending more and more time in Monte Carlo or with the Prince at their château.

This last year had been a particularly happy one for Princess Grace. Still incredibly beautiful, her face had gained a new kind of strength. She looked far younger than her fifty-two years. There were still bundles of film scripts on her desk sent by Hollywood hopeful of seducing her back to the film industry. Though the answer would always be 'no' she never could resist reading them. She had been offered one of the lead roles in the recent film *The Turning Point*, eventually played by Anne Bancroft and Shirley Maclaine. In a television film she did make to publicise Monaco it was clearly evident that the old magic was still there. Age had not withered her extraordinary womanly beauty.

In the early months of this year she and the Prince visited the Far East for the re-dedication of the cruise ship SS *Constitution* which had played such a romantic role in their life. It was in the *Constitution* that Grace Kelly had sailed for Monaco with her entire family to marry Prince Rainier in April 1956.

In August this year the Prince fulfilled a long awaited dream. He and the Princess sailed to Norway. 'It was absolutely perfect except that the air-conditioning in the ship brought on bronchitis which I am having trouble in getting rid of,' she wrote in a letter to me.

The family usually spend all of August at Roc Agel where the Princess used to relax doing her flower pictures. Because of all the travelling this year the holiday had been extended to the middle of September. On the morning of 14 September, Princess Grace made the decision to drive herself and Stephanie down to Monaco. She seldom drove and was always apprehensive of that particular bend in the road.

According to writer S. Jackson in his book *Inside Monte Carlo*, 'In the historic past a curse was put upon the reigning monarch of

Monaco that every marriage would end in disaster.'

Had the curse struck again? Amid all the horror and anguish of those last tragic days, the Prince's decision to have the life-saving machine turned off was his final gesture of love and respect for the woman who had transformed his life. Professor Charles Chatelin, the doctor in charge at the Princess Grace Hospital, explained to the Prince that apart from the physical injuries, Princess Grace's brain had been fatally damaged as a result of the accident. After consultation with Prince Albert and Princess Caroline, the Prince gave the order 'Let my wife die.'

There never has been a more radiant royal funeral as on the day they brought Princess Grace back to the cathedral where, amid showers of rose petals, she had been married. People came from all over the world—princes and princesses, heads of state and a galaxy of film stars who had remained friends over the years. Standing, dazed in grief, weeping into their handkerchiefs, were the citizens of Monaco who felt that they had lost not only their Princess but a very special friend.

No one present will ever forget the tearing agony of Prince Rainier nor the poignant grief of Princess Caroline as they followed the white, silk-draped coffin embroidered with the Grimaldi coat of arms through the narrow, cobbled streets followed by little girls and boys carrying hundreds of wreaths of flowers.

En route they passed the shrine of St Devote, the patron saint of Monaco, where the Princess had laid her small bouquet of lily of the valley after her wedding.

The service was filled with beauty, and the music with joy—just as Princess Grace would have wanted it. The hushed congregation and millions watching television round the world listened to the words of the Archbishop of Monaco, Monseigneur Charles Brandt, who is an old family friend:

'Lord we weep for our Princess Grace. And the brutality of her death added to our pain ... She was such a good person—so beautiful and so loved. She was an exemplary Christian. Not only were her husband and children crushed by tragedy but a whole people ... *au revoir* Madame, you have perfectly fulfilled your contract. Signed Monaco.'

Through our tears we shall never forget her. She touched our lives with gold.

Index

Academy Award (Oscar), 98-100, 149
Albert Alexandre Louis Pierre, Prince, 188, 189, 201, 205, 208-209, 210, 223, 226, 238, 245, 265, 269-270
Albert I, Prince (great grandfather of Prince Rainier), 131
Aldrich, Larry, 154
Alexander, 60
Alexandre (hairdresser), 17, 204, 229
Allen, Rupert, 66, 120-121
American Academy of Dramatic Arts, 45-47, 49, 51, 52, 56, 59, 68, 86
Anne, Princess, 221
Anouilh, Jean, 190, 191
Antoinette, Princess (sister of Prince Rainier), 158, 179, 181
Assembly Ball, The, 24
Association Mondiale des Amis de L'Enfance (World Association of Friends of Children), 194
Astor, Mary, 70
Astrology and Prediction by Eric Russell, 247
Aumont, Jean Pierre, 102-103, 105-107
Aumont, Marie-Christine, 105
Austin, Edith ('Auntie' Eddie), 124, 137, 141
Austin, Russell ('Uncle' Russie), 124-125, 137, 141

Bainbridge, John, 211
Baker, Josephine, 195-197
Baker (children), Marianne, Akio, Luis, Jarri, Jeannot, Moise, Marianne and Brahima, Koffi, Mara, Noel, Stellina, 196

Balenciaga, 255
Baltzell, Professor E. Digby, 24
Bamberger, Theron, 56
Banac, Madame, 181, 229
Bancroft, Anne, 47
Barbizon Hotel for Women, 49-52, 58, 103
Bardot, Brigitte, 55
Barelli, Aimé, 159-160
Barrault, Jean Louis, 107
Bel Geddes, Barbara, 50
Bellofatto, Mrs Angelo, 151
Benenson, Fira, 154
Benington College, 39, 44
Bennetts, Leslie, 256
Bergman, Ingrid, 42, 56, 106
Berin, Harvey, 154
Bethel Merriday, 61
Bevan, Aneurin, 67
Biddle Family of Philadelphia, 23
Birkner, Fred, 152
Blum, Phyllis (Mrs Julian Earle), 191, 223-225, 226, 228-229, 231
Bob Hope Show, 92
Bonaparte, Napoleon, 131
Borgnine, Ernest, 149-150
Boston, Father, 263
Bozzacchi, Gianni, 254
Brando, Marlon 14, 59, 99, 101
Branells, 154
The Bridge on the River Kwai, 266
The Bridges of the Toko-Ri, 94-95
Brigance, 154
Broadway Theatre, 100
Brown, Judge Dudley, 20
Buchwald, Art, 214

Bucks County Playhouse, 21, 56
Burton, Richard, 204, 248-249

Cadwallader Family of Philadelphia, 23
Callas, Maria, 216, 218
Carl Gustav, King of Sweden, 133
Caroline Louise Marguerite, Princess, 12,
    15, 17, 123, 176, 185, 187, 205, 208, 209,
    210, 223, 224, 225, 238, 240, 244, 245,
    255, 261, 262, 263-264, 265, 267, 269
Carten, Father John, 166
Cartier, 249
Cartier-Bresson, Henri, 168
Cassavetes, John, 46
Cassini, Igor, 103
Cassini, Countess Marguerite, 102
Cassini, Oleg, 102-105, 114-118
Cathedrale de Monaco, 206
Charles, Prince, 133, 247, 268
Charlotte Louise Juliette, Princess (mother
    of Prince Rainier), 132, 133, 139, 160,
    181
Château Marmont, 67
Chevalier, Maurice, 247
Chiron, Didi, 228
Chiron, Louis, 228
Christians, Mady, 58
Churchill, Sir Winston, 253
City of Boston, 18
Clements, Julia (Lady Seton), 199-200, 201
Clooney, Rosemary, 156
Coe, Fred, 61
Colby, Anita, 127
Coleman, Dr George, 157
Columbia Broadcasting Service, 236
Come Dancing, 270
Conant, Howell, 54, 90
Conlan, Peggy (sister—formerly Davis),
    15, 27, 28, 30, 31, 33, 34, 35, 37, 39, 41,
    43, 67, 82, 100, 138-139, 157, 159, 163,
    168
Connor, Hugh J., 49-50
Constantine, Eddie, 159
Cooper, Gary, 65, 68
Costello, Mary (grandmother), 18-19, 21
The Country Girl, 47, 56, 95, 96-98, 105,
    120, 124
Cousteau, Jacques Yves, 175, 273
Cowles, Fleur (Mrs Tom Mayer), 223,
    230, 241, 242, 255
Cowles, Gardner, 134, 136, 255
Craig's Wife, 21
Crawford, Joan, 255-256
Crosby, Bing, 64, 96, 97, 98, 145-146, 147,
    253
Crozier, William ('Bill'), 24
Cukor, George, 93
Cummings, John M., 217
Curie, Madame, 247
Cyrano de Bergerac, 86

Dahl, Arlene, 112
Daily Mirror, (New York), 156
Darcy, Virginia, 149, 163, 168
Davies, Marion, 96
Davis, Bette, 67, 68
Davis, Harper, 43-44
Davis, Marylee, 155
Davis, Meg, 155
Davis, Peggy, see Conlan, Peggy
Day, Doris, 52
de Gaulle, President Charles, 172, 220, 236
de Havilland, Olivia, 121
de Segonzec, Gladys, 121
De Valera, Eamon, 218, 271
Deo Juvante II, 149, 157, 168-169
Dewar, Lord, 20
Dial M for Murder, 84, 86, 235
Diba, Empress of Iran, 256
Dilworth, Mayor and Mrs Richardson, 140
Dior, Christian, 154, 254
Docker, Sir Bernard, 188
Docker, Lance, 189
Docker, Lady Norah, 188-190
Donat, Dr Maurice, 137, 138
Don't Feed the Animals, 40
Douglas, Kirk, 52
Doverdale, Lady, 241
Dressler, Marie, 20
Drouillard, Jean, 50
du Maurier, Sir Gerald, 85
Dylan, Bob, 67

Ecole des Sciences Politiques, 172
Ecole du Rosay, 171
Elitches Garden Theatre, 62, 66
Elizabeth, Empress of Austria, 152
Elizabeth, Queen Mother, 67, 247
Elizabeth II, Queen, 13-14, 17, 160, 187,
    222
Emmert, Ruth, 40
Expo 67, 206

Fahrney, Merry ('Madcap'), 103
Fairbanks, Douglas, Junior, 34-35, 89
Farouk, King, 225
The Father, 57-58, 61
Faye, Alice, 146
Feldman, Charlie, 81
Ferrer, Jose, 86
For Love of Money, 63
Ford, Ethel, 28
Ford, Godfrey ('Fordie'), 28-29
Ford, John, 57, 70, 72, 78
Foreman, Carl, 65
Foreman, John, 8, 11, 14, 58, 60-61, 75,
    127, 223, 241
Fourteen Hours, 62
France Soir, 155
Frankes (photographer), 92
Frederica, Queen of Greece, 133

Freeman, Mary (Mrs 'Kell' Kelly), 91
Frosch, Aaron, 249
Fryer, Bill, 237
Fuller, Frances, 47, 56

Gable, Clark, 67, 70, 72, 73-74, 75-76, 78 97
Gabor, Zsa Zsa, 103, 156
Gaither, Gant, 8, 127, 156
Galanos, James, 154
Galante, Pierre, 121, 122, 123, 124
Gallico, Paul, 127, 223, 242, 272
Gallico, Virginia, 242, 245, 272
Gam, Rita (Mrs Guinzburg), 77, 80-81, 92,
    153, 168
Garbo, Greta, 13, 14, 91, 93, 106, 135, 156
Gardner, Ava, 12, 14, 61, 70-71, 72-73,
    74-75, 76, 91, 166
Garland, Judy, 98, 156
Garson, Greer, 85
Gatti, 149
Ghandi, Mahatma, 67
Givenchy, 254
Goethe, 247
Goldwyn, Samuel, 81, 157
Grable, Betty, 146
Grace Kelly Fan Club, 62
Grace, Princess, 7, 8, 11, 12, 14-17, 18, 19,
    20, 21, 22, 23, 28, 29, 31, 35, 52, 54, 60,
    63, 67, 70, 74, 76, 79, 81, 93, 108, 111,
    113, 119, 126-128, 134, 136, 152, 154,
    161, 163-164, 165-169, 170, 176, 177-184,
    185-187, 190, 191, 192-198, 199-204,
    205-212, 213-222, 223-232, 233-240,
    241-247, 249, 250-258, 259-260, 262,
    264-266, 267-273
Graham, 239
Graham, Billy, 67, 247
Graham, Winston, 235
Granger, Stewart, 100
Grant, Cary, 109, 111, 114, 115, 116, 145,
    160, 204
Gray, Bettina, 127, 168
Green Fire, 92, 100
Green, Milton, 135
Green, Ruzzie, 55
Greenfield Jr, Mr and Mrs Albert, 155
Grimaldi Family, 15, 16, 131, 172, 245,
    251, 252, 268, 273
Guilaroff, Sidney, 78
Gilels, Emil, 203
Guinness, Alec, 15, 127, 128, 129
Guinzburg, Tom, 153

Hamilton, Mrs Jay, 149
Hamilton, Lady Mary Douglas-, 132
Hancock, John, 74
Hari, Mata, 247
Harlow, Jean, 70
Hartman, David, 46
Hartman, Don, 98

Hauser, Gaylord, 128
Hawkins, Peter, 8, 171
Head, Edith, 82, 88, 92, 96, 98, 109, 110,
    242
Hearst, Randolph, 96
Heine, Alice, 132
Hepburn, Audrey, 91, 94, 95, 107
Hepburn, Katharine, 145, 247
Hervet, Dr Emil, 184, 187
Heyes, Douglas, 238
High Noon, 62, 64-65, 67, 68, 70, 83
High Society, 60, 145, 147, 148, 149, 153, 156
Hill, Graham, 239
Hitchcock, Alfred, 57, 59, 84-86, 87, 88,
    93, 95, 109, 110, 111, 112, 114, 115, 116,
    120, 127, 155, 233-235, 236
Holden, William, 67, 94, 95-96, 99, 110
Holm, Celeste, 145-148, 149
Holman, Dennis, 19
Hopper, Hedda, 109, 116
Howdy Doody, 152
Hudgins, Morgan, 71, 150, 154

International Arts Festival, 16
International Flower Show, 16
Iran, Shah of, 256
Ivanovic, Vane, 9, 229

Jacobs, Arthur, 66
James, Henry, 93
Jeanmaire, Zizi, 98
Jehlinger, Charles, 46, 47
Johnson, Van, 85
Jones, Jennifer, 96
Jourdan, Louis, 127, 129

Kanter, Jay, 65-66, 77, 84, 111, 128, 129,
    130, 233
Kanter, Judy, 156, 168
Karloff, Boris, 67
Kaye, Danny, 148, 204
Kazan, Elia, 93
Keay, Douglas, 170
Kellerman, Annette, 148
Kelly, Ann (aunt), 21
Kelly, Charles (cousin), 152
Kelly, Elizabeth (aunt), 21
Kelly, George (uncle), 21, 47, 52, 55, 56
Kelly, Grace, 11, 13-15, 21, 23, 24, 26-36,
    37-39, 40-48, 49-54, 55-63, 64-68, 69-78,
    79-82, 83-89, 90-93, 94-101, 102-108,
    109-119, 120-125, 127, 128-129, 133-134,
    137-144, 145-147, 148, 149-150, 151-158,
    159-163, 165-166, 168-180, 203, 233, 234,
    253, 273
Kelly, Grace (aunt), 19
Kelly, Jack Henry (grandfather), 18, 21
Kelly, John B. ('Jack'—father), 18, 20, 22,
    24-25, 27, 30, 32, 34, 37-39, 40, 41, 43-45,

52, 58, 62, 67, 77, 116, 124, 137-138, 139, 140, 141, 142-143, 148, 152, 155, 156, 159, 165-166
Kelly, Mrs John B. (formerly Margaret Majer—mother), 21, 22-23, 25, 26-27, 28, 30-31, 32, 33, 34, 37, 40, 41, 42, 43-44, 45, 49, 52, 55, 58, 67, 76, 97, 116-117, 124, 137-139, 141, 142, 143, 148, 155, 159-160, 182, 184
Kelly, John B. ('Kell'—brother), 29-30, 31, 33-34, 37-39, 43, 52-54, 141, 143, 163
Kelly, John Henry (uncle), 18, 21
Kelly, Mary (aunt), 21
Kelly, Patrick (uncle), 22
Kelly, Patrick Henry (great-uncle), 20
Kelly, Walter (*The Virginia Judge*—uncle), 20, 52
Kendall, Kay, 100
Kennedy Family, 23, 27
Kennedy, Jacqueline, 103, 216-219, 272
Kennedy, John (father of President Kennedy), 118
Kennedy, President John F., 67, 216, 217-220
Kennedy, Pat, 118
Kennedy, Robert, 247
Kent School, 38
Kerr, Deborah, 85, 94
King, 'Nana' (Mrs Maureen Wood), 190-191, 208-209, 223-228, 230, 231
King of Kings, 234
Klecki, Paul, 203
Knickerbocker, Cholly (Igor Cassini), 103, 119
Koelle, Rusty, 34
Korbut, Olga, 34
Kramer, Jack, 37
Kramer, Stanley, 64

Lacoste, Nadia, 8
Ladd, Alan, 42
Lambert, Eleanor, 153
Landis, Jessie Royce, 128-129, 230
Langdon, Dottie, 35
Lanvin, 254
Lapinere, Elias, 122
The Lavender Hill Mob, 221
Lawford, Peter, 118
Lawrence, Gertrude, 67
Leader, Governor and Mrs George, 140
Le Vine, Lizanne (sister), 26, 27, 31, 33, 34, 37, 67, 100, 141
Leigh, Vivien, 7, 94
LeRoy, Mervyn, 70, 157
Lewis, Jerry, 149
Lewis, Sinclair, 61
Life, 155
Ligato, Dominic, 141
Lights Out, 57
Lindsay, Cynthia, 237-239, 240

Lipton, Sir Thomas, 20
Loiewski, Alexander, 102
Lollobrigida, Gina, 122, 204
London Evening News, 189
A Look at Monaco, 236-239
Loos, Anita, 88
Loren, Sophia, 14, 55, 94, 204
Louis II, Prince (grandfather of Prince Rainier), 169, 171, 192
Louvet, Juliette, 132
Loy, Myrna, 67
Lumet, Sidney, 153
Luther, Martin, 247
Lynden, Lionel ('Curly'), 237-238
Lyon, Mrs Ben, 148, 156, 168

MacMahon, Marshal, 221
Maguire, Mrs, 272
Mahin, John Lee, 70
Mailer, Norman, 134-135
Management Corporation of America, 234
Mangiapan, Émile, 254
Mann, Daniel, 93
Mannerheim, Countess, 70
Manx Mouse, 242-243
Marigny Theatre, 107
Markovitch, Igor, 203
Marnie, 234, 236
Marquise, 154
Massey, Raymond, 58
Maxwell, Elsa, 216, 218
Maxwell, Vera, 119, 242, 245-246, 255
McCardell, Claire, 154
McGraw, Ali, 267
McGuire, Dorothy, 50
Meisner, Sanford, 56
Menuhin, Yehudi, 197, 203
The Merchant of Venice, 45
Metro Goldwyn Mayer, 67, 69, 71, 78, 94, 96, 100, 101, 107, 109, 120, 122, 128, 141, 146, 147-148, 150, 154, 161, 233
Milland, Ray, 67, 84
Minnelli, Liza, 267
Minnelli, Vincente, 93
Mogambo, 57, 70-71, 77, 78, 79, 83, 86, 101, 103, 120, 246
Molnar, Ferenc, 127
Monroe, Marilyn, 12, 14-15, 91, 105, 135-136, 146
Montand, Yves, 105
Monteleagre, Felicia, 61
Montez, Maria, 105
The Moon is Blue, 83
Moorhead, Agnes, 146
Motion Picture, 106
Mountbatten, Lady Edwina, 67
Murphy, Bridie, 127
Music Corporation of America, 59, 61, 65
Myler, Worthington, 47

Nage, Sandor, 46
Neighbourhood Playhouse, 56
Neiman Marcus, 245
Newman, Paul, 14
Nicholas II, Czar, 102
Nicholson, Camper, 169
Niven, David, 89, 242
Norell, Traina, 154
North, Sheree, 146
Nova, Ludmilla, 243-245

O'Brien, Jack, 139-140
Oceanographic Museum, 175, 273
O'Donnell, Cathy, 50
Oechsle, Jack, 42
Old Academy Players, 40
Olivier, Laurence, 105
Olympia Theatre, 107
On the Waterfront, 99
Onassis, Aristotle, 135, 157, 172, 214-216, 218, 231, 253
Onassis, Jacqueline, *see* Kennedy, Jacqueline

Pamp, Maree, 168
Pantages Theatre, 99
Panton, Margaret, 114
Paramount Pictures, 82, 94, 98, 109, 111, 124
Paris Match, 155
Parsons, Louella, 109
Pascal, Gisèle, 122, 133, 175
Patachou, 107
Penn, William, 23
Perchance to Dream, 173
Perette, Suzy, 154
Perlberg, Bill, 94, 96, 98
Perrie, Ernestine, 60
Philadelphia Bulletin, 8, 123, 141
Philadelphia Country Club, 53
The Philadelphia Gentleman—The Making of a National Upper Class by Professor E. Digby Baltzell, 24
The Philadelphia Inquirer, 217
The Philadelphia Inquirer Magazine, 211
The Philadelphia Social Register, 24
The Philadelphia Story, 60, 145
Philadelphia's Playhouse in the Park, 62, 83
Philip, Prince, 256
Piaf, Edith, 67
Pierre, Prince (father of Prince Rainier), 132, 147, 158, 160, 266
Plaistow, Christine, 250, 252
Polignac, Duke of, *see* Pierre, Prince
Portanier, Judge Marcel, 186
Porter, Cole, 156
Prêtre, Georges, 203
The Prince and the Showgirl, 15
Princess Grace Foundation, 197

Quadras, Vidal, 266
Quentin Durward, 100

Radio Monte Carlo, 154
Rainier, Prince, 8, 14-16, 25, 29, 32, 35, 52, 59, 76, 87, 89, 102, 113, 118, 119, 121-125, 126-127, 128, 131-136, 137-143, 145, 147-148, 151, 155, 156, 157-158, 159-160, 162-163, 165-169, 170-176, 179, 180-181, 182-183, 184, 185-187, 190, 192, 194, 201, 203, 204, 206, 207, 209-212, 213-218, 221, 222, 223-232, 233-240, 242, 243, 245, 250-254, 259-264, 265, 266, 267-273
Rambo, Maree, 127
Ratoff, Gregory, 57
Ravenhill Academy, 35
Ray, Harry, 112, 113-114
Rear Window, 55, 86-87, 90, 94, 128, 235
Red Cross of Monaco (Croix-Rouge Monégasque), 15, 192-194, 254
Redford, Robert, 46
Redgrave, Lynn, 67
Renaud, Madeleine, 107
Reybold, Carolyn, 127, 139, 168
Reybold, Malcolm, 139
Rhine, Dr J. B., 127
Richards, Lexford, 60, 160
Richardson, Sally, 149, 168
Righter, Carroll, 143-144
Ring Round the Moon, 191
Riva, Maria, 61
Robert Montgomery Presents, 152
Roosevelt, President Franklin D., 22, 29
Rose, Helen, 128, 148, 154
Rostropovitch, Mstislav, 203
Rubin, Stan, 160
Russell, Jane, 146
Rutherford, Margaret, 7

S.S. *Constitution*, 154, 156, 157, 158, 159
S.S. *Independence*, 156
St Alphege Church, 202
St Bridget's Church, 22, 33, 53, 151
St Charles' Church, 123
Saint Dévote, 167
Schary, Dore, 101, 147-148
Schlee, George, 135, 136
Schoenbrun, David, 133
Schraffenberger, Nancy, 193
Schwarzkopf, Elisabeth, 203
Scott, Lizabeth, 59
Scott, Sir Walter, 100
Seaton, George, 94, 96, 97, 98
Selznick, David, 96
Shakespeare, William, 246
The Show Off, 21
Simpson, Adele, 154
Simpson, Wallis, 134
Sinatra, Frank, 71, 73, 74-75, 76, 105, 145 148
Sinclair, Mary, 61
Sinden, Donald, 72
The Sleeping Prince, 15

Smith, Constance, 57
Smith, Margaret Chase, 211
Smithsonian Institute, 246
The Snow Goose, 243
Société Anonyme des Bains de Mer et du
    Cercle des Strangers du Monaco, 214
Société des Bains de Mer, 213, 215, 216
Sollito, Maurice, 145
Sophia, Princess of Greece, 204
Spencer, Frank, 270
Spencer, Peggy, 270
Stacey, George, 184, 259
A Star is Born, 98
Stars on Sunday, 86, 197
Steele, Al, 255-256
Stein, Gertrude, 85
Stephanie Marie Elisabeth, Princess, 201,
    205, 209, 210, 264, 265, 270
Stevens School, 45
Stevenson, Robert Louis, 210
Stewart, James, 67, 86, 87, 90, 145
Stotesbury Family of Philadelphia, 23
Stowe, 171
The Student Prince, 173
Studio One, 47
Surtees, Robert, 72
The Swan, 15, 46, 127, 129, 152, 160

Tabor Academy, 38
Taxi, 57, 84
Taylor, Elizabeth, 12, 13, 14, 55, 91, 93,
    94, 100, 204, 248-249
That Kelly Family (A. S. Barnes and
    Company) by John McCallum, 19
Thompson, Bettina, 50
The Three Princes of Serendip, 127
Tierney, Gene, 50, 103
Tisserant, Cardinal Eugene, 206
Tito, President, 256
To Catch a Thief, 109, 113, 121, 128, 235,
    236
The Torchbearers, 21, 45, 56
Toumonova, Tamara, 159
Tovarich, 105
Tracy, Spencer, 46, 100-101
Tregere, Pauline, 154
Tribute to a Bad Man, 100
True Love, 147, 253

Tucker, Father, 123, 125, 134, 136, 137-139,
    140, 172, 182, 186, 212
Turngemeinde Athletic and Social Club, 22
Turner, Lana, 71
Tuttle, William ('Bill'), 78
TV Playhouse, 61, 62

Umberto, King of Italy, 204
Universal Pictures, 84
Universal Studios, 113

Valentina, 135
van Cleve, Edith, 59, 61, 63, 65
Vanderbilt, George, 128
Vashsewskaya, Galina, 203
Vassary, Tamas, 203
Victoria Eugénie, Queen of Spain, 204, 225
Vidor, Charles, 127
Voice of America, 154
von Falz-Fein, Ludmilla, *see* Nova,
    Ludmilla
von Matacic, Lovo, 203

Walpole, Horace, 127
Walters, Chuck, 145, 147
Warner Brothers, 84
Wasserman, Lew, 96
Waters, Alice, 34
Webster, Margaret, 24
Westmore, Wally, 112
Whisky Galore, 220
White, Gordon, 107
Whitney, Cornelius Vanderbilt, 160
Wikoff, Howard, 29, 43
Williams, Percy, 20
Wilson, Earl, 75-76
Windsor, Duchess of, *see also* Simpson,
    Wallis, 70
Windsor, Duke of, 134, 175
Wise, Prudence ('Prudy'), 80-81
Women's Medical College, 33
Wragge, B. H., 154
Wyler, William, 93

Zinnemann, Fred, 64, 65, 68
Zubin, Mehta, 203
Zuckerman, Ben, 153, 246